CAUSAL THINKING
IN THE CHILD

CAUSAL THINKING
IN THE CHILD

A Genetic and Experimental Approach

MONIQUE LAURENDEAU   ADRIEN PINARD, c.s.v.

Institute of Psychology
University of Montreal

Preface by
JEAN PIAGET

INTERNATIONAL UNIVERSITIES PRESS, INC. • NEW YORK

Contents

Acknowledgments ix

Preface xi

Introduction 1

Part I

The Problem of Precausality

I   Egocentrism and Precausal Thinking 7

II   The Existence of Precausal Thinking 16

     Controversial Evidence 16

     Conditions Affecting Causal Thinking 23

       Methods of Examination 23

       Type of Subjects 26

       Techniques of Analysis 28

III   The Infantile Character of Precausal Thinking ... 37

IV   The Existence of Stages in Intellectual Development   45

Part II

The Experiment

V   Preparation of the Experimental Questionnaires .. 57

     Criteria for the Selection of Questionnaires 58

     The Wording of the Questionnaires 61

	The Concept of Dream	62
	The Concept of Life	66
	The Origin of Night	68
	The Movement of Clouds	72
	Floating and Sinking	74
VI	**The Sample**	80
VII	**Conditions of Testing and Methods of Analysis**	90
	Conditions of Testing	90
	Examiners	90
	Form and Place of Testing	91
	Order of Test Administration	91
	Methods of Analysis	92
	Identification of Stages	93
	Age of Accession to Stages	94

Part III

The Results

VIII	**The Concept of Dream**	103
	Stage 0: Incomprehension or Refusal	104
	Stage 1: Integral Realism	106
	Stage 2: Mitigated Realism	112
	Substage 2A	115
	Substage 2B	116
	Substage 2C	119
	Stage 3: Integral Subjectivism	121
	Substage 3A	124
	Substage 3B	125
IX	**The Concept of Life**	131
	Stage 0: Incomprehension or Refusal	141
	Stage 1: Animistic Thinking Based upon Usefulness, Anthropomorphism, or Movement	144

Stage 2:   Autonomous Movement with Some
Residual Animistic Thinking 147
Stage 3:   Total Disappearance of Animistic
Thinking 150

X   The Origin of Night 160
Stage 0:   Incomprehension or Refusal 166
Stage 1:   Absolute Artificialism 167
Substage 1A: Finalistic Interpretations 169
Substage 1B: Finalistic and Artificialistic,
or Exclusively Artificialistic Interpretations ... 170
Stage 2:   Semiartificialistic and Semiphysical
Interpretations 171
Stage 3:   Absolute Physicalism 175
Substage 3A: Physicalism Still Tainted
with Finalism or Animism 176
Substage 3B: Physicalism Freed from any
Precausality 178

XI   The Movement of Clouds 182
Stage 0:   Incomprehension or Refusal 186
Stage 1:   Human or Divine Action 188
Stage 2:   Autonomous Movement, or Action of
Other Celestial Bodies 192
Stage 3:   Action of the Wind (or Movement
Regarded as Illusive) 197
Substage 3A: Correct Explanations, But
Still Tainted with Precausality 198
Substage 3B: Correct Explanations Freed
from Any Precausal Thinking 199

XII   The Floating and Sinking of Objects 204
Stage 0:   Incomprehension 206
Stage 1:   Precausal Explanations (Finalism,
Animism, Dynamism, etc.) 209
Stage 2:   Physical Explanations, but Tainted
with Illogical Reasons (Contradictions
or Misconceptions) 212

Substage 2A 213
Substage 2B 217
Stage 3: Physical and Always Coherent
    Explanations 221
    Substage 3A 222
    Substage 3B 225
XIII   Interdependence of Precausal Notions 231

Conclusion

Precausality Reconsidered   245

Appendices
A. Experimental Questionnaires 263
B. Statistics on the Child Population of Montreal 276

Bibliography 283

Author Index 289

Subject Index 291

Acknowledgments

This project has been supported by Federal-Provincial grants from the *Department of National Health and Welfare* and by grants from the *National Research Council of Canada.*

An investigation of this scope would not have been possible without the generous collaboration of scores of people (examiners, parents, children) and the complete cooperation of the *Montreal Catholic School Commission.* To each and every one of these collaborators, our most sincere gratitude. Special mention should be made of the particular contribution of one of our colleagues, Cécile Boisclair, who has been of great assistance throughout the experiment and who is referred to in this book as "the third scorer."

The task of translating into the English language an argument that had first been conceived and expressed in French raised problems which are practically insuperable. The manuscript has been translated and revised several times; yet it is still undoubtedly tainted with an inevitable and rather bizarre French flavor for which the authors offer their apology and assume full responsibility. Special thanks are due to Mrs. Lottie M. Newman who has accepted the difficult task of editing this manuscript and who, by her numerous suggestions, has contributed to the improvement of the text.

Finally, the assistance of the *Canada Council* and the *Social Science Research Council of Canada* in providing funds for the publication of this report must be gratefully acknowledged.

Université de Montréal
July, 1962

Preface

When our Geneva group heard the news that Monique Laurendeau, Adrien Pinard, and some of their Canadian collaborators proposed to design a new scale of intellectual development essentially based upon our operational tests, we felt a
real joy; for, although B. Inhelder and Vinh-Bang were already
engaged in a parallel task, it goes without saying that comparisons and eventual controls resulting from these endeavors
could but increase their common import. On the other hand,
while our investigations of the development of "operations"
proper (published between 1940 and 1958) had already led to
a series of replications and systematic verifications in Anglo-
Saxon and Scandinavian countries, it was the first time that so
broad and so original a global application of our hypotheses
was made known to us.

Accordingly, may I confess, without astonishing M. Laurendeau and A. Pinard, that I was taken by surprise and even
felt somewhat uneasy when I received the first of their im-
patiently expected books and realized that it did not yet have
any bearing on the operational aspects of development, but
dealt exclusively with the verbal forms of precausal thinking
in the child. It so happens that the precausal notions studied
in my first investigations (so long ago, alas!) had been recognized as valid by some authors, but much less so by others
who had at the time taken a very critical attitude. Why then,

in this case, revive antediluvian disputes and begin with these nonoperational aspects, which good contemporary accounts of our research work relegate, somewhat rightfully, to the last part?[1] As a matter of fact, the main reasons for the decision of our Canadian friends are altogether relevant. Realizing that the numerous publications on the problems of "precausality" led to two series of conclusions quite exactly contradictory, it was their estimation that these very contradictions gave rise, on the one hand, to a preliminary question on method of such a nature as to condition the methodological scope of their entire effort of standardization, and, on the other hand, to a preliminary fundamental question relative to the spheres to be included or not to be included in a complete series of tests on intellectual development. Indeed, had it been demonstrated that our findings on precausal thinking could not be replicated with the same methods, the latter would naturally have had to be rejected entirely in the sole favor of questioning procedures focused on the child's manipulation of concrete material. If, on the other hand, our results had been replicated, but in proportions varying too greatly with milieu, the domain of precausal thinking would have had to be discarded, not indeed as unauthentic, but as lacking the necessary frequency of occurrence and consistency.

In this respect, I must confess that had I been consulted, I would perhaps have attempted to dissuade my friends from such a return to precausality, not because I no longer believe in it, but because today verbal thinking seems to me marginal to real thinking which, even though verbalized, remains until about eleven to twelve years of age centered upon action. I surely do not hold that in order to solve the problem it is sufficient to say, as H. Wallon does, that when the child speaks of

[1] See, for instance, Guido, Petter: *Lo sviluppo mentale nelle ricerche di Jean Piaget* (Preface by C. Musatti), Firenze (Ed. Univ.), 1960, 495 pp., Part III, Chap. 2 and 3.

celestial bodies, of clouds, or of origins, he is only manipulating "hyperthings" instead of conceptualizing the actual "things" which are the object of his actions. Be that as it may, the fundamental fact remains that children ask questions spontaneously and that their "whys" bear precisely, with surprising frequency, on these "hyperthings" (indeed, Wallon himself repeated a series of our questions in his *Origines de la pensée chez l'enfant*). But it is nonetheless true that thinking divorced from action is not operational at all until the level of formal or propositional operations (eleven or twelve to fifteen years of age) has been reached, and that exclusively verbal thinking therefore no longer seems to be sufficient for the investigation of the child's thinking: it provides a series of instructive indications, which must, however, be related to other findings derived from operational tests proper.

This is indeed, it goes without saying, the point of view of M. Laurendeau and A. Pinard. Why, then, did they deliberately publish their data on precausality first? Of course they had, as we have just seen, excellent reasons for beginning their general study with the investigation of this problem; but why deal with this subject in their very first publication?

I admit that I was soon won over by their presentation which, to the qualities of an excellent factual study, adds those of a remarkable critical and methodological analysis. When reading their book in its present arrangement, one discovers rapidly that its three parts were conceived in the order II, III, and then I, and that Part I is so vivid because in it there is a discharge of tensions accumulated during the elaboration of Parts II and III. It was then with this release from conflicting strains that they chose to mark the beginning of their successive accounts.

In other words, M. Laurendeau and A. Pinard began with experimentation, unhurried and unprejudiced. Knowing that certain authors had reached contradictory results, they took all possible precautions in the examination of their 500 subjects ranging from 4 to 12 years of age, and did not attempt to predict whether their findings would corroborate, or invalidate, my own observations. They did, of course, start with a favorable prejudice with respect to specifically operational tests, since in fact they had decided upon undertaking this standardization. But they had taken no definite *a priori* stand on precausality and were just as ready to drop it from their final synthesis as to include it.

In fact, they have met with results agreeing much better with my former observations than the diverse findings of other authors might have led one to anticipate. But as their results were gradually taking shape, they were faced with a problem which then raised a question concerning their own methods as well as mine: how could the contradictions between the preceding authors be explained? M. Laurendeau and A. Pinard were indeed well aware that it would not be enough for them to add to the record some new results in agreement with those of Dennis and Russell, and others, who had corroborated mine, and in contradiction with Deutsche, Hazlitt, and others, who had contested mine. In order to end up with a valid standardization, much more has to be done: it becomes necessary to determine precisely the method of questioning, the method of analysis, and the method of interpretation in such a way that one will understand, not only the why of the results obtained, but also the why of divergent results when the procedure and criteria happen to be different.

Here, then, Part I finds its logical place with all its momentum and the frequent verve displayed by our two Canadian authors as the result of a long inner debate with opponents of mine who might also have become theirs. In the perspective of years long past, I confess to feeling a certain gratification at the reopening of a trial at which my former judges are now arraigned, and by new unexpected partners as talented as they are well informed. But all sentiment aside, the remarkable result of this critique of critics is that M. Laurendeau and A. Pinard have solved the methodological problem with which they were faced. They have shown that if a first group of authors failed to rediscover precausal explanations in significant frequencies, while a second group definitely confirmed their existence, the difference was due not only to rather naïve substitutions of criteria (thus Deutsche confuses phenomenism with physicalism, or Hazlitt accepts simple automatic generalizations as indications of logical structures!), but mainly to the very method used in the quantification of results. Authors who are favorable to the hypothesis of precausality analyze their results by individual subjects, each child thus being judged according to the internal coherence of his answers, while the opponents of the hypothesis simply quantify their data, object by object, without regard to the subject's point of view.

Apart from thus providing a good example of methodological criticism, the book by M. Laurendeau and A. Pinard is no less interesting for its own fundamental conclusions. Reconsidering the problem of the succession of stages—a succession which may be based either on a process of direct filiation as in the case of "operations" deriving from action, or on one of substitution—the authors agree with me that the transition from artificialism to natural explanations constitutes an instance of succession by substitution: when a child accepts the idea that a lake has been dug by a river after he had already attributed the digging to the shoveling of workmen, his final belief is not derived from his initial one, but is substituted for it, even if, intermediate between the two beliefs, there is evidence of finalistic thinking, such as the idea that the town had to exist before the natural lake, because lakes must be beside towns. But, as M. Laurendeau and A. Pinard so correctly maintain and as I have always admitted myself, substitutions are always very partial and are necessarily registered in a context of filiation. The very gradual transition from finalism (which is the principal motive of artificialism) to mechanistic explanations is thus based upon a process whereby operations are derived from action through direct filiation; but this process is made possible by a progressive decentration which eliminates the egocentric features of the subject's action (thereby its finalism) in favor of coordination as such, which is the source of objectivity. In short, the evolution of precausal thinking, even in its marginal and verbal forms, is one of the essential phases in the development of causal thinking. From a mere assimilation to the subject's discrete actions, causality is progressively raised to the level of an assimilation of external sequences to the very coordination of actions, and thereby to operations, as deductive structures applicable to physical and temporal sequences.

Geneva   JEAN PIAGET
February, 1961

Introduction

A few years ago, the Laboratory for the Study of Child Development of the Institut de Psychologie de l'Université de Montréal undertook the intensive study of a group of 700 children in order to ascertain the existence and sequence of stages of mental development. The complete program will eventually result in the publication of a new developmental scale, better adapted to the prevailing concepts of the nature of intelligence. Yet, the project is not limited to this practical objective. These experiments also seek to elucidate the theoretical problem of the genesis of intelligence by retracing, in the light of Piaget's findings, the main phases of the mental development of children from a different cultural milieu.

This genetic study is meant as an experimental one: it is based on the systematic observation of a group of children undergoing an examination that satisfies the minimal conditions of objectivity and standardization required by the experimental method. To achieve its aim completely, such an investigation should deal with the same group of children tested regularly at successive and relatively short intervals. A longitudinal study of this kind is not easily practicable, especially if one considers the duration of the complete examination, the great number of subjects required, the age intervals to be dealt with, and the necessary limitations in time and personnel under which such an investigation must take place.

Accordingly, one should stick to a cross-sectional study, which allows for the parallel examination of several groups of children of various ages. Moreover, this methodological approach is more convenient for the elaboration of a normalized scale of mental development. In short, this combined developmental-experimental study constitutes a systematic replication of Piaget's main experiments, under conditions perhaps better adapted to stricter methodological requirements. It should show to what extent the stages of mental development described by Piaget apply to a slightly different sociocultural milieu, and it should also serve to validate or invalidate their accuracy. In the same way, the assessment of various fragmentary studies on certain particular aspects of Piaget's theory—studies conducted in different countries and under conditions not readily comparable—should become easier. Finally, this study will provide the statistical or normative complement, which is still lacking in Piaget's wealth of observations and which can give them increased significance in the fields of pure research as well as applied psychology.

The present report is limited to the study of the child's conception of reality and causality. Only the symbolic forms of causality are considered, and solely at those ages when the child becomes capable of satisfactorily imparting his thoughts to others, that is from the age of four. The development of infantile concepts of reality and causality does not occupy a very considerable place in Piaget's studies. The only two books (1926, 1927) explicitly devoted to this subject belong to the very first part of his psychological work. They date back to the period when he investigated the child's mental organization with the aim of discovering some characteristics which could form the basis for the elaboration of an explanatory system. Piaget considers these publications as essentially preliminary. Very recently, he even went so far as to use the expression "un peu adolescents" ("somewhat adolescent") in referring to them (1959, p. 10). No doubt he was then still under the strong influence of some of his masters, and his very first hypotheses should be regarded as the mere outline of a theory which he intended to state more and more precisely. However, even though they may hold a rather small place in his written scientific production and belong to a period already somewhat remote, these investigations on the various forms of the representation of the world surely retain an immediate interest. The contemporary psychological literature is studded with articles and books reformulating Piaget's hypotheses in various ways. There are many studies purporting to verify the existence and the importance of precausal thinking. It is indeed rather astonishing to find that these very first books by Piaget are by far the best known and—for that very reason—the most contested. This phenomenon can undoubtedly be explained in different ways. Besides being the first to have been translated into many languages, these books are most readily accessible to the nonspecialist, primarily because demonstrations were not yet based on the logistic schemata he now uses. Moreover, the concepts studied in these works venture well beyond the context of child psychology, or that of the psychology of thought processes, into related domains such as anthropology, social psychology, and clinical psychology. It is then readily understandable that these books should have received so wide a distribution.

Among the authors who have made an attempt to test some of Piaget's conclusions, many have ended by disagreeing profoundly with him. In fact, the results obtained from varied populations and through the same type of questionnaires (whether identical or at variance) by no means always corroborate Piaget's observations. Some have used this circumstance to express scornful skepticism of his generalizations, or have even discarded his theory as a whole. Such an attitude is really inadmissible. Piaget's investigations on precausal thinking do not constitute a valid sample of his entire work, even though they form an integral part of it. On the other hand, disagreements are often superficial and arise rather from mutual misunderstanding than from objective incompatibility. All these comparative studies are indeed too dissimilar to warrant the drawing of definitive conclusions.

The present investigation intends to raise once again the problem of the existence of various forms of precausal thinking. Among the twenty-seven questionnaires directly derived from Piaget's work and used in the complete project, five deal specifically with the child's representation of the world. The analysis of the results obtained through these five tests from a large sample of children of various ages will probably provide more decisive answers for the solution of the very controversial problem of what the child's beliefs are.

PART I

The Problem of Precausality

The first chapter of this section aims at a precise description of the relationships which Piaget's theory infers between the egocentrism of the child and the various manifestations of precausal thinking.

Piaget's system has been extensively criticized. These criticisms involve three major issues: they question the very existence of precausal thinking, its exclusively infantile character, and finally the concept of stages of intellectual development. Since these three topics encompass almost all the criticisms raised by specific problems, the present discussion will be limited to them. They will form the subject matter of Chapters 2, 3, and 4, respectively.

CHAPTER I

Egocentrism and Precausal Thinking

Piaget's scientific work is so well known that a detailed summary is unnecessary. It is sufficient to remember its most essential elements. However, in drawing attention to only a few aspects of his whole work, there is the risk of falsifying the perspective of a system in which not a single element is useless for a perfect understanding of the whole. Being aware of the limitations inherent in a compendious synthesis, the reader will compensate for major oversights by referring to the analysis Piaget has presented in his two books dealing specifically with the child's intellectual attitudes toward reality: *The Child's Conception of the World* (1926) and *The Child's Conception of Physical Causality* (1927).

Intellectual development as a whole can be defined as the passage from an initial state of egocentrism to a state of total objectivity. The discovery and progressive coordination of the various perspectives implied in this slow process of decentration have to occur at three successive levels, and thus give rise to a triple timelag, which Piaget clearly underlines in his study on the thinking processes of the adolescent (Inhelder and Piaget, 1955). In the first place, at the sensorimotor level the child starts by confusing his own activity with that of the external world before he slowly comes, through a series of successive stages, to the practical dissociation of these two poles. The appearance of symbolic thinking brings back the egocentrism which had already been overcome at the sensorimotor level. Henceforth, it is at the level of representation that a relative undifferentiation will be observed between the child's own viewpoint and that of others, as well as between the internal and the external world. Not until the advent of concrete operational thinking will the way be open to a second decentration allowing the coordination of these different viewpoints by the child. Finally, with the appearance of the reflective processes specific to formal thinking, the child must face a third type of egocentrism whereby he is unable to differentiate his own perspective from that of the social milieu to which he must adapt. Learning to think productively on a strict reality basis and to develop a genuine social reciprocity requires a third effort toward decentration, which will last throughout adolescence and will culminate in the achievement of perfect objective thinking.

Thus, the study of the child's representation of reality dealt with here refers only to the second form of decentration which begins with the appearance of symbolic thinking. Even though the manipulation of causality, space, time, and object is already perfectly organized at the level of immediate physical activity (Piaget, 1936, 1937), the intelligence of the child who is beginning to use symbolic thinking is once again subjected to an initial lack of differentiation between the self and the outside world. At first, this lack of differentiation relates to the various possible viewpoints: in leading the child to believe in the exclusiveness of the personal and momentary perspective, it leaves him open to prelogical and intuitive forms of reasoning. This lack of differentiation also covers the multiple dimensions of reality, and as such gives rise to endless confusions about what is internal and external, subjective and objective, physical and mental, about the ideas and the objects, the sign and the significate, etc. Egocentrism induces the child to draw for himself a very specific image of the world, which Piaget qualifies as realistic in opposition to the objectivity characterizing adult intelligence.

Objectivity consists in so fully realising the countless intrusions of the self in everyday thought and the countless illusions which result—illusions of sense, language, point of view, value, etc.— that the preliminary step to every judgment is the effort to exclude the intrusive self. Realism, on the contrary, consists in ignoring the existence of self and thence regarding one's own perspective as immediately objective and absolute [Piaget, 1926, p. 34].[1]

By objectivity we mean the mental attitude of persons who are able to distinguish what comes from themselves and what forms part of external reality as it can be observed by everybody [Piaget, 1927, p. 241].

At first the child has no image either of his self or of the external world as such. These two universes are compounded into one single reality, each one contributing to the other to the same degree. The external world shares the characteristics of the self (awareness, purposiveness, etc.). These two worlds take shape gradually through more and more definite elaboration. Differentiation comes about in a parallel way: the child gives a structure to the external world inasmuch as he becomes aware of his own self, and, reciprocally, he builds this self-image as he becomes conscious of existences different from his own.

[1] In the case of quotations, the year refers to the date of original publication, and the page number to the English edition, when it exists.

The period of total egocentrism is hard to grasp, being characteristic of an age at which it is impossible to question the child in a systematic way. Accordingly, it is only through the accumulation of all types of observations that Piaget (1945) succeeded in demonstrating the universal existence of this phenomenon among children less than four years of age. When the child becomes able to communicate with others, he has already reached some degree of that dissociation which will keep on establishing itself until it becomes what it is in adulthood.

At each step in the process of dissociation these two terms evolve in the sense of the greatest divergence, but they are never in the child (nor in the adult for that matter) entirely separate. From our present point of view, therefore, there is never complete objectivity: at every stage there remain in the conception of nature what we might call "adherences", fragments of internal experience which still cling to the external world [Piaget, 1927, p. 244].

In the young child, the adherences are many and varied, pervading all his notions of reality. Their importance as well as their intensity fade away with the evolution of intelligence. They cling to fewer and fewer notions and are gradually replaced by objective conceptions, possible only for a mind which has become conscious of its subjective existence and aware of the multiplicity and relativity of possible viewpoints.

The analysis of the concepts of reality and causality reveals the existence of five major forms of realistic adherences. We shall discuss them under the general term of "precausality," thereby generalizing the use of an expression which Piaget introduced to represent chiefly the explanations intervening between those based on pure psychological and those relating to pure physical causality. In the present study, this term will include all forms of explanation antecedent to the ones depending on physical and objective connections.

Phenomenism is the most primitive form the child uses in his representation of reality. It is the establishment of a causal connection between phenomena which are contiguous either in space or in time, or between facts which, for the subject, bear some resemblance or relation. Being ignorant of the eminently subjective nature of such connections, the child is prone to link everything to anything. For instance, the color of an object may explain its floating, the heat of the sun may be the reason why it is classified as a living object, etc. However, reality sometimes forces upon the child some privileged connections. The events frequently associated in his perceptions will more often be causally related, and the more striking aspects of reality will be retained in preference to less obvious properties. Consequently, one should not be surprised to observe that most children establish quasi-universal connections at a given phase of their evolution.

According to the nature of the relationships involved, this first form of precausal thinking manifests itself under the guise of pure phenomenism, feelings of participation, or magical beliefs. Pure phenomenism exists when the assimilation is imposed by the objects themselves. In the feeling of participation, the relation the child perceives is more personal: he relies upon impressions of similarity, or upon any other subjective feeling, in order to form relationships readily transformable into causal connections. Objects very remote in space or time will thus participate with each other and exert a mutual influence. For instance, the shadow of an object may be explained by the darkness of the night which comes to stay under this object, and, in a reciprocal fashion, the night is the gathering up of many shadows. When one of the terms of the relationship is located in the child, or in human beings in general, magical beliefs are added to the feelings of participation: thus, the relationship between night and sleep takes, in the eyes of some children, such importance that the desire for sleep is sufficient to bring about the advent of night. And again, the relation between the movement of celestial bodies and that of man leads to the belief in the efficacy which human displacements have for the direction of the movements of celestial bodies.

Finalism is the second form of precausal thinking. In this perspective, reality is conceived as a world organized along well-determined plans and almost always centered upon human activity. Each object has a function which, by itself, amply justifies its existence and its properties: thus, a ship floats in order to carry people from one country to another, the clouds move in order to carry rain to other regions, etc. The finality implied in these conceptions of nature is not, as a matter of fact, restricted to the usefulness of objects. The child often relates the origin of phenomena to motives of a psychological or moral nature, as if he were imagining an organizing agent capable of subduing individual wills: accordingly, dreams happen in order to entertain or punish the dreamer; large mountains exist for the benefit of adults and the smaller ones for that of children; ships float because they must; etc.

Artificialism, the third form of precausality, draws its principle from finalism which it complements by positing the explicit action of a maker at the origin of things: either God or men are held responsible for the existence of all objects, natural or artificial, observed in the external world. When God is part of these explanations, He is grossly humanized and compares with a giant or a magician. In short, artificialism draws all its analogies from human industry. This human supremacy is derived from many factors: the two most important seem to be, first, the analogy of the parents' action in relation to the child since his birth; and second, the anthropocentrism natural to the child, which leads him to transform finalistic expressions ("made for men") into artificialistic ones ("made by men"). Thus, lakes and rivers are at first explained in a utilitarian way: they exist because boats must sail on water. Soon, the interpretation is completed by an artificialistic theory: men have dug rivers and lakes in order to move about from one place to the next.

Animism and *dynamism* represent the fourth and fifth forms of precausal thinking and come to support the child's conception of nature. Through animism, the child gives life and consciousness to surrounding objects, and through dynamism, he grants them an energy similar to man's muscular strength which makes them capable of all sorts of efforts and motions. For instance, clouds are conscious of their displacements, and they may choose their own course and execute their movements without any assistance. Confused in the beginning, animism and dynamism will finally dissociate: animism will vanish first, while dynamism will still remain for some time.

The apparent systematization linking all these manifestations of precausal thinking has no existence in the mind of children. On the contrary, the child's thinking is disconcertingly incoherent. Even when faced with a group of similar problems, the child will not respond consistently.

We were able, within each sphere, to establish special stages, but it would be extremely difficult to establish inclusive stages for the reason that during these early years the child is still very incoherent. At the age when the child is still animistic, artificialist, or dynamic in his way of thinking on some points, he has already ceased to be so on others. He does not reap the benefits of a progress in all the domains where this progress is bound eventually to make itself felt. Corresponding stages are at varying levels, because the influence of one belief upon another takes place unconsciously and not thanks to a conscious and deliberate generalization. Thus child thought is in no way organised. There are, of course, certain remarkable correlations between one given achievement and another. . . . But this is not the sign of discursive and reflective logic, it merely indicates the existence of a certain coherence between the warring parts of an organism which is unable as yet to release instantaneously such synergy as may exist [Piaget, 1927, p. 292].[2]

That the child's answers often seem to spring from a rigorous system is largely due to the questioning itself, which forces the child to formulate explicit beliefs heretofore unexpressed and still relatively uncommunicable. The examination situation introduces artificial and dangerous elements. It stimulates the child into becoming conscious of mental attitudes which are not yet conceptualized, but which are mere images or motor impressions. The questions bring about, so to speak, the systematization of a way of thinking which itself is not systematic. A cautious interpretation of the results is thus in order. Among other things, it is important not to consider the child's verbalizations as the expression of a real theory, or of a deliberate conviction. Most often the child creates a myth to overcome momentary difficulties and is easily led by his imagination into whimsical elaborations. But this is not pure verbalism. The details of the explanation must no doubt be neglected, but the general meaning of the protocol does not fail to reveal the orientation of the child's mind and the process of his thinking.

It is, as always, open to question exactly how far the children believe what they are saying and at what point they start romancing. But the important thing is to realise that they have nothing with which to replace this artificialism. Whether they

[2] The last sentence of this quotation has been somewhat condensed and modified through the process of translation. To avoid any possible confusion, the original text is quoted: "Seulement c'est là l'indice, non pas d'une logique discursive et réfléchie, mais de la cohérence d'un organisme dont les parties s'entretiennent mutuellement, en gros, sans éviter les heurts et les chaos partiels ni rendre instantanée la synergie dans la mesure où elle existe" (Piaget, J. La causalité physique chez l'enfant. Paris: Librairie Félix Alcan, 1927, p. 329).

THE PROBLEM OF PRECAUSALITY

make up the details or not they can only explain things by having recourse to human activity and not to things themselves [Piaget, 1926, p. 313].

In short, whatever the nature of the child's interpretation of reality, one should disregard particular and accessory elements in order to focus upon the common theme of all myths created, while bearing in mind that a large number of properly infantile notions remain imperceptible in their uncommunicability.

CHAPTER II

The Existence of Precausal Thinking

Of all the problems raised by the study of precausal thinking, the most important is undoubtedly that which questions the very existence of this form of thinking. This type of criticism is directed at the very structure of Piaget's theory. The present chapter will first review the controversial evidence, and will then seek to explain it.

Controversial Evidence

It is a fact that the replication of Piaget's experiments, or the examination of children through comparable methods, does not always elicit the primitive answers characteristic of precausal thinking.

Johnson and Josey (1931-1932), for instance, found no animism, finalism, artificialism, or egocentrism among six-year-old children. Yet they used, without change, all the techniques described by Piaget. Askar (1932) discovered only a few rare examples of animistic thinking among rather young children; his group of 714 subjects ranged from five to twelve years of age. Isaacs (1930), relying on the simple observations of children, noted that precausality was quite exceptional among children, and was akin to anything the adult could call upon when obliged to face problems exceeding his cognizance. On the other hand, she observed in these children a genuine interest in things of the physical world. The explanations given by the children were almost always adequate and clearly formulated. Mead (1932) observed no spontaneous animism among Manus children. She even emphasized the fact that some children readily rejected explanations suggested in animistic terms. Jahoda (1958b) too found very few animistic expressions in the explanation African children gave of a mechanical apparatus (a gramophone).

Deutsche (1937) added to a few questions taken directly from Piaget some ten simple physical experiments which children were asked to explain. She found that most explanations call upon physical and naturalistic concepts. Some types of precausal thinking never came to the fore, and others appeared so seldom that they could not validly be subjected to even a very rudimentary statistical analysis. In fact, only four types of explanations recurred frequently enough to warrant attention. Among these, only two were typical of precausal thinking: phenomenism and dynamism. The other two, mechanistic and logical explanations, already belonged to causal thinking and, as a matter of fact, accounted for most of the explanations offered, that is, approximately 62 per cent of the total responses.

Jones and Arrington (1945) have reached practically the same results by using Deutsche's problems with Negro and white American children. According to Deutsche, Huang in 1930 seems to have obtained similar results. Confronted with simple physical problems, natural phenomena, or feats of legerdemain, children resorted to naturalistic and physical explanations, even though simple and naïve, rather than to precausal relationships. Huang (1943) has indeed made that same observation in various ways over and over again. On the basis of previous investigations made in 1930 and 1935 and of an extensive review of other work in the same field, he postulated the existence of some forms of precausality, among which animism and dynamism were especially noted for their frequent appearance in the literature. On the other hand, some types of precausal thinking described by Piaget did not seem really to exist. Huang called particular attention to causality through participation, which he claimed never to have observed in the course of his experiments. Moreover, even under its animistic and dynamistic forms, precausal thinking would be neither typical, nor prevailing, nor universal among children. It would not even be exclusive, but would simply coexist with causal thinking. The instances of precausal thinking he was able to observe among his own children were very rare and often ambiguous. In his opinion, this would be the reason why manifestations of precausal thinking were readily noted: they were so infrequent and striking that they could not escape attention. Physical and naturalistic explanations were so commonplace that they were not even noticed. The illusion of the prevalence of precausal thinking would thus be accounted for.

In 1945, Huang and Lee noticed that only in a small proportion of cases did children regard inanimate objects as living; and even when they did so, they very often denied them anthropomorphic traits, such as the capacity to will, or to feel pain. Then Huang and Lee reverted to an idea already suggested by Bruce (1941) and proposed that the hypothesis of a general animistic tendency in the young child be rejected. The genesis of ideas would be explained rather by a principle of differentiation: at the start, the child would be in a so-called neutral state, which is not animistic; then, gradually, the animate-inanimate dichotomy would develop and become clearer, owing to definitions and mutual contrasts. Before reaching perfect differentiations, the child will most certainly make errors. The more an object shares the typical properties of living things, the greater will be the tendency to confuse it with these. But this should be seen as nothing more than an error analogous to that of a bird fleeing from a scarecrow. Nobody would indeed pretend that a bird is animistic; the scarecrow is not seen as a living thing distinct from the farmer: it is merely confused with him. Thus, in the same way, the child's primitive thinking would be neither animistic, nor precausal, but undetermined. Originating in this state of undifferentiation, two forms of thinking would develop in a simultaneous and parallel way: physical or causal thinking proper, and animistic, moralistic, dynamistic, or any other form of precausal thinking, patterned, according to Huang, upon social schemata and born of a contact with living beings. Huang does not understand why this paracausal thinking would constitute a universal tendency in the young child and would not be simply generated by social relationships, since, phylogenetically, physical concepts precede the magical, moralistic, artificialistic, or animistic explanations. As a matter of fact, the animal adapts to its physical environment and manipulates relationships within this physical world without forming, on this account, animistic, moralistic, or artificialistic conceptions. Why then should it not be the same ontogenetically? Why should not the child, during the first seven or eight years of his life, reach at least the functional level of the most rudimentary organisms? If all intellectual conceptions derive from experience—that is to say, from an adaptation of the organism to its environment—it would then seem normal that the concepts related to the physical world be above all of a physical nature.[1]

[1] It is amazing to note that so keen an investigator as Huang could be taken in by a gross confusion between the level of representational thinking, the only one directly involved in the present context, and the widely accepted level of sensorimotor adaptations, which directs the physical behavior of all animals and which children have already outgrown at the age of about two.

Children from seven to ten years of age have also been subjected to Huang's questionnaire by Klingberg (1957), who obtained similar results. He, in turn, challenged the existence of a general animistic tendency among very young children. Pananimism, he added, has never been verified empirically, since, according to Piaget himself, it appears at such an early age that children cannot be questioned successfully. Even before the age of seven, the child's thinking does not, as a matter of fact, seem to be fundamentally different from that of an adult. Although children may seem animistic, nothing proves the existence of primitive thinking as Piaget understood it, that is, completely animistic thinking. Of course, it should not be concluded, however, that the child experiences no difficulty in making a distinction between the living and the nonliving. On the contrary, such errors are frequent; but instead of progressing from universal animism toward a greater objectivity, mental development would be characterized rather by the transition from a state of total ignorance to a more accurate knowledge of reality.

Briefly, when it is impossible to find one or several types of precausal thinking described by Piaget, the idea of an essential difference in the thinking of child and adult is given up more or less completely or explicitly. In lieu of a typically precausal thinking in the child, it is considered preferable to assume the existence of a progressive differentiation of concepts, or that of a continual accumulation or development of knowledge. The differences between adults and children become purely quantitative differences, a state of affairs which is tantamount to a setback, because this was precisely the prevailing conception at the time Piaget propounded his explanation. Besides, are these hypotheses of differentiation and accumulation of knowledge really opposed to that of precausal thinking, or can they be substituted for it? As Jahoda (1958a) so aptly noted, these two new hypotheses postulate, at the start, the existence of an undetermined or neutral state, or of an initial state of ignorance, the definition of which is indeed completely avoided. Now, it is hard to imagine what this state of neutrality really represents when the child meets with reality. The only valid interpretation would imply, for instance, that undifferentiation causes the child to behave in a similar way when confronted with animate or with inanimate objects. This is precisely one of the main characteristics of animism, and consequently one of the most obvious forms of precausal thinking.

The ultimate rejection of this mode of thinking in the child is the more debatable when one considers that a number of investigations did seem to establish its existence. In addition to Piaget's experiments, there is the series of investigations carried out by Russell and Dennis, whose results unfailingly support the existence of various types of precausal thinking and various stages of animism, realism, or artificialism. The stages described by Piaget are met with again among children of normal intelligence (Russell and Dennis, 1939; Russell, 1940a; Dennis, 1942) as well as among mentally deficient adults or children, among children of American culture as well as among Zuni (Dennis and Russell, 1940) or Hopi (Dennis, 1943) children. When a child attributes life to inanimate objects, there is a close correspondence between this animism and some anthropomorphic manifestations (Russell, 1940b). Finally, a net decrease of the types of precausal thinking is always noted together with an increase in chronological or mental age. With reference to the particular case of animism, the one type of precausal thinking most frequently studied by Dennis and Russell, its almost complete disappearance is noted around the age of twenty (Russell et al., 1942). In 1938, Lerner (see Jahoda, 1958a) had observed a still more rapid decline of animism: very high around the ages of six or seven, it disappeared almost completely around ten or eleven. With a standardized questionnaire, perhaps even less systematic than those used by Dennis and Russell, Bruce (1941) nevertheless obtained the same results with a group made up of Negro and white children from a certain region of the United States: the four stages describing the evolution of animism were easily recognized. Klingensmith's results (1953) demonstrated the presence of genuine animism, despite the existence of a marked timelag between the manifestations of animism and anthropomorphism. Havighurst and Neugarten (1955) also found a high percentage of animism among the children of ten American Indian tribes. In a group of preschool children, Grigsby (1932) retraced Piaget's seventeen types of causality and, among these, the nine types of precausality. For her, therefore, there was no doubt about the reality of precausal thinking. Finally, Ausubel and Schiff (1954), while trying to study the influence of previous learning on the understanding of a simple physical phenomenon, found that the younger the child was, the more easily he accepted an explanation based on a false principle of causality. Briefly, the younger the child, the greater the tendency for him to consider two concomitant phenomena as causally related. It is therefore impossible not to acknowledge, even though the authors fail to do so, one of the most frequent types of precausal thinking, namely, phenomenistic causality. Zietz (see Huang, 1943) also made a similar observation when he noted among his pupils many instances of what Piaget calls circular theories. These circular theories consist in the consideration of causes and effects as totally reversible, and are thus clearly characteristic of precausal thinking.

In view of all these results, it is quite legitimate to conclude with Dennis (1942) that precausal concepts are truly autogenous and universal, since they can be observed among children who have never been trained to use them, as well as among children belonging to very different cultures, regions, and countries. But is this conclusion not in opposition to that inferred from the work of Deutsche, Huang, and Klingberg? In order to understand what may lead to such divergent results, it is indeed pertinent to examine, in studies of this type, the various conditions affecting the manifestation of causal thinking.

Conditions Affecting Causal Thinking

The factors influencing causal thinking naturally fall into three categories, depending upon the method of examination itself, the subjects examined, or the techniques of analysis.

METHODS OF EXAMINATION

It has often been noted that some techniques of questioning are perhaps better suited than others to bring out the real thinking of the child. It is also repeatedly claimed that some examiners are too easily given to guiding the child's reasonings in a preferred direction. With barely concealed malice, Huang (1943) feigned surprise in noting, on this point, that almost all investigations revealing precausal thinking had been conducted by European psychologists. British and American psychologists, excepting perhaps Russell and Dennis, almost never observed any manifestation of that primitive form of thinking. Isaacs (1930) even declared that those children examined by Piaget were subjected to conditions detrimental to the manifestation of their real ability. In her opinion, Piaget's clinical method is inadequate, the questions being too difficult or too suggestive. The child is often more capable than he shows himself to be when answering Piaget's type of questionnaires, since the questions appeal more to his imagination than to his intelligence. According to Deutsche (1937), the individual method forces the child to answer at any cost. Her reading of Piaget's work leaves her with the impression that his technique prompts the child to have recourse to imagination and to pure chance. The answers the child gives without spontaneity are easily tainted with precausality; but, then, nothing proves that he is thinking of natural phenomena in precausal terms. When in some experiments children tend to apply a specific type of precausal thinking to many different concepts, this is imputed to perseveration on the part of the child (Bruce, 1941; Huang, 1943). For instance, the fact that Russell (1940b) observed close concordance between concepts related to animism should not have led him to conclude that the child has general notions about life. His standardized questionnaire does not allow for the exploration of the real meaning of the child's answers. Therefore, the more plausible explanation, according to Bruce or Huang, would have been that he was dealing with a mere perseveration phenomenon.

It cannot be denied that the examination technique can influence the nature of the information gathered. Experimental proofs of this influence have often been sought. Bell (1954), for instance, obtained a smaller number of animistic answers when questionnaires used in the experiment offered a multiple choice rather than a simple alternative. Questions suggesting animism, supernaturalism, or dynamism bring out more precausal responses than other questions; and again, a question beginning with "why" is more suggestive than one thus formulated: "How is it that . . . " (Nass, 1956). Special instructions inviting, for instance, answers in the manner of those of a biologist or a poet can modify the frequency of precausal answers (Simmons and Gross, 1957).

Are these variations in the examination techniques sufficient to explain the divergence of results in the above-mentioned investigations? It would seem not, since the same techniques do not necessarily yield the same results. Piaget's individual method, when used by other psychologists, may fail to prompt the child to think in a precausal way. For instance, Askar

(1932) obtained an extremely low percentage of animism among children of five, six, and seven years of age. In the same way, Johnson and Josey (1931-1932) did not find any of the characteristics of precausal thinking among six-year-old children. The experiments by Russell and his co-workers (1942) show that the group administration of a questionnaire yields results comparable to those obtained through individual questioning. If one were to believe Askar, it would even be legitimate to conclude that group administration elicits more animism than the individual method. Yet, other investigators tend to ascribe to the use of a group technique the fact that so few manifestations of precausal thinking are expressed (Deutsche, 1937). Moreover, contrary to Piaget's expectations, the standardization of an experiment does not necessarily impoverish the results (Russell and Dennis, 1939). In short, no matter whether the examination technique is of the individual or collective type, very rigidly standardized or left to the examiner's free initiative, it does not seem decisively to determine the trend of the results. In consequence, the explanation of the divergences displayed in the results and conclusions of various investigations must be sought elsewhere.

Can the content of the examination possibly exert a decisive influence? This is implied by Isaacs (1930) when she states that in Piaget's technique the questions require too much knowledge, and thus call more upon the child's imagination than upon his intellectual resources. Deutsche (1937) takes up the same argument. Her experimental results seem to indicate that the type of reasoning is determined more by the nature of the question than by the age of the child, or by his level of general ability: different questions bring out a very variable number of causal or precausal answers, and the same child changes his type of reasoning with each of the questions. In addition to this, Nass (1956) notes that the number of precausal answers is larger or smaller according to whether the questions refer to phenomena familiar to the child, or to phenomena the cause of which is not accessible to the child's experience. Finally, Huang and Lee (1945) point out with some insistence that the percentage of animism varies with the type of objects involved. For them, this is another reason to reject the generality of various types of precausal thinking, and to consider Piaget's conclusions as invalid. Briefly, the occurrence of so-called precausal answers would be due to the fact that the problems given to children by some investigators are too difficult. These primitive answers would not correspond to the real thinking of the child, but would derive rather from his imagination and be the result of a simple experimental artifact.

Although apparently legitimate, this reasoning involves a number of illogical inferences, which we shall take up later. Let us emphasize at once, however, that the comparison of the problems used in various investigations does not support the hypothesis according to which the divergence of results derives from the difficulty or the content of problems. The same questions very often lead to dissimilar results. Johnson and Josey, Deutsche, Huang, Dennis, Russell, etc., all used Piaget's problems at one time or another, and yet they did not obtain similar results. When, for example, Dennis or Russell repeated Piaget's questions concerning the concept of life, they encountered many instances of animism. On the other hand, with the same problems, Huang, or Johnson and Josey found very little or no evidence of animism. Under these conditions, it can hardly be claimed that the questions asked determined the child's answers.

TYPE OF SUBJECTS

A second factor which could explain the diversity of results relates directly to the characteristics of the subjects submitted to this type of examination. Is it possible to identify some constant distinguishing factor either among subjects capable of precausal thinking, or among those who seemingly use this mode of thinking only accidentally? Even a superficial examination of various groups of children warrants the immediate rejection of some possibilities. The sex of children does not have any bearing: boys and girls always give explanations at a comparable level. Some differences are noted among subjects of varying socioeconomic strata (Deutsche, 1937), but these differences are relatively slight and often lack significance. It is indeed difficult to evaluate the equivalence of socioeconomic strata among samples drawn from populations which often differ in almost every other respect. Chinese or Africans, for instance, are hardly comparable to Americans or Europeans. It seems, however, that the number of subjects examined is almost always sufficient to provide an adequate representation of the various strata existing in each of the populations involved. When the number is not large, subjects of the middle strata are usually sought. Briefly, with few exceptions, the samples studied are sufficiently similar for valid comparisons. Neither does the cultural environment seem to have any influence on the results. Dennis and Russell, for instance, found much precausal thinking among American children, while Deutsche saw practically none. Mead (1932) observed no evidence of animism among children of an American Indian tribe, while Dennis and Russell, working with comparable tribes, arrived at completely opposite conclusions.

In fact, in the various investigations considered here, only one characteristic seems consistent enough to deserve attention: the age of the child. It is indeed worth noting that the great majority of investigators, undoubtedly for the sake of convenience, restrict their sample to schoolchildren, thus using subjects of at least six years of chronological age. Moreover, since the questionnaires are frequently administered to groups, the examiners must wait until the children can read and write, which further raises the minimal age of examination to eight or nine. Now, as a matter of fact, a certain relationship seems to exist between the presence of precausal thinking and the age of subjects: the more negative the results, the older the children submitted to the experiment. Deutsche, in particular, who voices much skepticism concerning the hypothesis of precausal thinking, draws her major conclusions from the examination of subjects all between eight and sixteen years of age. Under these conditions, how can she be amazed that she discovers so little evidence of precausal thinking? In the formulation of his hypotheses Piaget always claimed that precausal thinking, in its purest and most general form, exists only during the very first years of childhood, and recedes rather rapidly after the age of seven or eight. If precausal thinking persists after that age, it does so only occasionally, and chiefly in reference to phenomena which are still beyond the child's ability to understand.

The age of the subjects thus appears, in some cases, to constitute the major reason for the presence or absence of precausal thinking, but it cannot sufficiently explain all the divergences noted. Exceptions are too numerous to be simply dismissed. For instance, it is incomprehensible that Johnson and Josey did not find any trace of precausal thinking among children of only six years of age, or that Huang and Lee encountered very few animistic answers among children from three to eight, when Dennis and Russell still found a high percentage of these answers among subjects of twelve or thirteen. Hence, age can explain the exceptional character of some conclusions, but for a complete solution of this problem it is necessary to look elsewhere.

TECHNIQUES OF ANALYSIS

The last point to be considered deals with the techniques used by the various authors in their analyses of results. Here will probably be found the most important causes for the divergences observed. But this is also the most difficult factor to appraise, because the necessary details for the evaluation of the procedures of statistical analysis, or simply the evaluation of criteria for the classification of answers, are never completely given. Some indications, however, often make it possible to reconstitute, at least in a general way, the methods of analysis that may have been used.

First, when the various classifications adopted by each of the authors are examined, one can surmise the presence of much confusion over the meaning of the terms used. Precausal thinking, which in fact receives various names from those who study it, does not always seem to have the same connotation. Deutsche, for instance, takes exception to Piaget's classification; she claims that its application is too difficult: his seventeen types of causal thinking are too loosely defined, which makes them hard to distinguish, and the personal judgment of the examiner plays too large a role to provide minimal objectivity. Deutsche then suggests replacing this classification, judged inadequate, by a much simpler schema with only two categories: answers with a materialistic content in which explanations refer only to the activity of some material substance; and answers with a nonmaterialistic content involving a person, a spirit, or some force in the explanation of a material change. In this classification, only the answers belonging to the second category would correspond to precausal thinking. An examination of the type of answers Deutsche includes in each of these categories immediately discloses a fundamental error, sufficient to cast doubt upon a major part of her analyses and conclusions. Among the answers of the first category, the more mature ones, she places the explanations in terms of phenomenistic relationships, that is, explanations referring to a concomitant phenomenon which at times may hold no true causal relationship with the fact to be explained. Thus, to account for the fact that the flame of a candle dies out when covered with a glass jar, some children will simply refer to the smoke, or to the jar itself. Following Deutsche's criteria, these children are to be classified in the first category with those who give the correct explanation. It is nevertheless obvious that they do not understand the phenomenon at all, and merely link together two successive perceptions. They associate at random any elements of a situation and consider these associations as causal. The fact that the associated elements happen to belong to the material world gives the impression of objective causality. But is this not the very manifestation of a specific type of precausality preponderant among children, and which Piaget calls phenomenism? In lumping together these explanations with the more sophisticated answers, Deutsche clearly shows that she does not understand Piaget's position, and one may validly wonder whether similar errors were not committed in connection with other forms of precausal thinking. Not identifiable without referring to the original data, classification errors of this kind may easily explain the fact that so few instances of primitive thinking have been reported. A similar confusion seems to prevail in the case of Herzfeld and Wolf (see Huang, 1943), who exclude from all their tabulations the merely descriptive answers, even though these constitute approximately one third of the answers given by the six-year-old children examined. Huang's reports on his own experiments indicate that he also would have excluded phenomenistic, or descriptive answers from other categories of precausal thinking.

It is indeed a somewhat delicate matter to raise questions concerning the validity of all these authors' classifications and the legitimacy of their conclusions on the basis of just a few clues. But the criticisms of Piaget's theory are convincing only to the extent that they are based on comparable data. To us it seems, at least in a few cases, that this condition has not been met. A scrutiny of the original data would possibly help to eliminate this uncertainty, but this is not feasible. Only new experimentation can provide the elements necessary for the evaluation of this explanatory hypothesis.

The more strictly statistical aspect of the analysis of results also suggests other reasons for questioning the validity of some conclusions. If small differences are omitted, two general techniques of analysis can be identified. The *first* one consists in the global evaluation of all of the child's answers to a group of problems, all aiming at the determination of the presence or absence of a certain type of primitive thinking. In their questionnaire concerning animism, for instance, Dennis and Russell did not study in detail the answers given to their twenty problems, but instead sought to identify, through the examination of the answers and explanations given, the criteria used by the child in his classification of this or that object as living or nonliving. According to that technique, even a correct answer can be classified at a lower level if its apparent value is derived solely from the fact that the criterion used by the child does not happen to include the particular object under consideration. For instance, an answer in which a *stone* is denied life because the child does not see its usefulness is not necessarily a better answer than that in which the *sun* is endowed with life because the child acknowledges its heating or lighting functions. The really primitive character of such a criterion can therefore leave the subject, despite some apparently good answers, at an inferior level regarding the concept of life. With this method of analysis, which is the exact replication of that of Piaget, Dennis and Russell have no trouble in identifying the various types of infantile primitive thinking.

The *second* technique is much more analytical, and more closely resembles the item-analysis methods used in test construction. It consists in determining, for each question, the frequency of answers belonging to the precausal level. Thus Huang and Lee (1945), Klingensmith (1953), and Klingberg (1957) compute the number of animistic answers relating to each one of the objects dealt with in their questionnaires. Each time the child attributes life, or an anthropomorphic trait, to an inanimate object, an error is noted. The data derived from such an analysis do not relate to the behavior of each child answering a series of questions, but to the reaction of a group of children to each one of the objects mentioned during the examination. Instead of showing how many subjects regard a certain number of inanimate objects as endowed with life, this technique will yield only the total percentage of errors for each particular object, thus making it impossible to discover directly whether these errors, when applying to various objects, are made by the same or by different subjects.

The comparison of the results obtained by these two techniques brings into focus a phenomenon which is indeed remarkable for its permanence, even though it seems to have escaped the attention of all those (Deutsche, 1937; Huang, 1943; Strauss, 1951; Voeks, 1954; Jahoda, 1958a, 1958b) who have at times tried to explain the disagreement between the various investigators. Yet it is obvious that the use of the first technique by Russell (1940a, 1940b), Dennis and Russell (1940), and Bruce (1941) has always yielded results similar to those of Piaget, while the second technique has consistently led authors like Deutsche (1937), Huang and Lee (1945), Jones and Arrington (1945), Klingensmith (1953), and Klingberg (1957) to opposite conclusions. Here is surely another explanation of the various reports of conflicting data: the technique of analysis obviously has a strong influence on the results to be expected.

But, then, what of the respective validity of these two techniques? Perhaps they are not equally applicable to the analysis of precausal thinking. The question may be raised, for instance, as to whether the first technique does not unduly, and in too artificial a way, bring out the manifestations of pre-causal thinking. It could be, on the contrary, that the second technique has an attenuating or masking effect on these manifestations. As a matter of fact, there are two main reasons for believing that the second technique does not allow for the disclosure of the subject's real level of thinking. In the first place, this technique completely neglects the reasons invoked by the child in justification of his answers. It is based strictly on the subject's first answer, that is, "yes" or "no." Huang himself regards as dangerous a procedure which dispenses with an inquiry into the real meaning of the answers. Many reasons may at one time or another induce the child to answer in a particular way, and these reasons are not all related to his intellectual activity. Unless the child is brought to justify his answers, it will never become possible to discriminate between those that are based upon a real reasoning process and those related simply to chance, fantasy, perseveration, or to what Binet and Simon (1908, p. 326) called "*n'importequisme*" ("anythingness"). Moreover, the identification of the truly correct answers from among those still linked to some precausal mode of thinking is made possible only through the examination of the reasons given by the child. Indeed, it must be fully understood that even primitive reasoning can often lead to a true-to-reality conclusion. These are important factors for which the second method of analysis does not afford an explicit and direct control.

Secondly, due to its exaggeratedly analytical character, this technique neglects a fundamental aspect of Piaget's explanation. In attempting to study problems independently from each other, one pays no attention to the child's attitude toward the questionnaire as a whole. Now, all children belonging to an intermediate level, that is, those who function neither at the pure precausal level nor at a perfect causal level, will answer in very different ways according to the problem offered. Facing a relatively simple question, or a question close enough to their daily experience, they remain capable of causal reasoning, while a more difficult question immediately brings them back to a more primitive mode of thinking. In spite of some correct answers, these subjects obviously still reason in a precausal way when confronted with an unusual or unexpected difficulty. In order to make a correct diagnosis concerning the child's real level of thinking, it is absolutely necessary to use a series of questions analyzed globally, for even perfect answers are often steeped in a context of very primitive thinking. An analysis based only on the results obtained on each individual item of a questionnaire does not reveal anything about the actual phenomenon and easily fosters the illusion that there is only a very small proportion of precausal answers. Thus, because Huang and Lee (1945) find that some objects are very seldom regarded as living, they are led to deny the generality of the animistic tendency: the *pencil*, for example, is taken to be alive in only 9.5 per cent of the cases, the *stone* in 9.8 per cent, the *river* in 17.2 per cent, etc. On the other hand—and Huang does not lay more stress than he must on this fact—some objects are very frequently considered as living: the *moon* and the *watch* are said to be living in proportions of 72.2 and 72.1 per cent each. If it can be assumed that the subjects who give life to the moon and to the watch are the same ones, this means that 72 per cent of Huang's subjects offer evidence of animism, at least in two instances in the course of the examination. Piaget would certainly not hesitate to regard this fact as a sure indication of primitive thinking. Since the subjects who give life to the various objects are probably not the same ones, the number of children manifesting some animism, at least once during the examination, should greatly exceed the three quarters in Huang's sample. Seen in this perspective, Huang's results stand in clear contradiction with his conclusions. The same remarks apply indeed to the conclusions of all those who have used this same method of analysis. Considering the assurance with which Piaget's theory has been summarily rejected, we may well deplore the fact that the severity of the criticism of these authors too often exceeds the acuteness of their analyses. It would have been so much more natural to adopt Piaget's own technique, since all these investigators were admittedly aiming at the verification of his hypotheses. In short, when the results of different experiments are to be compared, a minimum of constancy in the manipulation of experimental procedures must be preserved. Otherwise, chances are that artificial differences will appear, which are mainly due to the heterogeneity of methods.

In conclusion, the problem of the reality of precausal thinking is far from being definitely solved. The investigations of Piaget, Dennis, Russell, Grigsby, Lerner, and Havighurst and Neugarten support the assumption that such a mode of thinking exists in the child; but there remains a greater number of experiments yielding contradicting results. The examination of the various factors capable of explaining these conflicting data leads to hypotheses which cast some doubt mostly on the negative conclusions. When no instance of precausal thinking is observed among children, the reason is frequently that the subjects examined are too old; or else that the concept of precausality does not have the same connotation for different investigators; or, finally, that the techniques of analysis cunningly do away with indications of primitive thinking. The mere formulation of these hypotheses, however, does not solve the problem; it merely allows us to state it in more specific terms. The real solution would call for a return to the initial data; only a fresh re-examination of the protocols would make the assessment of these explanatory hypotheses possible. Since this is not practical, the only remaining course is

to undertake a new experiment which will provide the data
necessary for the evaluation of all opinions concerning this
fundamental problem of the existence of precausal thinking.

CHAPTER III

The Infantile Character of Precausal Thinking

Even if we assume the existence of precausal thinking, we must still ask whether this mode of thinking is truly characteristic of the child, or whether, as suggested by Hazlitt (1930) and Huang (1943), it is not simply a method used by both children and adults of approaching certain problems, a method which would coexist with more mature types of reasoning. This second question raises a problem, perhaps of less consequence, but nonetheless troublesome for Piaget's theory. A rather large number of investigations have revealed the presence of very persistent traces of animistic thinking among adults, and even among old people. These data cast some real doubt on the infantile character of this mode of thinking and, through generalization, on that of all modes of thinking hitherto considered as primitive.

For instance, Hazlitt reports that whenever adults are confronted with unfamiliar problems, they make the same errors as children. She therefore comes to the conclusion that Piaget has clearly exaggerated the difference between the logic of the child and that of the adult. Replicating with adults Piaget's experiments on verbal understanding between partners, Abel (1932) also observed much juxtaposition, syncretism, and reversal of order between causes and effects, all traits specific to prelogical thinking. Huang, Chen, and Yang (see Huang, 1943) found that Chinese children and adults of sixteen to thirty years of age gave the same type of answers: phenomenism and naïve physicalism. But it is the work of Dennis and Mallenger (1949) which has cast the most serious doubt on one of the best-defined forms of precausal thinking, namely, animistic thinking. Moved by the desire to know how adults would answer questions analogous to those usually given children, they presented a group of old people of seventy and over with a questionnaire concerning the concept of life. To their great surprise, 75 per cent of these subjects ascribed life to a few inanimate objects. Following this first experiment, Dennis (1953) gave the same questionnaire to a group of college and university students and obtained similar, although less pronounced, results. As may well be imagined, these data have been regarded with skepticism; yet, they were instrumental in creating an interest in the study of this problem. Thus Crannell (1954), Bell (1954), Lowrie (1954), Voeks (1954), Dennis (1957), and Simmons and Gross (1957) have repeated analogous experiments, always with college and university students, often even with their own students, and have finally been led to the same observations: there always is an impressive number of subjects who classify some inanimate objects with living beings.

Among these authors, only Lowrie and Voeks refuse to see in these answers a manifestation of real animistic thinking. It is, however, difficult to know whether their criticisms also apply to animism as observed among children, since their investigations deal exclusively with adult subjects, and their conclusions do not, at least explicitly, go beyond the scope of

this restricted group. On the basis of the analysis of the protocols, and the observations made during the course of the experiments, they reach the conclusion that the fact of attributing life to an inanimate object is not a sure indication of
animism. The ambiguous character of this hypothetical animism is frequently manifested through some spontaneous
remarks from the subjects. For instance, in Voeks's experiment, half of the students attributing life to the *ocean* admitted that they included in the word *ocean* all beings living
therein. Or else some subjects stated that the *sun* was alive,
but they immediately added that the word "alive" did not
have the same meaning as applied to human beings. Such responses cannot easily be compared with those of children and
involve much more subtle distinctions. A child who regards
the *sun* as endowed with life relies upon the fact that it gives
light and heat, or upon the fact that it moves about in the sky.
If questioned about the *ocean*, he probably would also refer
to its usefulness, or its movement, to say it is alive. Even
though it is difficult to prove it, the analysis of all these experiments creates the clear impression that adult animism does
not have the same meaning as that of children. Accordingly,
Voeks and Lowrie are seemingly justified in attempting to
tone down the dramatic aspect of some conclusions, by looking for the factors which would explain the occurrence of
these animistically flavored answers.

The arguments called upon are numerous, but of unequal
value. Lowrie is convinced that errors of classification are not
indications of real animism, since the subjects, when justifying their answers, never attribute a soul, a mind, or a con-
science to inanimate objects which they regard as living. The
errors would stem rather from the fact that the students are
profoundly ignorant about the criteria of life, an ignorance
which is singularly stable since even a series of lectures, aiming at the development of their understanding of the distinc-

tion between the living and the nonliving, failed to prevent these errors. According to Lowrie, real animism is consequently reduced to the attribution of anthropomorphic properties to some inanimate objects, a delimitation which considerably restricts the extension usually given to the term. On the other hand, the observation that students are ignorant of the criteria for distinguishing living and nonliving does not per se constitute an explanation. This is a mere statement of fact which is equivalent to the assertion that students make errors of classification. But it is not a statement that can be used to refute the existence of adult animism.

Voeks, in denying the animistic character of the errors made by her subjects, points to the fact that these subjects do not call upon biological criteria (e.g., capacity to grow, to reproduce, to die, etc.). According to her, real animism is rare. When an inanimate object is said to be alive, one should speak of animism only if these biological criteria are invoked. All other cases would not involve genuine animism, but could be explained by other factors. For example, an object may be said to be alive because it has some attribute of a living organism. When the attribution is not that of a specific biological characteristic, Voeks infers that it is not an instance of real animism, but of a simple lack of logic. Indeed, because a living object may have some practical use, or because it is capable of motion, the subject sometimes falsely concludes that any useful or mobile object is alive. It is not easy, however, to understand why such an error would not be an indication of genuine animism. At any rate, it is impossible not to realize that the logical confusion implied in this form of animism, which Voeks rejects, is almost identical with Piaget's description of the child's animistic reasoning. Briefly, Voeks's argument, quite contrary to its objective, is tantamount to a denial of the genuineness of the child's animism, and thus reserves to the adult the only possible form of real animism. In fact, only adults are capable of using specific biological criteria to justify their animistic answers. The very recourse to these criteria represents a highly sophisticated form of thinking, which, in any case, does not yet exist in the child. Piaget (1926) is very explicit on this point:

> . . . for adult common sense, two types of criterion aid this distinction [between living and inert bodies]. First, the fact that living bodies are born, grow and die. But curiously enough none of the children we tested ever invoked this criterion. Sometimes, indeed, the child told us that plants "grow" (poussent) but this was for him a way of regarding them as endowed with spontaneous movement, and the movement of growth was thus conceived as of the same order as the movement of the clouds or of the sun [p. 229].

Voeks's intentions are much better served by the other factors she has noted. The apparent animism in some answers could often be explained by a lack of information, a flaw in reasoning, or a semantic confusion. For instance, the subject for whom a *pearl* is alive because it belongs to the living oyster shows an obvious lack of knowledge. On the other hand, the subject who attributes life to the *sun* on the factual basis that it is essential to life gives evidence of a rather lame type of reasoning. Finally, many animistic answers can be ascribed to the ambiguity of the word "living." Many of Voeks's subjects admit that "living" simply means "real" or "existing." One should not therefore be surprised that these subjects consider inanimate objects to be alive. It is to be noted, moreover, that the word "living" is used in a multitude of metaphorical expressions: we speak of a living language, a living faith or religion, a living portrait, etc. Besides, as noted by Lowrie, the language used by adults is studded with anthropomorphic terms, without any implication of real belief in anthropomorphism. The learned adult is particularly sensitive to such analogical language, and it is probable that many answers given by students are misleading reflections of this use of figurative speech.

These last arguments are indeed very pertinent, but they offer only an indication of the real explanation. In all the foregoing cases, it seems that the animism observed among adults was artificially induced by the various experimental conditions, and consequently does not at all correspond to that existing in the child. The reasons for such an explanation are numerous. In the first place, the questions given to adults always differ greatly from those given to children. Most of the time, the list of items presented includes only inanimate objects. Some objects are especially difficult (e.g., *seed, atom*), and could even give rise to many a philosophical discussion. When the items used are more trivial (e.g., *pearl, sea, flower, sun,* etc.), the problem is then readily made more complex by questions concerning the existence of some anthropomorphic traits in these objects (e.g., *does the pearl feel the flow of water, does the sea know the location of ships, does the fading flower feel somewhat depressed,* etc.), and the subject is generally not informed that he must make a distinction between metaphorical and scientific language. It also happens that due to the way some questions are formulated, certain elements induce the subject to look for refined distinguishing criteria. Thus the subject, who is first questioned about the possible life of an *unlit match,* and immediately thereafter about that of the *same match which had just been lit,* is almost forced to give a different answer; he will then have recourse to some subtle way of reasoning, which he will thereafter attempt to apply to subsequent objects. Especially with a questionnaire of this kind, which always favors negative answers even in the case of real living objects, it is normal for the subject to hesitate before answering invariably in the same fashion. Ordinarily, when the questions offer a simple choice between two possible

THE PROBLEM OF PRECAUSALITY

answers, care is taken to provide for some alternation in the sequence. This is why, in such instances, the subject who is familiar with the classic type of questionnaire will soon notice that his answers are always the same, and will immediately take advantage of a more equivocal object to modify the direction of his answers. Experimental conditions sometimes induce the operation of this factor. Some experiments have in fact taken the form of an academic examination. In such a context, it is easy enough to understand why a student does not dare resist all suggestions made by the teacher. He does not suspect the naïve turn of the questions asked, and, as Lowrie remarks, he tries not to be caught in the snare.

In conclusion, another point should be stressed to show that the child's animism does not have the same meaning as that of the adult. Most investigations of children have disclosed that the different modes of precausal thinking disappear with the increase in chronological age. Even in Deutsche's and Huang's work where manifestations of these modes of thinking were sometimes very rare, the same phenomenon could be observed. If the animism found among adults were of the same nature, this phenomenon would be difficult to explain. How would it be possible to understand why Dennis and Russell, for instance, at first observed a decrease in the animism of children as they grew up, and then, in subsequent investigations with adults, noted the reappearance and persistence of animism? Short of postulating the existence of an unprecedented type of evolution specific to this aspect of mental development, they should at least have surmised that animism in the child and in the adult does not have the same connotation.

The question could be raised why none of these authors, in order to explain the fact that adult subjects give "animistic" answers, has thought of resorting to the convenient hypothesis of a regression to infantile modes of mental functioning, as the case is likely to be with some older subjects who have become senile or have started to deteriorate mentally, or in general with adults suffering from various pathological states or subjected to momentary conditions of stress (e.g., extreme fatigue, highly charged emotional situations, etc.). But this omission is, in our opinion, easily understandable when one considers the astonishingly large number of "animistic" answers yielded by adults and also when some thought is given to the concept of regression itself. It is a fact, on the one hand, that the percentages reported by the various authors are much too large—they reach about 50 in most cases and may even go up to 75 or 95—to be attributable to such specific factors as senility, mental deterioration, psychological stress, pathological conditions, and the like. On the other hand, it is not possible to invoke the phenomenon of regression in this context without admitting *ipso facto* that the type of behavior under consideration has already been extinguished in the normal adult; this would be the equivalent of conceding the very fact which this argument meant to question, that is the infantile character of precausal thinking. And even if it were granted that the process of regression is actually involved in some cases of adult animism, it should be emphasized that regression is not to be confounded with the mental oscillation observable in the normal children of intermediary stages and, most of all, that adult "regressive" behavior is never the mere replica of the corresponding behavior in the normal child, in spite of evident similarities between them.

CHAPTER IV

The Existence of Stages in Intellectual Development

This is not the place for a minute discussion of the highly debatable question of the existence of stages in mental development. Yet this thorny issue, even though not specific to precausal thinking, cannot be completely evaded. Three main reasons may account for the frequent hesitations and even refusals to admit the existence of stages: the considerable overlapping in age found in all types of answers; the apparent continuity suggested by the absence of gaps or plateaus in the developmental curve; and, finally, the relative inconsistency with which the same subject will explain the same phenomenon.

No attempt will be made to consider all the factors involved in this complex concept of stage, nor shall we attempt to provide a definite answer to this difficult problem. The conclusions reached at the Geneva symposium (Osterrieth et al., 1955), devoted specifically to taking stock of our present knowledge of this matter, demonstrate with sufficient clarity the utopian character of such a pretense. The discussion concluded with the explicit acknowledgment that psychology did not yet have enough empirical data to validate or invalidate the hypotheses supporting the use of this theoretical tool of analysis. It is nevertheless legitimate to study the arguments most commonly offered by those who deny the reality of developmental stages which Piaget proposed on the basis of his research on children's thinking.

The first argument emphasizes the overlapping of these so-called stages in the age series (Deutsche, 1937; Bruce, 1941; Huang, 1943). Whenever they occur too frequently to be attributed to mere chance, the various types of answers described by Piaget come from children of all ages. The development of causal thinking should therefore not be conceptualized in terms of stages. At no age is it possible to classify all answers in the same category, and each age level amost always includes answers belonging to other stages. Some types of answers are in fact so frequent that they lose all discriminative value. In short, a legitimate use of the concept of stages would, according to these authors, almost require that all children of the same age give the same type of answers. Such reasoning is, to say the least, peculiar. It is tantamount to assuming that all children of the same chronological age should have the same level of intellectual maturity. Is it necessary to emphasize the arbitrariness of such a postulate, when psychology constantly accumulates new evidence demonstrating the existence of tremendous individual differences in the mental functioning of children of the same age, and in the rhythm of each child's development? The concept of stages rather involves, on the contrary, some foreseeable overlapping in the age series, if these stages are really to reveal intellectual progress. For instance, when a given stage represents the normal maturity of ten-year-old children, it means, in the first place, that only a certain percentage of ten-year-old children are in this stage; in the second place, that this stage of functioning has also been reached by precocious children of nine or eight years of age; and, finally, that some retarded children of eleven or twelve years of age have not yet reached this stage. It would indeed be abnormal if all children of the same chronological age were at the same stage of development. The optimum span of such overlapping is rather difficult to determine; yet a relatively simple statistical technique, already used for the solution of an analogous problem (Laurendeau and Pinard, 1957), could possibly be applied here. Using the data of the normal distribution curve, one has only to count the number of children who reach the intellectual maturity specific to each age level one year, two years, etc., in advance of or later than the norm. Such a tabulation would show that the overlapping of stages is large. One would then have to compare the results of the various investigations in order to check the extent to which the span of overlapping conforms with the theoretical norm, or goes beyond it. Such a study would be of great interest, but need not be considered here because the aim of the argument outlined above is precisely to exclude any overlapping, an argument which in any case cannot be maintained.

Russell (1940a, 1940b) could have raised a much more subtle objection. By grouping his subjects according to mental age (Kuhlman-Anderson test) rather than chronological age, he obtained a correlation of .59 between mental age and the stage of animism. So even under these conditions, there is a noticeable overlapping: children of the same mental age do not all give the same type of answers. Would one, then, be justified in concluding that stages are not a good indication of intellectual maturity, or that they do not correspond to the various phases of mental development? A person who accepted such a conclusion without reservations would have to have a rather blind faith in the value of the mental ages provided by intelligence tests. This is not the place to question the validity of these commonly used measurements. Their analytic and artificial character has been emphasized too often to require further reiteration. As Piaget and Inhelder, for instance, pointed out on several occasions, these tests measure only the end product of intellectual activity, but they completely disregard the internal dynamics of mental operation. One would be ill-advised to draw definite conclusions, on the basis of test results, about the quality of the reasoning process or about the fundamental nature of intellectual maturity. Therefore, the comparison of the mental age of children, as determined by the usual type of psychometric test, with the various stages to which they belong according to a diagnostic examination such as that of Piaget, should not be expected to yield a very high correlation. Those two types of instruments explore partial, and also very different, aspects of the child's mental activity, and neither instrument can by itself form the basis for valid conclusions regarding the totality of what is conventionally called, by a term very difficult to define, the level of intellectual maturity. Briefly, it is unwarranted to make the *a priori* assumption that results formulated in terms of mental ages rather than in terms of stages of development yield more information about the maturity of a child.

The second argument closely resembles the first one and can be refuted in the same way. The fact that there is a gradual progression of mean percentages, spaced out through the age series, has led some writers (Deutsche, 1937; Huang, 1943) to believe that causal thinking, for instance, develops continuously, that is, without revealing the gaps that the very concept of stages involves. But this impression is due precisely to the inevitable overlapping that has just been discussed. For one particular subject, the passage from one stage to another may be somewhat abrupt; but since these changes do not always occur at the same moment in all subjects, these individual spurts become less evident when the children are grouped. Accordingly, the mean rhythm of evolution does not always reflect individual rhythms. Only a longitudinal study could provide precise information on the rate of progress of successive stages. Such a study is not yet available; therefore, the second objection is no more valid than the first one.

The third argument is used more often. A large number of investigations have shown that the level of answers varies according to the nature of the problems to be solved. Dennis (1942), from observations made on his daughter, noted that artificialism did not vanish simultaneously in regard to all objects, but persisted longer in regard to those items the origin of which the child had to make up. Deutsche (1937), Huang and Lee (1945), Klingensmith (1953), Klingberg (1957), and also Russell and Dennis in all their investigations end up with similar results. But while some of these authors (Russell and Dennis) accept this fact as a normal phenomenon, others (Deutsche and Huang) use it as a new argument to reject the concept of stages. As a matter of fact, for Deutsche and Huang, the various types of causality are too specifically linked with the nature of the questions; consequently, the level of answers is determined more by the content of the problems than by the child's age. Thus, causal thinking would not be a general attitude, because the child's explanations do not always indicate the same type of reasoning. In support of this contention, Deutsche (1937, p. 94) noted that the correlations yielded by the split-half method (odd-even) were relatively low: .73 and .74 for each of the two parts of her questionnaire. This is a very debatable argument. Such coefficients could as easily be taken to demonstrate the existence of a relatively high degree of consistency in the answers. Indeed, three pages earlier, when discussing the reliability of her questionnaire, Deutsche had no qualms about deriving great satisfaction from the same coefficients: in fact, she found them to be rather high, granted the fact that the questions were neither standardized nor ranked according to difficulty. However, one cannot logically consider the same coefficient as a proof of both consistency and inconsistency.

In this point of view, one would attribute a general mode of thinking to the child only if he attacked all sorts of different problems by invariably reasoning in the same way. If, at times, he thinks in a primitive fashion, and at other times like an adult, his primitive answers are the result of a simple experimental artifact, namely, the excessive difficulty of the problems. The argument could easily be reversed; the fact that some problems are extremely easy or very familiar could be used to explain the adultlike answers given by the child. The understanding of an easy question does not require a high level of development. On the other hand, if the child is too familiar with a question, he may recall ready explanations which actually allow him to dispense with the use of his real thinking abilities and with demonstrating his spontaneous level of reasoning. In short, when one wants to find out a child's true capacities, it is always preferable to confront him with new and sufficiently difficult problems to avoid restricting him to inferior forms of reasoning.

In any case, it is completely illogical to demand that the child always reason exactly in the same way when attacking different problems. Such a requirement would certainly run counter to Piaget's conception of stages. Carried to extremes, this argument would imply, for instance, that the child considered all objects as alive until the time when all traces of animism should abruptly disappear. The existence of a general animistic tendency in the child would be recognized only if a sudden change occurred in the course of development, without evidence of any intermediate stage between absolute animism and its complete disappearance. The evolution which Piaget describes calls, on the contrary, for a series of stages intervening between those two extremes. These stages correspond to levels of conceptualization which come increasingly closer to objective thinking, and their presence is indicated by a progressive decrease in the initial animism. It is therefore quite natural that the first objects which lose their animistic character are precisely those with which the child is most familiar, which he has handled frequently, and the lifelessness of which he has most readily experienced. Animism would thus persist for a more or less prolonged period depending upon the nature of the objects. At the end of this evolution, the only animated objects are those which the child knows less about, and which are more distant and divorced from his concrete experience. This, however, is no reason for denying the generality of the initial animistic tendency. The same argument, moreover, applies to each type of precausal thinking. Artificialism will disappear sooner in relation to those objects whose real nature the child can ascertain through experience. Similarly, the disappearance of dynamism will be delayed to the extent to which the lifelessness of things is difficult to grasp. This fact no doubt is responsible for the illusion that the type of reasoning is specifically determined by the nature of problems. In fact, it is not the problem which imposes a mode of reasoning on the child, but rather his actual level of development, and this level depends as much upon his intellectual maturity as upon his experience with objects in his environment. Contrary to Isaac's opinion, such a conception does not necessarily attribute too much importance to maturation: maturation is a necessary condition of development, but is not per se sufficient. The child's intellect must also interact with surrounding things. It is to the extent to which the external world comes to clash with concepts already established in his mind that the child will be forced to modify these concepts and thus develop intellectually. In relation to familiar objects in his immediate environment, the child's conceptions will become objective sooner, and this phenomenon will manifest itself externally in the level of his reasoning which will vary according to the problem.

To summarize, none of the arguments offered can justify the rejection of the concept of stages. On the contrary, this concept readily accounts for observations of overlapping age levels, for the absence of plateaus in the mean developmental curve, and even for a certain variability in the level of answers given by the same child.

In conclusion, let it be noted that the crucial problem has never been approached by any of those who have chosen to reject the concept of stages. The real problem concerns the constancy in the sequential order of the child's various forms of behavior. This constancy constitutes the fundamental character of any stage scale and, among the five criteria offered by Piaget, it is the one most generally accepted as necessary in all the theories of stages developed to this date. Piaget (see Osterrieth et al., 1955) gives the following definition of this primordial character:

> . . . in dealing with stages, the order of successive types of behavior is to be considered as constant, that is, a given characteristic will not appear before another in a certain number of subjects, and after another in a different group of subjects. When there is such alternation, the characteristics involved therein cannot be used to identify stages [p. 24].

In order to verify the existence of this criterion, one must inevitably resort to a longitudinal study. This is no doubt the reason why those who have rejected the theory of stages have always deemed it sufficient to bring in accessory motives, which often were only pseudo motives. Russell is the only one who, when studying the reliability of his questionnaire, offers partial data on the succession of stages: a second examination of his subjects, after a three-month interval, revealed that 64 per cent remained in the same stage; among the 24 per cent who showed any progress, 54 per cent progressed only one stage further, 34 per cent two stages, 9 per cent three stages, and 3 per cent four stages. From this, Dennis cautiously concludes that the scale of animism propounded by Piaget is most probably a real scale, that is, a scale according to which the subjects successively go through all stages of animism as they get older. This is only a partial corroboration, however, and the final demonstration calls for longitudinal studies.

PART II

The Experiment

Although deliberately limited and therefore incomplete, our discussion so far has clearly shown that the initial issues have by no means been solved. None of the objections raised against Piaget's thesis escape criticism, and all points of view remain debatable. The experiment to be described aims at the clarification of most of these questions and, as far as possible, we shall attempt to draw definite conclusions. Its three immediate objectives are (1) the verification of the existence of precausal thinking, (2) the control of the sequence of the stages described by Piaget, (3) and the determination of the age at which each stage is reached. While the experimental design adopted here is limited to the consideration of these specific problems, it nevertheless provides some answers to questions beyond the scope of this study, and some of these issues cannot be totally neglected. Let us mention, for instance, the problem of the exclusively infantile character of precausal thinking, or again the critical problems of the transitivity of stages and the continuity of intellectual development.

The following section is specifically devoted to the description of the experiment proper. Its three chapters deal respectively with the preparation of the questionnaires, the selection of the sample, and finally the conditions of testing and the methods of analysis.

CHAPTER V

Preparation of the Experimental Questionnaires

Aiming at the verification of Piaget's conclusions, the present study is but a systematic replication of his main experiments, under conditions conforming more closely to the requirements of the experimental method. It seems altogether useless to try to invent new experiments, which would indeed make comparisons impossible. Were there serious reasons for believing that Piaget's findings depend solely upon the nature of the questions submitted to the child, it would be in order to formulate new problems. But, as already noted, this hypothesis of Deutsche and Huang is not supported by the facts. Moreover, it must be admitted that Piaget has drawn so largely upon the possible repertory of the most instructive topics that it would be uselessly burdensome, if not impossible, to work out equivalents. In spite of these deliberate limitations, the present experiment still offers many points of interest justifying such a replication: the examination of children from a milieu different enough to refute the objection that answers have a regional character; the use of a larger group in order to counteract idiosyncrasies inherent in a child's explanations; and such rigorous objectivity in formulating the questions, as to preclude decisive or undue influences on the part of the examiner.

Criteria for the Selection of Questionnaires

The number and variety of the experiments presented by Piaget in his two main books devoted to precausal thinking (1926, 1927) made the choice extremely difficult. There are at least forty different questionnaires, all of them most ingenious. An attempt to repeat them all would have been purely utopian. To be able to stress, more than Piaget himself has done, the magnitude and the variety of the groups to be examined, it was a practical necessity to reduce the original number of experiments. It is also important to point out that this investigation formed an integral part of a project of much larger scope; this project aimed at retracing the main phases of the development of reasoning in all the basic domains of thought. Accordingly, the child's precausal beliefs could not be given excessive importance in relation to all the other aspects of mental development.

It therefore seemed reasonable to restrict the number of tests to the exact number of concepts to be studied, provided these tests constituted a reliable sample of Piaget's investigations of the child's various beliefs. Thus, instead of using the wealth of tests that Piaget employed to check, and by variety countercheck, observations proper to each one of these several beliefs, we considered it sufficient to use for each of them a single questionnaire, but drawn up with the care required to yield the valid results hoped for. Piaget's work may readily be divided into six sections, reviewing, in turn, the child's realism, animism, and artificialism, his explanation for mechanical and natural movement (dynamism), and finally his prediction and understanding of certain elementary physical laws. Of these six sections, only the tests on mechanical motions had to be eliminated *a priori*: these tests, as Piaget himself admits, are subject to hazard and their usefulness is questionable for an examination which, among other things, is meant to be normative. More particularly, there seems to be a very marked difference between the interest boys and girls show in such questions, and consequently in the level of the explanations they offer. In fact, with respect to the understanding of mechanical problems, girls seem to be two to three years behind the boys. Of course, this timelag does not diminish the significance of the answers obtained: the solutions offered by girls and boys always remain a source of valuable information concerning the child's thinking. In all probability, systematic experimentation would even demonstrate that these mechanical concepts follow the same evolution in both sexes, though they appear earlier in boys than in girls. If, however, one is interested in determining the age at which the various stages of intellectual evolution are reached, it is legitimate to eliminate at the start those questions which are known to elicit differences between boys and girls.

This does not mean that sex differences should be ignored; they could, on the contrary, even make the subject of a specific investigation. But in a partly normative study of mental development, factors extrinsic to the child's reasoning powers, such as a special interest in certain kinds of problems or greater experience with them, must be avoided, lest they obscure the subject's abilities and reduce the scope of the results. Take, for instance, a problem which is solved, on the average, at the age of seven by boys and of nine by girls. In order to establish the normal age at which this problem is understood by children in general, the two groups of subjects would be combined: the result would be a mean age of eight, which in reality would be incorrect for both groups. It is therefore preferable to choose problems in which boys and girls manifest the same interest from the beginning, and in relation to which they have had comparable personal experiences. If, in spite of such precautions, the analysis of results reveals differences between the sexes, it is then easier to conclude that these differences derive from factors intrinsic to mental operation. If the results obtained from boys and girls do not differ, it must obviously be recalled that care has been taken to eliminate, *a priori,* such extrinsic elements from the tests as would have been likely to lead to differences attributable to sex. Under such conditions, objections would necessarily have to be made to extending findings derived from the tests to problems of a more specialized content relating to attitudes or interests specific to one sex.

After having eliminated all items involving mechanics, one still must select the most illustrative type of problems in each of the other five topics. Various theoretical as well as practical criteria codetermined this choice. On the one hand we preferred to retain those tests which, according to Piaget's data, provide particularly clear-cut indications of an evolution, but which are nevertheless spread enough in time to remain observable in spite of inevitable gaps in the sampling. On the other hand, we rejected all those questions which bear upon phenomena that are too complex or of no interest to younger children, or which are likely not to be equally familiar to all. Problems requiring the manipulation of too delicate or too cumbersome material also had to be eliminated. Finally, all things being equal, a preference was given to those of Piaget's tests which had also been used by other investigators. Thus, it was possible to benefit from their experience, and to minimize the risk of making basic errors in the construction of the questionnaires. The use of problems that have been employed in many different studies also permits us to broaden the scope of the conclusions, because it multiplies the number of possible comparisons. The five tests finally selected are shown in Table 1. It is quite apparent that all the phenomena investigated

Table 1

List of questionnaires

Name	Objective
The concept of dream	Realism
The concept of life	Animism
The origin of night	Artificialism
The movement of clouds	Explanation of natural motions
The floating and sinking of objects	Prediction and understanding of elementary physical laws

are very familiar to children, no matter from what milieu they come, and are likely to arouse about the same interest and curiosity in all.

The Wording of the Questionnaires

The wording of experimental questionnaires is not a simple task. In order to permit a valid comparison with Piaget's results, the examination technique must remain as close as possible to his. On the other hand, the tests were eventually to be included in a psychometric scale; moreover, all the examiners do not have the training required for a valid application of the clinical method in its purest form. For these reasons Piaget's questionnaires had to be standardized, but in a way that would nevertheless preserve the essentials of their diagnostic value. The inquiry had to be systematic enough to insure uniform and objective examining conditions, and yet allow sufficient flexibility and differentiation to avoid rigidity and imprecision. To reach this objective, the most effective procedure consisted in first drawing up a repertory of possible answers, and in formulating the questionnaires accordingly. The material gathered by Piaget and other investigators already afforded solid ground to work on. Then, a preliminary experiment with some thirty subjects of various ages provided for the verification of the provisional catalogue of answers and for occasional additions as required. Starting from these data, it was relatively easy to prepare questionnaires likely to disclose the real thinking of the child and, so to say, to exhaust his reasoning capacities. These questionnaires are thus rather new in kind and stand about midway between Piaget's free interrogations and the objective technique of traditional tests. The child's answers regulate in great part the direction of the examination, but all questions asked by the examiner are formulated in advance. Indeed, most of the time, the words used are vague enough to conform to all possible cases and, when this presentation proves inapplicable, the examination provides as many subgroups of questions as there are possible answers. In order to bring out the quality of the child's reasoning, the questionnaires never stop at first answers; the child is always led on to justify or explain his assertions, through a set of subquestions, counterquestions, and even suggestions which aim at probing, so to speak, the limits of his understanding. The description and a brief content analysis of the final form of the five questionnaires will provide a sufficient illustration of these varied processes. The complete questionnaires are given in Appendix A.

THE CONCEPT OF DREAM

The child's realism leads him to a lack of discrimination between the various levels of reality, for instance, between what is subjective and objective. Hence we are interested in finding out how he conceives of the dream phenomenon, which is a pre-eminently subjective phenomenon, though its subjectivity is at first far from obvious. To realize this fully, one need only recall the emotional upset a nightmare can produce in children, and even occasionally in adults. According to Piaget, the young child, because his mind is still realistic, attributes the origin of the dream to causes which are often vague, but always external to the sleeper. Moreover, the dream is located in the room, or in the very place where the events occur. Since the dream is something seen or heard, the eyes and the ears are considered its organs. Children often even agree that it is possible for others to see their dreams, as long as they happen to be in the room at the right moment. To find out to what extent the child objectifies the dream, Piaget questions him thoroughly on four essential points: the origin, the location, the organ, and the cause of the dream. In the course of the conversations, he sometimes adds questions on the very substance of dreams and on their reality. The content of the present questionnaire follows this general plan, because it seems to cover all the aspects of the problem and also permits a valid diagnosis of the child's conceptions.

The wording of the questions requires special care. It is not easy, particularly in such a field, to find expressions entirely free of suggestions, and at the same time sufficiently definite for the child to grasp their exact meaning. The strategy resorted to consists in asking, first, a very general question; should the child evade it, or misinterpret its meaning, the questioning becomes more and more direct. Thus, the conversation begins with deliberately vague statements: "*You know what a dream is? . . . Do you dream sometimes at night? . . . Now, tell me, where does a dream come from?*" These questions on the origin of the dream soon become more and more insistent: "*Where are the dreams made, where do they come from? . . . Do they come from inside of you, or outside of you?*"

The more suggestive questions, it will be noted, usually give several options, thus still leaving the subject free to state his personal beliefs. The choices presented correspond exactly to the conceptions the great majority of children spontaneously formulate. This strategy may admittedly have its faults, but it is nonetheless the most capable of insuring the objectivity of the questionnaire. At certain points, however, the formulation is intentionally made very suggestive, and induces the subjects to state their convictions more strongly, whether they agree or not with the given suggestion. The last questions on the origin of the dream are examples of this tactic: *"Who makes the dream come? ... Is it you or someone else? ... Who is it?"*

The same procedure recurs when the child is questioned on the location of dreams: at first vague statements, and then more and more suggestive questions. But, in this instance, it is no longer possible to find formulations equally effective with the children who locate the dream in the head and with those who locate it in the external world. Therefore, it becomes necessary to prepare in advance two series of different questions. In the first alternative, the objective is to discover if, in spite of this interiorization, the dream remains something material: *"If we opened your head while you are dreaming, if we looked into your head, could we see your dream? ... Why do you say that we could (or could not) see your dream? ... Then where in your head is your dream?"* With the children who externalize the dream, the insistence is first on finding out if there has been any misunderstanding of the meaning of the terms. In locating the dream in his room, the child may sometimes refer to the dream illusion through which he becomes a spectator, "as if" the dream were a spectacle before him, in his room. Therefore, he is asked: *"Is it in your room (on the wall, etc.) for real, or is it only as if it were there? Or does it only seem to be there?"* If the child keeps on externalizing his dreams, he will then be led to doubt his explanations. "*When you dream, are your eyes closed or open? . . . Then, where is your dream? . . . When you dream that you are playing in the street, where is your dream? . . . In the street, or in your room?*" The last questions on the location of the dream are asked of all children, whether they have located the dream inside or outside. They are meant to bring out a further confirmation of the child's answers: "*Is there something in front of you when you dream? . . . When your mother is in your room, can she also see your dream? And I, if I were in your room, could I see your dream? . . . Why do you say that I could (or could not) see your dream?*"

Questions on the organ and the substance of the dream are more easily understood by children, and do not consequently require varied formulations: "*What do we dream with? . . . What is a dream made of?*" Yet, to dispel any possible misunderstanding of the meaning of these questions, or to incite hesitating subjects to look for an answer, deliberately absurd suggestions are given: "*Do we dream with our hands? . . . With what then? . . . Is a dream made of paper? Of what then?*" During the conversation, the child is led to narrate one of his dreams, which provides an occasion to question him on the cause of the dream: "*Why did you dream of that? . . . Then, do you know why we dream, why there are dreams?*" Finally, in order to discover the degree of reality of the dream, one asks: "*When, during the night, you dream that you are playing, are you really playing? . . . Is it the same as when you play for real? . . . Is it the same as when you play during the day? . . . Then, are our dreams true?*"

No doubt many questions, especially some of those dealing with the reality of the dream, remain very ambiguous. In spite of many preliminary tests, it has not been possible to attain formulations equally accessible to all children. These difficulties do not seem, however, to justify the *a priori* rejection of some parts of the questionnaire. At least when the questions are well understood, they retain all their usefulness. The results of the experiment alone will show whether they should be retained in the questionnaire.

THE CONCEPT OF LIFE

The second questionnaire aims at the exploration of the child's animism, namely, his tendency to consider all objects as living, endowed with consciousness, intentions, feelings, etc. It is not possible in only one questionnaire to reach all these aspects of animism. Thus, it is preferable to limit the experiment to the problem which seems to be the most central, that of life, and to study it as thoroughly as possible. How extensive is the child's concept of life? Piaget, Russell and Dennis, as well as all those who have admitted the existence of animistic thinking in the child have equally observed the same evolution of this tendency to attribute life to inanimate objects. With the youngest children, anything useful is alive: life is simply identified with the function or activity of objects. Then comes the period during which life is confused with movement: all moving objects are alive, regardless of where their movement originates. Thus *clouds, birds, trains, bicycles* are said to be living, while the *table*, the *mountains*, the *trees* are not regarded as alive because they are devoid of movement. The third stage can be recognized through the distinction between immanent and transmitted movement: those objects endowed with autonomous movement are the only ones to be considered alive even though this movement may often be illusive. Thus, the *sun*, the *wind*, sometimes even *clocks* or *airplanes* are claimed to be living because their movement does not seem to be directed by any other object. Finally, it is in the fourth stage only that life is reserved to animals and plants, and often exclusively to animals.

The technique of questioning, worked out by Piaget and

replicated almost always without change by investigators interested in the same problem, is alluring in its extreme simplicity. Indeed, all there is to do is to name a series of objects, to ask the child each time whether the object is a living one, and why. Obviously, the diagnostic value of the questionnaire depends on the selection of the objects. Thus, it is important to make sure that the list contain the items necessary to bring out the essential features of the child's various conceptions about life.

The questionnaire prepared for the purpose of the present investigation starts with a very general question largely intended to make sure of the subject's understanding of the term "living": "*You know what it is to be living (to be alive)? . . . What does it mean? . . . Can you name some things which are alive?*" The examiner notes the child's answers to these nondirective questions, and then presents him with the various items of the questionnaire, asking each time if the object concerned is alive (or living) and why. The list includes 21 objects altogether: 7 living objects (2 plants and 5 animals) distributed at random among 14 inanimate objects. All inanimate objects have some activity or usefulness, but a few are markedly motionless (e.g., *table, mountain, lamp*), while others are usually associated with movement (e.g., *automobile, airplane, wind*). To allow the child to make a distinction, if he is capable of doing so, between autonomous and transmitted movement, the series of mobile objects includes some objects in which the origin of the respective movements is not equally evident. Thus, in the case of the *bicycle*, the *pencil*, or the *bell*, the origin of movement is easily perceptible. The movement of the *watch*, the *automobile*, the *airplane*, or the *clouds* is already more puzzling, but things like the *sun*, the *wind*, the *rain*, and the *fire* are more likely to baffle the child and to lead him to believe in their autonomous movement.

A questionnaire of this kind seems quite adequate for the

identification of the four essential phases of the evolution of the concept of life. There is of course no *a priori* assurance that the child will always classify objects according to plan. Hence, the way in which he justifies his answers must be relied upon to reveal his real criterion of discrimination. In order to test the stability of the criteria the child uses, five particularly insinuating questions are added at the end of the questionnaire; these may lead a subject who lacks conviction to reject his previous answers. For instance, the child is asked: *"Take the wind and a bicycle, is one of them more alive than the other? ... The rain or the fire? ... A fly or a cloud? ... Why?"* Such suggestive questions are obviously very dangerous, but they serve the purpose, especially with negative answers, of reassuring the examiner about the child's real belief.

The objects selected are all very simple and familiar to the child. None of them call for specialized knowledge, nor do they involve the ambiguity that too frequently occurs in items of examinations for adolescents and adults. The question could be raised why, instead of being exclusively verbal, the questionnaire should not bear on objects actually presented to the child. It would indeed have been possible, as Russell and Dennis (1939) did, to include concrete objects that the subject could manipulate during the conversation. But the findings of these authors so closely resemble those of Piaget that the two techniques may be taken as equivalent. It must be remembered also that the objects named in the present list are all very concrete and never go beyond the familiar world of the child. Under these conditions, the simpler procedure was deemed preferable.

THE ORIGIN OF NIGHT

Artificialism in the child consists in the belief that everything is the result of human industry. For the majority of objects surrounding the child, this belief is corroborated by the facts.

In order to evaluate the inclusiveness of this conception, the child must be questioned on the origin of the few objects which he does know, but which are not man-made. This particular investigation is thus limited to natural phenomena: sun, wind, clouds, rain, night, rivers, meteors and the like, are all so many occasions for the child to manifest his artificialistic tendencies. Out of all these possible themes, the explanation of the phenomenon of night has been selected for the present investigation. All children are equally capable of noting its existence, whereas such familiarity would not necessarily apply to all natural phenomena, for example, rivers, lakes, or some meteors.

In the child's explanation of the origin of night, Piaget has observed that artificialism is first manifested in a finalistic form. The child explains the phenomenon of night by the mere fact that it is useful for man's sleep. When the questions become more insistent, he attributes its origin to the intervention of God or of man, but he is unable to describe the mechanics of this intervention. At a second stage, finalistic reasons have not yet vanished but are supplemented by a system aiming at explaining how night is effected: a large black cloud steered directly, or ordered from a distance, by God or man, moves in to fill the atmosphere. These clouds most frequently come from the smoke of chimneys, trains, or industrial plants. At the next stage, artificialism recedes almost completely to make room for a physical, but still imperfect, explanation: the clouds are still the cause of night, but do not constitute the substance of darkness any longer; their only role is to hide daylight. In short, night is a shadow produced by the clouds forming a screen in front of daylight. It is only during a fourth stage that the disappearance of the sun is brought in to explain the phenomenon of night.

The actual beliefs held at these different stages are too varied for a single questionnaire to elicit satisfactory findings.

Hence, three different sections have been prepared which explore, respectively, each of the three main explanations: sleep, the clouds, and the disappearance of the sun. Thus the inquiry begins with questions of a general bearing, meant to facilitate the child's spontaneous explanation and to prepare the way to one of the three particularized questionnaires: *"You know what the night is? Tell me, what is night? . . . Why is it dark at night? . . . Where does the dark come from, at night? . . . What makes it night?"* In accordance with the child's response to these preliminary questions, the conversation goes on in any one of the three foreseen directions. The examiner of course is guided by the child's reasoning and changes to another section as soon as a different type of explanation is given spontaneously by the subject.

The first section deals with finalistic interpretations. Its object is to test the strength of the child's convictions. To make him aware of the weakness of his explanation and to goad him into seeking another, if he can, the examiner confronts him with situations where the relation of sleep to night does not apply: *"Do you sleep, sometimes, during the day? . . . Is it dark when we sleep in the daytime? . . . Then, why is it dark at night? . . . Are there times when it is night and you do not sleep? . . . Then, how is it that it is dark when we do not sleep?"*

The second section is designed to discriminate, among explanations of the intermediate levels, those wherein the clouds are the substantial cause of night (second stage) and those wherein they merely mask the light of day (third stage): *"The clouds at night, are they white or black? . . . Can white clouds make it night? . . . At night, is it black clouds which take the place of white ones, or white clouds which turn black?"* To urge the child to find an explanation on a higher level, the question is even added: *"Why, when there are clouds in the daytime, is it not dark like at night?"*

The third section, reserved for subjects who explain night

by the disappearance of the sun, is designed to test the genuineness of this explanation. The fact that the child refers to the sun is not always a sure sign of a true causal or physical relation. Some children, for instance, because they have noticed an infallible correlation between the sun's disappearance and nightfall, will mention the disappearance of the sun, in the course of the conversation, with the naïve idea that the sun, like human beings, merely goes to bed when night comes. Since it is essential to identify these answers, which are still very animistic and also probably tainted with artificialism, the examiner becomes insistent: *"Can you explain how it becomes dark when the sun is gone? . . . Where does the sun go when it is night? . . . Why does the sky become dark at night? . . . When it rains, do we see the sun?"*

With all the subjects, the inquiry ends with questions which aim at helping those capable of doing so to understand the phenomenon: *"Can we make the night in this room? If I pull the blinds down, will it be dark? . . . Then, how is it? Where does the dark in the room come from? . . . And the dark outside, what is it?"*

The question could be raised why the questionnaire was limited in advance to the investigation of only three categories of answers. Some may see in this practice a risk of missing other possible types of explanation. However, on the basis of pre-experimental data, one can conclude that this risk does not exist. For every time a child has attributed the origin of night to factors not included in the questionnaire, for instance, to the moon or the stars, it is obvious that his answer derived rather from mere associative processes than from a genuine explanation. As the inquiry went on, the child was always led to choose one of the foreseen directions spontaneously. This is why examiners are instructed to go on with the conversation, even when the child does not immediately give the expected answers. They simply repeat, in the form of questions, the assertions of the child himself: *"Tell me how (. . .) goes about making the night?"* In any event, the questions the examiner may add are always noted down so that, if unexpected explanations occur, they may be included in the protocol.

THE MOVEMENT OF CLOUDS

According to Piaget, the child's various conceptions of the world always involve the element of attributing some energy or power to objects. If the world is indeed composed of conscious animated objects, bent on achieving some purpose, these objects then possess the necessary power to fulfill their mission, the capacity to move by themselves, and the like. For a better understanding of the extent of this tendency, which Piaget calls dynamism, it is essential that the child be questioned on the movement of objects which do not in fact possess intrinsic dynamism. Here again, objects in nature offer the most promising field of investigation and, among them, the movement of clouds is the most familiar to children. The movement of celestial bodies is too slow to be perceived, and all children do not have the same opportunity to notice the movement of streams or rivers.

Since dynamism permeates all children's representations, it is not surprising that magical, animistic, artificialistic, or finalistic tendencies become manifest in their explanation of the movement of clouds. Thus, in Piaget's view, the young child's conception of the world is at the same time magical, animistic, and dynamistic: it is human beings who, as they move about, make the clouds move, and the clouds, obedient, follow their least change of place. This explanation is later modified and becomes more markedly artificialistic, while remaining animistic: the clouds are now ordered to move by men (or by God), or they are directed in much the same way as an automobile is driven. At the next stage, artificialism either recedes or is transferred to heavenly bodies. Explanations are then pervaded with finalistic elements, which are added to the still persisting animism and dynamism: the clouds move by themselves; or they are subjected to the will of the sun, the night, the rain, or bad weather. In the fourth and fifth stages, the wind is the basic element of explanation. Dynamism, however, still survives during the fourth stage, since the cloud itself generates the wind necessary for its displacement.

Here again the variety of answers is too wide to permit the elaboration of a single inclusive questionnaire. The strategy of the questionnaire on the origin of night must therefore be repeated: the inquiry starts with general questions in order to discover the spontaneous explanations of the child and to guide the remainder of the conversation. The three sections developed investigate respectively: explanations with magical content (first stage), artificialistic or purely dynamistic explanations (second and third stages), and finally, physical explanations implying the intervention of the wind (fourth and fifth stages). In each section, the child is brought around to specifying the content of his answer: *"Can you, yourself, make the clouds move? ... And at night, when everybody is asleep, do the clouds move? ... Why do the clouds sometimes move fast and sometimes move slowly? ... What does he (God, the sun, etc.) do to make the clouds move? ... Do the clouds move by themselves, alone, or is there something to make them move? ... Where does the wind come from? ... When there is no wind, can the clouds move by themselves?"*

Further, whatever system the child adopts, it is important to find out whether he regards this movement as conscious and intentional: *"Do the clouds know they are moving? ... Why do you say they know (or do not know)? ... Can the clouds go where they want? ... Why can they (or can they not) go where they want?"* If the child does not bring the wind at all into his explanations, the examiner ends the conversation with a suggestion intended to probe the limits of his understanding:

"Can the wind make the clouds move? ... Why do you say that the wind can (or cannot) make the clouds move?" The child who accepts this suggestion is then questioned about the role of the wind, its origin, etc.

FLOATING AND SINKING

The study of the child's understanding of physical laws provides information about both his logic and his mental representations. Hence, the inclusion of a problem of this kind in the present study has a twofold interest. This test not only completes the observations derived from the other tests, but makes it possible to establish the necessary relationships between two complementary aspects of the thinking process, and to explore the strictly formal level of reasoning. The efforts made by the child to induce a general law from the observation of certain facts reveal the development of a closer and stricter operational logic. On the other hand, the content analysis of the explanations shows that, anterior to its elaboration, the physical law is compensated by precausal representations. According to Piaget, the preoperational explanation of the floating of bodies is characterized by two distinct phases. First, the child relies on finalistic, moralistic, or animistic reasons: bodies float because they are made for floating, because they abide by their maker's will, because they prefer remaining on the surface of the water, etc. Later, the child calls upon factors apparently more objective, but still bound to precausal representations which reveal the intuitive character of his reasoning: the weight, the shape, the size, or the movement of bodies explain their floating or sinking. All these factors, however, derive from a basic dynamism as disclosed in the child's numerous explanations that are at variance with the facts: an object floats if heavy, that is, if it has the strength to stay above the water; an object sinks if too small, or if its shape does not allow its remaining on the surface, etc. As soon as operational thinking occurs, this type of error disappears almost completely. From then on, any light object will float and any heavy object will sink, but the concept of weight retains an entirely qualitative and absolute meaning. Some bodies are heavy and others light by nature: every wooden object will be light, every metallic one will be heavy, regardless of the respective size of these objects. At a certain level of development, this concept of specific weight is coupled with an explanation involving density: the heavier bodies are fuller or contain less air. At no time, however, does it come to the mind of the child to establish the proper relationship between the weight of an object and that of the corresponding volume of water. At first, he pays attention only to the comparison of the weight of bodies with that of the *total* volume of water, a consideration that betrays the presence of residual dynamistic thinking. He will grasp the concept of relative weight only much later when he becomes capable of formal mental operations.

The technique elaborated for the investigation of this question consists in presenting, as a first problem, a series of small objects to be deposited on water: a *miniature boat*, a *large marble*, a *small wooden bead*, a *small marble* (equal in size to the bead), a *nail*, a *wooden peg*. Before each object is released, the child is asked to predict whether it will float or not; when the experiment has been made, he must explain what he has just seen. The material is chosen in such a way that recourse to irrelevant properties (e.g., absolute weight, size, color, shape, etc.) leads the subject into contradictions. If he realizes this, he must seek better explanations.

The second problem emphasizes certain contrasting phenomena; the child is led to explain why, of two objects of the same shape, but unequal in size (a *nail* and a *wooden peg*), the smaller goes to the bottom; or why, of two objects, equal in size and shape (a *small marble* and a *wooden bead*), the first goes to the bottom while the second remains on the surface. If the child merely alludes to the substance or the material of the objects, more insistent questions are asked: *"Why does it stay on the water, when it is made of wood? ... Why does it go to the bottom, when it is made of metal (glass)?"* Then follows a still more subtle comparison: *"Which is heavier: a large boat or a small marble? ... Then, why does a large boat remain on top of the water, and a small marble goes to the bottom?"*

To find out whether the child grasps the correct relationship involved, that between the weight of an object and the weight of the corresponding volume of water, the examiner simply presents him with two receptacles equal in size, one filled with water, and one with wood, and asks: *"Which is heavier, do you think, the one filled with water or the one filled with wood? ... Why do you think it is the one filled with wood (or the one filled with water)?"*

Finally, in the last problem, the child has to mold a piece of plasticine in order to make it float on the water. If he does not succeed, the examiner himself molds the plasticine in the shape of a crucible and asks him: *"Why does it float, do you think, when it is made like that? ... What makes it float, now? ... Why does a ball go down, and this now remains on top of the water?"* This technique is particularly instructive. The child is called upon to participate directly in the experiment, and this never fails to intensify his interest. Further, the various means he uses in his attempt to make the plasticine float are most informative, for they concretely convey the hypotheses which the child cannot always formulate verbally. For instance, a subject who attempts to make smaller and smaller pieces float undoubtedly refers floating or sinking to the absolute weight of the object; on the other hand, a subject who servilely seeks to re-create the shape of a boat (mast, keel etc.) bases his reasoning on an intuitive type of criterion (shape, length, etc.).

• • •

Of the five questionnaires described above, the last one only requires the use of concrete material. The first four are exclusively verbal, the examiner limiting himself to questions and using no material object to sustain the child's attention. The appropriateness of such a procedure may be questioned. In the case of an examination dealing with young children, it seems preferable to avoid exclusively verbal tests. Is it not better to try to render the situations concrete and have the child reason from materials which he can manipulate? Whenever possible, the most concrete techniques are indeed indicated; but, in the present context, they are not easily applicable. The investigation of the child's representation of the world necessarily involves phenomena, undoubtedly well known to him, but impossible to reproduce in a laboratory situation. Hence, unless purely verbal tests are accepted, the investigation of this really fundamental aspect of thinking would have to be abandoned. Besides, a verbal test is not, by definition, exclusively abstract. In the present case, the themes of the questionnaires remain essentially concrete: clouds, night, and dreams are all realities which the child can perceive or experience personally. This is why the child is seldom confused when these themes are introduced. And, if need be, the examiner can easily put some questions more concretely. During the test on the movement of clouds, for instance, he may take the child to a window and have him observe the phenomenon. When questioned on dreams, the child is asked to narrate his most recent dream, a procedure which can only enhance his interest in the whole set of questions. In actual fact, the test on the concept of life seems to be the most abstract, because life as such is not a direct object of perception. It might then have been of advantage to make the questionnaire more concrete by the use of some real objects; and in this case, moreover, it would have been possible to do so. However, as already emphasized, the results of previous studies do not show noticeable differences between the strictly verbal techniques (Piaget, 1926) and those involving the actual presentation of the objects referred to in the course of the questioning (Russell and Dennis, 1939). There is nothing particularly surprising about this, for these objects, though only verbally presented, are always well known to the child, and their actual presence would provide no additional information, nor make the task more concrete. The situation would no doubt be different if the list included items unfamiliar to the child, or items of highly specialized and often equivocal information such as some authors have chosen to introduce by questioning the child on objects like *atoms* or *arable land*. The present questionnaire refers only to very simple objects: a *cat*, an *automobile*, a *bell*, a *lamp*, a *table*, a *bicycle*, etc. It seems useless therefore to attempt to present these items in their concrete form. To avoid unduly limiting the scope of the examination, it would be necessary to resort to prints or miniature reproductions. Such substitutes could not be used in the case of living beings without giving rise to ambiguities, which would seriously obscure the meaning that the child attaches to his concept of life.

A last point must be emphasized on account of its possible repercussions on the validity of the whole investigation. The questionnaires were constructed with a very definite purpose, that of verifying the existence, in the development of each of the concepts under study, of the stages predicted by Piaget. It may be asked whether such a procedure does not involve the grave danger of a bias in the interpretation of results. This risk is admittedly present, but it could not possibly be avoided. Without a working hypothesis or, if preferred, without preconceived ideas, it is impossible to elaborate a detailed questionnaire. The few general questions which may serve to introduce the topic are certainly not sufficient to establish the stability and the generality of the child's beliefs. Unless the

THE EXPERIMENT

main themes of the examination are anticipated, the examiner would have to be given *carte blanche* and he would have to let himself be guided completely by the child's answers. This would mean a return to Piaget's pure "clinical" method, the objectivity and uniformity of which have so often been contested. In this field even more than in similar fields, it is essential to know from the beginning what is to be verified to avoid getting lost in an inextricable maze. Awareness of the danger of bias can minimize its possible ill-effects. Accordingly, the construction of the present questionnaires was based on a complete revision of past investigations, as well as on a preliminary experiment aimed precisely at delimiting the repertory of the main beliefs of children. Moreover, the first questions that introduce the several tests—and this is particularly true of the tests on dreams, the origin of night, and the movement of clouds, which are the most open to suggestion—are designedly neutral and nondirective, in order to elicit the child's spontaneous beliefs and, at the same time, to give him an opening for unforeseen types of explanation. When the subjects' first answers are readily classifiable into the predetermined categories, the remainder of the questionnaire serves only to establish the authenticity of these answers. When, exceptionally, first explanations belong to a new type, the examiner records the child's specific answers, and then tries to explore their real meaning by transposing, at need and in the light of his experience, the text of the standard questionnaire. The examination thus sheds some of its rigor and uniformity, but it nevertheless reaches its main objective, that of revealing the child's spontaneous beliefs.

CHAPTER VI

The Sample

Piaget's critics usually argue that the excessive rigor and dogmatism of his system are not at all compatible with the frailty of the sampling from which it is derived. For the most part, Piaget does not specify the number of subjects examined and, particularly in his first books, this number does not seem large enough to support his conclusions. His description of stages always includes the age at which a given stage is normally reached; but it is not uncommon to find instances in which the examples quoted refer to children whose chronological age differs considerably from the norm. The verbal precautions occasionally used by Piaget (e.g., "subject particularly retarded," "subject very precocious") do not entirely reassure readers accustomed to more meticulous practices. Nor does his selection of experimental subjects seem to have been made according to very strict procedures. Children were questioned at random, as circumstances permitted, or, again, the availability of subjects served as the deciding factor in selection. The possibility of extending his conclusions to general populations, probably much more heterogeneous than his samples, thus becomes quite problematical.

In order to avoid the same criticism of the results of the present study, a completely representative sample of the population under investigation had to be assembled. The technique adopted was that of a stratified sample, selected according to the following criteria.

1. *Chronological age.* The subjects ranged between four and twelve years. The very nature of the experimental questionnaires imposed this choice of age. It is, in practice, ineffective to use almost exclusively verbal tests with subjects younger than four. Even at that age, children still experience great difficulty in communicating and in focusing their attention for any length of time on the same problem. On the other hand, it seemed superfluous, at least provisionally, to extend the experiment beyond the age of twelve, because the main manifestations of precausal thinking should, if the results of previous authors are generally to be trusted, normally disappear around the age of eleven or twelve. Because intellectual development proceeds much more rapidly in early years, the age intervals used were set at six months for ages below five, and at twelve months for ages ranging from five to twelve. The sample thus included ten age levels and fifty children for each of these levels.

Each child was examined on the date which was the nearest possible to his birthday. The maximum deviation from the birthday anniversary was limited to a month either way for children from four to five years of age, and to two months for children from six to twelve.

2. *Sex.* The sample consisted of an equal number of boys and girls. Once reduced to required proportions, the slight differences reported in the census data between the total number of boys and girls became negligible.

3. *Occupational level of the parents.* The census data (*Bureau fédéral de la statistique*, 1955) classify the total population of Montreal children into two age groups (children below six years of age, and children of six to thirteen years of age), and into twelve categories distributed according to the occupation of the head of the household. Three of these classes

Table 2

Distribution of subjects according to
parents' occupational level

Occupational level		Age groups	
Identification number	Description	4 to 5 (3 subgroups)	6 to 12 (7 subgroups)
1	Proprietary, managerial, professional	10	12
2	Clerical	4	3
3	Commercial, financial	4	4
4	Manufacturing, mechanical, construction, transportation, communication	25	24
5	Service	3	3
6	Laborers	4	4
Total (per age subgroup)		50	50

(agricultural, mining, and fishing) had such a small number of subjects that they were eliminated at the very beginning. By combining the more homogeneous categories, it was then possible to reduce to six the final number of occupational levels to be considered. The resulting classification is shown in Table 2. This table also gives the distribution of the subjects according to the parents' occupational level for each age subgroup, between four and twelve years. These figures were obtained by reducing the statistical data of the total population to the proportion of fifty subjects for each age level (see raw data: Appendix B, Table 25).

4. *Familial environment*. Only the children living in their own family were included. The education received by children raised in institutions (asylums or orphanages) is too often prone to produce some retardation in mental development, and thus to falsify findings expected in a normal population.

5. *Physical condition*. Children suffering from serious physical defects were eliminated, since such infirmities can affect their performance in unpredictable ways.

6. *Siblings*. This factor was controlled among preschool age children. It is quite possible that the presence or absence of siblings may influence the rhythm of mental development. If this influence exists, it is surely more operative among children who do not benefit from daily contact with schoolmates. Available statistics do not permit the desired precision on this matter. The census groups children into five classes according to whether families include an only child, two children, from three to five children, from six to eight, or more than eight children. For the present purpose, the control of the number of children in the family did not require such minute subdivisions. Since the influence of this factor was more noticeable among small families, it became possible to reduce the number of categories to three: a group of only children; children who have only one sibling; and children belonging to larger families. Statistics, however, are much less informative on the relationship between the children's age and the type of families to which they belong. Indeed, they merely give inclusive

figures, that is, for all children from zero to twenty-four years of age. The proportion of only children and of children with only one sibling is presumably greater at lower than at higher ages. For lack of precise data on this particular relationship in the familial group, a theoretical distribution of percentages had to be inferred from certain demographic data, though they were incomplete.[1] Reduced to the proportions of a sample of fifty subjects for each age level, the errors of inaccuracies of such gross statistics became almost negligible. Hence, the distribution of the percentages finally adopted (see Ap-

Table 3

Distribution of preschool sample by age,
occupational level of parents, and
number of children in the family

Age	Number of children in the family	Occupational level						Total
		1	2	3	4	5	6	
4:0	1	2	1	1	4	1	1	10
	2	4	1	1	7	1	1	15
	3+	4	2	2	14	1	2	25
4:6	1	2	1	1	4	0	1	9
	2	3	1	1	7	1	1	14
	3+	5	2	2	14	2	2	27
5:0	1	2	1	1	4	0	1	9
	2	3	1	1	6	1	1	13
	3+	5	2	2	15	2	2	28
6:0	1	2	0	1	3	0	0	6
	2	4	1	1	6	1	1	14
	3+	6	2	2	15	2	3	30

[1] Unpublished information supplied by Jacques Henripin, Ph.D., University of Montreal.

THE EXPERIMENT

pendix B, Figure 2) set the global averages indicated in the census at the age of four and a half for the category of only children, six for the children with only one sibling, and five and a half for children with more than one sibling. The adoption of these distributions then allowed the weighing of the raw data and the choice of exact proportions.

Table 3 presents the results of these various calculations for each age level and each occupational level. The source data are given in Appendix B (Tables 26 to 28, and Figure 2). It may seem peculiar that the term "preschool" here includes six-year-old children, although the school attendance law in force for the Montreal region sets the age of admission precisely at six. But, in actual practice, all children are not admitted to school as soon as they reach the minimum age. The working principle for actual admission requires a minimum age of five years and eight months at the beginning of the school year: all children younger than this in September must wait until the beginning of the next school year for admission, even though many reach the required age before that time. The exact proportion of children attending school when they reach their sixth birthday is hard to discover, since available statistics do not cover this point at all. It was therefore simpler to retain for the six-year-olds the same criteria for selection as those applied at the preschool level. Chances were that the six-year-old subjects would be so divided as to reproduce approximately the proportion of those attending school.

7. *Academic level.* For school-age children, the control of academic level replaced that of siblings. It is reasonable to assume that social interaction through school contacts is sufficient compensation for the advantages of relations with siblings. The control of academic level also insured, for each age level, the presence of a proportionally exact number of precocious, normal, and retarded children.

Table 4

Distribution of school sample
by age, sex, and school grade

Age	Sex	School grade									Total
		1	2	3	4	5	6	7	8	Ungraded	
7:0	G	14	11	0	0	0	0	0	0	0	25
	B	15	10	0	0	0	0	0	0	0	25
8:0	G	2	13	10	0	0	0	0	0	0	25
	B	2	14	9	0	0	0	0	0	0	25
9:0	G	0	3	13	9	0	0	0	0	0	25
	B	1	3	12	9	0	0	0	0	0	25
10:0	G	0	1	4	13	8	0	0	0	0	26
	B	0	1	4	11	8	0	0	0	0	24
11:0	G	0	0	1	5	12	7	0	0	0	25
	B	0	0	2	5	11	6	1	0	0	25
12:0	G	0	0	0	2	5	11	6	0	1	25
	B	0	0	1	2	6	10	5	0	1	25

The only relevant statistics on this point are those supplied by the School Commission (*Commission des écoles catholiques de Montréal*, 1956).[2] The data they provide do not cover the entire population, however, since children attending special or private schools (kindergartens, etc.) are not included. Yet it must be pointed out that, on the one hand, these private schools do not release statistics on the composition of their classes and that, on the other hand, the proportion of children attending these schools is, in fact, very small. The *Montreal Catholic School Commission*'s data could therefore be applied

---

[2] Since practically all French-speaking children of Montreal attend Catholic schools, these statistics are the most adequate and carry no possible danger of bias.

Table 5

Distribution of preschool sample (200 subjects) by age, sex, occupational level of parents, and number of children in the family

Age	Number of children in the family	1 %	1 N	1 B	1 G	2 %	2 N	2 B	2 G	3 %	3 N	3 B	3 G	4 %	4 N	4 B	4 G	5 %	5 N	5 B	5 G	6 %	6 N	6 B	6 G	Total N	Total B	Total G
4:0	1	18	2	1	1	20	1	1	0	19	1	1	0	16	4	2	2	17	1	1	0	15	1	0	1	10	6	4
	2	35	4	2	2	33	1	0	1	35	1	1	0	28	7	3	4	29	1	0	1	25	1	1	0	15	7	8
	3+	47	4	2	2	47	2	1	1	46	2	1	1	56	14	7	7	54	1	1	0	60	2	1	1	25	12	13
	Total		10	5	5		4	2	2		4	3	1		25	12	13		3	1	2		4	2	2	50	25	25
4:6	1	17	2	1	1	19	1	0	1	18	1	1	0	15	4	2	2	16	1	1	0	14	1	0	1	10	5	5
	2	34	3	2	1	32	1	0	1	34	1	1	0	27	7	4	3	28	1	0	1	24	1	0	1	14	7	7
	3+	49	5	2	3	49	2	1	1	48	2	1	1	58	14	7	7	56	1	1	0	62	2	2	0	26	13	13
	Total		10	5	5		4	1	3		4	3	1		25	13	12		3	1	2		4	2	2	50	25	25
5:0	1	16	2	1	1	18	1	1	0	17	1	0	1	14	4	2	2	15	0	0	0	13	1	1	0	9	5	4
	2	33	3	2	1	31	1	1	0	33	1	1	0	26	6	3	3	27	1	0	1	23	1	0	1	13	6	7
	3+	51	5	2	3	51	2	1	1	50	2	1	1	60	15	8	7	58	2	1	1	64	2	1	1	28	14	14
	Total		10	5	5		4	2	2		4	2	2		25	13	12		3	1	2		4	2	2	50	25	25
6:0	1	15	2	1	1	17	0	0	0	16	1	1	0	13	3	2	1	14	0	0	0	12	0	0	0	6	4	2
	2	31	4	2	2	29	1	1	0	31	1	1	0	24	6	3	3	25	1	1	0	21	1	0	1	14	7	7
	3+	54	6	3	3	54	2	0	2	53	2	2	0	63	15	7	8	61	2	1	1	67	3	2	1	30	15	15
	Total		12	6	6		3	1	2		4	3	1		24	12	12		3	2	1		4	2	2	50	26	24

Table 6

Distribution of school sample (300 subjects) by age, sex, occupational level of parents, and school grade

Age	Sex	Occupational level						School grade								Total
		1	2	3	4	5	6	1	2	3	4	5	6	7	Ungraded	
7:0	G	6	2	2	12	1	2	14	11	0	0	0	0	0	0	25
	B	6	1	2	12	2	2	15	10	0	0	0	0	0	0	25
8:0	G	6	2	2	12	1	2	2	13	10	0	0	0	0	0	25
	B	6	1	2	12	2	2	2	14	9	0	0	0	0	0	25
9:0	G	6	2	2	12	1	2	0	3	13	9	0	0	0	0	25
	B	6	1	2	12	2	2	1	3	12	9	0	0	0	0	25
10:0	G	7	2	2	12	1	2	0	1	4	13	8	0	0	0	26
	B	5	1	2	12	2	2	0	1	4	11	8	0	0	0	24
11:0	G	6	2	2	12	1	2	0	0	1	5	12	7	0	0	25
	B	6	1	2	12	2	2	0	0	2	5	11	6	1	0	25
12:0	G	6	2	2	12	1	2	0	0	0	2	5	11	6	1	25
	B	6	1	2	12	2	2	0	0	1	2	6	10	5	1	25

to the entire school population, and, for lack of comparative figures, it could be assumed that precocious, normal, or retarded children were distributed in more or less the same ratios in both public and private schools. Table 4 shows the distribution of subjects in the school sample according to age, sex, and academic level. The statistics used to work out these various proportions are those for the school year 1955-1956 (see Appendix B, Tables 29 and 30).

To summarize, it may help to present in table form the exact characteristics of the children tested, at each age level, in both the preschool (Table 5) and the school group (Table 6) of the total sample. For children of preschool age, the sample provided for simultaneous control, but for the other children, no statistics gave the proportion of precocious, normal, or retarded children for each occupational level; in the absence of such data, a sample with parallel controls was indicated for this latter group. With this type of sample, the number of subjects required, for each occupational level and again for each academic level, had to be settled beforehand. When the time came for recruiting subjects, all that was required was to verify whether each subject met the specific conditions imposed by each of these two factors. In short, each subject had to meet two independent sets of conditions and the relationship between the two sets was left to chance. Table 6 is therefore divided into two sections: the first one shows the distribution of subjects according to age, sex, and occupational level; the second distributes the same subjects, but now according to age, sex, and academic level. Thus, each subject is represented twice in this table and is classified according to two different points of view.

CHAPTER VII

Conditions of Testing and Methods of Analysis

This chapter deals, first, with the conditions of testing and, secondly, with the statistical techniques used in the analysis of results. It thus supplements the technical data reported above. In addition, the discussion of the postulates involved in the statistical techniques affords an indispensable introduction to the description of results, which is the subject of the third part of this study.

Conditions of Testing

The necessary information on conditions of testing may be summarized under three headings: examiners; form and place of testing; and order of test administration.

EXAMINERS

All the examiners were graduate psychology students. Already familiar with psychometric techniques through laboratory courses, they also received additional intensive training in order to become even more deft in the difficult art of questioning children. After a thorough study of the rationale, instructions, content, and material of the examination, they were required to practice with pre-experimental subjects and were not admitted to work on the experiment proper until their skill had been verified by a complete and minute examination. In order to insure objectivity in the experimentation, care had obviously to be taken to preserve uniformity of procedure.

FORM AND PLACE OF TESTING

All the subjects were examined individually. With school children, the testing took place at school and during school hours, in an appropriate isolated room. All preschool children were examined in their home. A child of this age can hardly adapt successfully and without some anxiety to the situation of a psychological examination if he is suddenly removed from his familiar environment and if he does not at least sense the proximate and reassuring presence of one of his parents. As may be readily anticipated, there are at times serious drawbacks to testing the child at his home. Whenever possible, the examiner asked to be left alone with the subject. The passive presence of the mother occasionally proved useful, or even necessary. In spite of these precautions, certain experimental conditions sometimes escaped strict control. In poorer families, especially, the external conditions of available space, lighting, temperature, furnishings, and the like required the examiner to exercise considerable ingenuity in order to conduct the tests satisfactorily, and to preserve the motivation of the child.

ORDER OF TEST ADMINISTRATION

The five questionnaires studied in this report were scattered through a much larger battery comprising twenty-seven subtests. Except for those tests which clearly proved to be too easy or too difficult and had to be omitted at age limits, the entire battery was administered to subjects of all age levels. The time devoted to the examination of each subject reached an average total of ten hours distributed into four to eight sessions, depending upon the age of the child and the conditions of testing. The order of test administration did not have to be rigorous, because all these tests are independent and because the factor of learning has practically no effect since the solution of one problem cannot be transferred to the specific solution of another problem. In the lower ages particularly, the instability of the child's reactions and the fluctuation of his momentary interest precluded the use of a strict schedule, and required extreme flexibility on the part of the examiner. He had only to follow certain general instructions: after a verbal test, a nonverbal test; after a tiresome test, an attractive one; and the like.

In spite of all deliberate efforts to maintain objectivity and uniformity, it could not have been possible to foresee all the difficulties or errors likely to crop up during the experimentation. Accordingly, the examiners kept in constant touch with the supervisors of the project. The difficulties they met were considered in group discussions and, when necessary, the examination underwent minor changes in instructions or material.

Methods of Analysis

The analysis of results had to cope with two main questions: the search for stages characterizing the evolution of precausal thinking, and the determination of the age level at which each one of the stages is reached. In dealing with the first problem, it is necessary to verify whether the stages of precausal thinking described by Piaget are found in the present sample under approximately the same form and with sufficient consistency. As to the second problem, which refers to the developmental rhythm suggested by Piaget, but so often contested, it can directly be solved by computing the exact age at which the majority of children reach each one of these stages.

IDENTIFICATION OF STAGES

The search for stages and the scoring of the tests took place concurrently as parts of the same analysis. This task required a close examination of all protocols and an inclusive classification of all types of responses. Each protocol was scored as a comprehensive unit, since a separate answer has importance not per se but only to the extent that it is part of a whole which is likely to indicate a verifiable trend toward a specific mode of reasoning. All answers, whether right or wrong, were studied and interpreted. In fact, wrong answers are often more significant and throw more light on the true level of the child's explanations.

These various types of responses were then arranged into a scale of levels, which was provisionally based on Piaget's stages. When these stages did not prove adequate for the classification of all answers, appropriate modifications were made: additions, combinations, eliminations, reformulations, and the like. For instance, if a particular type of response not reported by Piaget occurred frequently enough and if it seemed to be indicative of a truly original phase of mental development, a new stage was added to Piaget's scale and inserted at the appropriate level. On the other hand, if one of Piaget's type of responses was too rarely met with to constitute an independent level of explanation, it was considered preferable to combine these responses with others of an equivalent level.

Independent scales of responses or stages were thus prepared for each one of the five questionnaires, and all protocols were scored according to these scales. It then became possible to decide on the precausal nature of the lower stages by analyzing the content of the protocols, and to assess the generality of the phenomenon by computing the frequency of such primitive responses.

The developmental sequence of the various levels of thinking is indicated by the age of accession to stages, that is, the age at which children normally reach the successive levels of that evolution. This does not require complicated or refined statistical techniques. All that is needed is to find, in the actual distribution occurring at each one of the stages, the critical point at which the percentage of subjects is high enough to corroborate definitive accession to the corresponding level of responses. The age at which this frequency is met for the first time is, in fact, the age of accession to the stage. However simple, this technique is based on certain postulates which must be considered briefly, in order to avoid any possible misunderstanding.

The first postulate concerns the criterion of accession to stages or, in other words, the frequency required to determine that a stage has been reached. Most authors dealing with this problem, such as Piaget and Inhelder, have adopted the statistical criterion first proposed by Binet, and later accepted by most American psychologists: a stage is considered to have been reached at a given age when 75 per cent of the children of that age fall in this class. A study of its rationale and of its implications does not seem, however, to justify the use of this criterion. It appears to be much more legitimate to set it at 50 per cent. In fact, when speaking of the age of accession to a stage, reference is made to a mental, and not to a chronological, age. Indeed, at each age level, only 50, and not 75, per cent of the subjects have a mental age equivalent of or superior to their chronological age. All the remaining subjects show retardation. Slight as it may be, this retardation nevertheless indicates clearly that these children have not yet attained the mental development corresponding to their chronological age. In working out the age of accession to a stage, only such children whose mental age corresponds to at least their chronological age, that is, only 50 per cent of the children of that age should be taken into account. True, a child showing only a slight retardation obviously still belongs among children of average or normal intelligence. But the requirement that 75 per cent of children of a given age be scored at a certain stage, before one can conclude that this stage has been reached, results in classifying half of the retarded children as normal, which seems to be excessive; or it results, in equivalent terms, in accepting implicitly that the proportion of retarded children is only 25 per cent for each age level, which seems no less questionable in the light of usual data on the normal distribution of intelligence.

The adoption of either one of these criteria may seem a purely conventional matter. Yet the choice must not be made arbitrarily since it may have serious repercussions on the interpretation of results, especially when these are consulted for individual diagnoses on mental development (retarded, precocious, interrupted, etc.). When the criterion of 75 instead of 50 per cent of success is accepted, the age of accession will necessarily be set later than it should be, and the interpretation in terms of months and years of precociousness and retardation will become either too strict or too generous. The prevailing confusion surrounding this problem derives no doubt from the fact that, in designing a scale of development of the Terman or Binet type, certain logical and statistical arguments demand the use of problems which are, as a matter of fact, solved a few months before the age to which they are assigned. Consequently, the success percentages used to determine the level of a test are always higher than 50, and vary from 60 to 75 depending on the ages (Laurendeau and Pinard, 1957). Moreover, in the construction of developmental scales, the requirement that at least 75 per cent of the subjects of a given age pass an item successfully for this item to be set at that age would lead, against all logic, to the placement of items at an age at which they are not yet solved. In fact, the localization of items (or stages), and the determination of the age of success on these items (or of the age of accession to these stages), constitute two distinct problems and require two different techniques.

For all these reasons, in this investigation the 50 per cent criterion was used to assess the age of accession to stages. In order to take into account, to a certain extent at least, the variability of the distributions, and thus to increase the stability of the calculated ages of accession, a gross method of linear interpolation was applied. This means that an average was taken between the age located directly at the true point 50, and the age located at a point 50 estimated, this time, on the basis of points 25 and 75. In the case of truncated distributions, this last estimate was based on the figures closest to points 25 and 75.

Needless to say, when we compare our data concerning ages with those reported by Piaget, we shall take the necessary precautions, because the techniques used are not exactly the same. It must also be emphasized at this point that Piaget and Inhelder hardly ever make any systematic attempt at determining with precision the age of accession for each one of their stages. Especially in their later books (Piaget, in Osterrieth et al., 1955, p. 34; Inhelder, 1956, p. 85), they even expressly guard against setting these stages at definite ages, stressing the fact that these ages may indeed show noticeable differences according to sociological milieu. However, they never fail to suggest at least approximate ages for each one of their stages. They do this solely by consulting the age distributions taken as a whole. They may say, for instance, that a given stage is reached between five and seven, without stating more explicitly that it is rather at five, at six, or at seven. Sometimes, on the other hand, they will strictly, and almost blindly, apply the 75 per cent success criterion, without any consideration for the total distribution. This may even lead them to say that a stage is not yet reached at a given age, because only 73 or 70 per cent of the children of that age are at that stage! In spite of these reservations, the comparison of the results of the present study with those of Piaget is still very instructive, even though the computation of the age of accession to stages is not designed expressly for that purpose.

The second postulate implied in the determination of the age of accession to stages refers to the necessity of using cumulative frequencies. It would obviously be insufficient to consider only the total number of the children of each age who are located at each one of the stages. For each age, as a matter of fact, the precocious children have gone past the stage characteristic of their age, and this proportion of precocious children should always be added to that of the normal children. Let us suppose, for instance, that the raw percentages of children of a certain age are distributed as follows: 50 at stage 1, 30 at stage 2, and 20 at stage 3. At first glance, these results might lead one to believe that stage 1 is characteristic of that age, since this is where the desired proportion is found. Such an interpretation would obviously be erroneous. Stage 1 is not reached by only 50, but indeed by 100 per cent of the children, because those located at stages 2 and 3 have also reached at least stage 1. To conform to the facts, percentages must be cumulated, thus giving the following figures: 100 per cent at stage 1, 50 at stage 2, and 20 at stage 3. These hypothetical results are henceforth interpreted as follows: all the subjects have reached at least stage 1, 50 per cent at least stage 2, and only 20 per cent have reached stage 3. It thus becomes much clearer that stage 2, and not stage 1, is characteristic of that age.

In order to be valid, however, such a cumulation must meet the fundamental condition of transitivity. Answers classified in primitive stages must genetically occur earlier than those found in later stages; in other words, the successive mastery of inferior levels must be postulated in order to conclude that the final level has been reached—a condition not easily verifiable. The best, if not the only way, to identify the order of stage succession within a developmental scale is a longitudinal study. In a cross-sectional study, the available techniques can yield only a partial and indirect solution of this problem. For a given concept, this solution can be achieved satisfactorily enough by: (a) the calculation of the median age of the children included in each one of the stages; (b) the consequent setting up of a chronological seriation of stages; and (c) a comparison of this chronological seriation with the one previously predicted on purely logical and theoretical grounds. Indeed, a similar procedure is resorted to in certain techniques of item analysis used for the elaboration of developmental scales. It constitutes, for instance, the essential element of Thomson's method, which has been used by Doll (1953) for the seriation of the items of his social maturity scale. The fundamental postulate in this type of analysis is simple and, it would seem, very acceptable: the younger the children who give a certain response, the lower is the level of development corresponding to that response. It must be noted, however, that this technique could not, by itself, confirm the hypothesis whereby each individual must of necessity pass through inferior stages before reaching the last one. For want of a longitudinal study, the conclusions can apply only to the group of children of each age level, considered collectively. If, however, the chronological and the psychological sequences of stages are parallel for the total group of children, it may well be assumed that the same relation exists in the individual child.

In short, the technique of analysis adopted, once all the

protocols had been scored, consisted in calculating the median age of the children who were located at each one of the stages. When the scale of median ages corresponded to the scale of stages, the transitivity of the various levels was assumed, and then the frequencies were cumulated for each age group in order to arrive at the age of accession to each one of the stages.

To avoid any possible misinterpretation of the results, a final reservation must be made concerning the use of these median ages. Unless these ages are drawn from complete distributions, they lose part of their meaning. These distributions must extend from the age at which no subject has yet reached the most primitive stage of the concept considered, to the age at which all subjects classify at the most mature stage. The age limits of the present sample do not allow for the observation of these extreme levels. The fact that, at the age of four, some subjects have already reached the most primitive level of a given concept makes it impossible to determine the real starting point of the evolution of this concept. It may also happen that the percentage of children located at the most mature stage has not yet reached 100 at the age of twelve. This is why more refined statistical analyses, such as, for instance, the calculation of the variability in the age series, did not seem indicated. These restrictions have two telling effects even upon the avowedly crude method of median ages. The first effect is a notable reduction of the intervals between these ages, with the resulting danger of dissimulating real differences, especially when the development happens to be spaced over a very limited number of years or when the distributions are exceedingly truncated. The second effect is to deprive these median ages of any absolute meaning, thus excluding the possibility of drawing conclusions concerning either the exact age at which each stage is reached, or the real distance between these various stages. A merely relative meaning is to be assigned to these median ages, in the sense that their seriation provides information only on the hierarchy of stages. In any case, this was the one and only practical objective of this part of the analysis.

PART III

The Results

The first five chapters of this part deal with each of the experimental questionnaires. For each test, the analysis provides a description of the stages identified in the protocols and sets the age of accession to these various stages. The sixth chapter presents a synthesis of the preceding data: it stresses their most general features and discusses the common elements of the various manifestations of precausal thinking.

A preliminary remark is in order. In an investigation of this kind, the scope of the conclusions depends largely on the validity of the classifications. In order to attenuate the difficulties inherent in a classification by stages and to increase the objectivity of the scoring, it was decided that each protocol should be assessed and classified by both authors working jointly. Debatable cases could thus be discussed and decided by mutual agreement. After this first classification, a third judge, already familiar with this type of analysis and widely experienced in the examination of children, made a revision of every one of the 2,500 protocols. This third scorer had not been involved in the task of defining the stages and, when verifying the classification, he had to rely upon the sole description of the characteristics of each stage. The results of this verification are most reassuring, since altogether only 3 per cent of the protocols were considered to have been incorrectly classified. The scoring of the questionnaire on the origin of night has given rise to the most instances of disagreement (3.8 per cent). In general, however, only minor changes were suggested: out of 75 protocols classified differently, 56 have been judged misplaced by only one stage, 6 by two stages, 4 by three stages, and 9 were considered unclassifiable. These results support the validity of the classification used in the present analysis.

CHAPTER VIII

The Concept of Dream

The responses collected in the examination on the concept of dream may be classified into four main categories. The first one contains the most primitive types of reaction, those characterized by a total incomprehension of the examiner's questions or by a flat refusal to undergo the examination. The other categories represent the three essential phases that mark progressive understanding of the phenomenon: absolute realism, mitigated realism, and integral subjectivism. These three levels of response seem to correspond closely to Piaget's stages in spite of minor differences between the two types of categories. However, we considered it necessary to make new divisions within these three general groups. The protocols of children belonging to the same stage show indeed a wide diversity which cannot be overlooked. This variation may be especially observed in the transitional stages. Thus, the mitigated realism of the second stage includes all the possible steps between the total reification of the dream, attenuated by unskillful efforts at interiorization, on the one hand, and the almost complete subjectivation of the phenomenon, together with a residual expression of realism, on the other hand. To indicate the differences in such a global interpretation and to introduce greater homogeneity in the classification, it became indispensable to discriminate substages within the more general phases.

STAGE 0

Incomprehension or Refusal

Stage 0 includes all children who refuse, or are considered inapt, to answer the questions. At no time do these children show any sign of real understanding. Most of the time, they merely accept any suggestion as the interview goes on, or else they simply break away from the examination for some other interest. Here is an example:

12 (5:0):[1] "You know what a dream is?—*Yes.*—Now, tell me, where does a dream come from?—*I don't know.*—Where are the dreams made; they come from where?—*I don't know.*—Do they come from inside of you, or from outside of you?—*From outside.* —Who makes the dreams come?— [. . . .]—Is it you, or someone else?—*Somebody else.*—Who?—*I don't know.*—While you are dreaming, where is your dream, where does it go on, in what place is it?—*I don't know.*—Is it inside of you or in your room?—*In my room.*"

Protocols of this type contain no indication of understanding: the child gives no evidence whatsoever of spontaneity, and it is only when answering questions presented in the form of suggestions that he may risk a choice between the two parts of the alternative offered. Moreover, this choice always falls

---

[1] The first figure indicates the number of the protocol, and the second one, in parentheses, the child's age in years and (:) months.

on the second suggestion, which almost invariably reveals a total absence of personal conceptions or convictions. Answers belonging to this level are not always easily identified. Many subjects confuse the dream with some related phenomena, such as night or sleep. Even though some such answers may appear well adapted to the questions on dreaming, the examiner must be careful not to be taken in by this illusion. The following protocol is a good illustration of this confusion:

30 (4:0): "You know what a dream is?—*It's people in the bed.*— Now, tell me, where does a dream come from?—*In the bed.*— Where are the dreams made; they come from where?—[. . . .]— Do they come from inside of you, or from outside of you?—*Outside of me.*—Who makes the dreams come?—[. . . .]—Is it you or some one else?—*Somebody else.*—Who?—*Jesus in Heaven.*— While you are dreaming, where is your dream, where does it go on, in what place is it?—*In the bed.*"

Besides these frequent and somewhat logical confusions between dreaming and sleeping, there are others more unusual and more superficial, based essentially on word assonance. For instance, the French word for dream (*rêve*) is sometimes assimilated to that of "rat" or "Revel" (the commercial name of an ice sherbet very popular among children). Finally, the questions on dream readily lead to various fabulations, often induced by the element of fear which usually accompanies nightmares. Thus, some subjects will speak of *"the big bad wolves,"* or *"the cops chasing gangsters,"* or *"the bad men who frighten little children,"* or *"who bite little babies,"* and the like. In such circumstances, it is almost always fruitless to carry on with the examination: the child pays no attention to the questions except, once in a while, to catch a word that will allow him to elaborate further on his fanciful descriptions.

STAGE 1

Integral Realism

As in Piaget's scale, the subjects belonging to stage 1 express their complete belief in the reality of dreams. The origin of the phenomenon is still often rather vague, but it is always external to the child. The most popular beliefs are that the dream comes from *"the night," "the dark," "the window," "the trains," "the moon," "the lights," "my bed,"* etc. These explanations are usually coupled with an artificialistic cause: God, the Blessed Virgin, the devil, or the sandman fabricate the dreams and then send them to man. This artificialism is sometimes very complex since the child tries to explain the concrete mechanics of this fabrication. Other subjects, however, merely mention supernatural intervention. The examiner may be tempted to regard this artificialism as a simple confirmation of the belief in the external origin of the dream. However, this does not seem to be the only possible explanation. Far from being characteristic of the most primitive beliefs, the recourse to divine or supernatural beings may be observed at all levels. Indeed, even among children who hold the strongest convictions about the subjectiveness and individuality of dreams, a reference to the action of a divine power may often occur.

Even though this artificialism is almost always expressed in the same way, it undoubtedly changes in meaning throughout the course of the child's evolution. For young children, divine intervention is often assimilated to a real fabrication comparable to manual work performed by man. It may happen, then, that artificialism merges with a belief in the reality, or the external origin, of natural phenomena. With older children, however, divine action is dehumanized and the recourse to the omnipotence of God becomes necessary only as a last resort, that is, when naturalistic explanations are no longer satisfactory to the child and he is led to look for a more distant cause. Piaget (1926) does not hesitate to compare this artificialism with that which permeates Aristotelian physics. It is well known that, according to Aristotle, the origin of all things is due to the action of a first cause, and yet the acceptance of this fact does not prevent the search for the physical laws regulating natural phenomena. Briefly, for the realistic child, the less elaborate forms of artificialism would constitute one means among others for expressing his belief in the external origin of dreams. For a child of greater maturity, on the contrary, artificialism would most frequently be equivalent to an admission of ignorance: incapable of giving a natural explanation of the dream, he calls upon the being to whom, according to what he has been taught, must be attributed the origin of all things. In its present form the questionnaire, unfortunately, does not clearly register this distinction. Hence, to avoid errors of interpretation, it seems preferable to ignore these artificialistic explanations, whatever their form, and to classify the children on the basis of the information yielded by other parts of the examination.

For the child belonging to stage 1, the events that occur in the dream have an origin external to the dreamer and also take place in front of him: *"in my room," "on the wall," "in the window," "in front of me," "in the pillow," "just by our side,"* and the like. It is therefore not surprising to hear most children state that their eyes are open while they are dreaming. On the other hand, those who know that their eyes must be closed to sleep, and hence to dream, find themselves up against their own contradictory statements—a fact, however, which does not seem to shake their convictions.

12 (4:6): "Is it in your room for real, or is it only as if it were there?—*For real.*—When you dream, are your eyes closed or open?—*Closed.*—Then, where is your dream?—*In my room.*—

How is it that you see your dream, if your eyes are closed?—*I don't know."*

Yet some children do try to find a solution to this problem by locating the scene of the dream as close to the dreamer as possible, while still leaving it on the outside.

27 (5:0): "[Contends in the first place that the dream is located outside, somewhere in the room.] When you dream, are your eyes closed or open?—*My eyes are closed.*—Then where is your dream? —*Under my blanket."*

Children belonging to this stage usually agree that those who happen to be in the dreamer's room while the dream is taking place can see the spectacle.

28 (4:0): "Your mother, when she is in your room, can she also see your dream?—*Yes.*—And I, if I were in your room, could I see your dream?—*Of course.*—Why do you say that I could see your dream?—*Because I think it's still there."*

Some subjects, perhaps already aware of the individuality of the dream, do not therefore agree that it may be seen by someone else, but the reasons they allege do not diminish its integral realism.

47 (4:6): "Your mother, when she is in your room, can she also see your dream?—*No, she turns the light on; when she turns the light on, the dream goes away."*

25 (6:0): "Why do you say that I could not see your dream?— *Because it is in my pillow."*

21 (5:0): "Why do you say that I could not see your dream?— *Because you are not asleep.*—If I were asleep?—*You could see it."*

The reaction of this last subject is particularly interesting, since it is also observed equivalently among children belonging to primitive as well as to more mature stages. In some instances, the subject simply means that in order to dream one must sleep, without inferring the possibility that two persons could share the same dream. For other subjects, on the contrary—and the last case quoted is a clear example of this—the simple fact of sleeping in the same room seems sufficient to produce the same dream in all the sleepers. This is not surprising since the objects or the persons in the dream are located in the room.

Questions about the organ, the cause, the substance, and the reality of dreams elicit little additional information from subjects belonging to stage 1. For the most part, children do not understand the meaning of the questions and are ready to accept whatever suggestions are offered, no matter how improbable. Questions about the cause of the dream seem particularly baffling. Questions bearing on the reality of the dream are too equivocal to yield uniformly interpretable answers. As for the organ of the dream, it is often confused with its origin. The child will say that he dreams *"with the moon," "with the clouds," "with the rain," "with God," "with my bed,"* and the like. A few children propose *"the eyes"* or *"the face"* as organs of the dream. Such answers merely indicate their belief in the exteriority of the phenomenon: the dream is a spectacle to be looked at. Finally, the child is also rarely capable of offering appropriate answers to questions bearing on the substance of dreams; but when he does, there are always manifestations of realistic beliefs typical of this stage: the dream is made of *"cloth," "dough," "wall plaster," "wood," "skin,"* and the like. Here again, the same lack of differentiation between dreaming and reality prevails: if the content of the dream includes people, it is made of *"skin"*; if it involves objects, or if it is seen on the wall, it is made of *"wood," "cloth,"* and so on. It is thus quite natural for children belonging to this stage to accept the possibility of touching their dreams.

16 (4:0): "Can we touch dreams?—*Yes, they do not move.*"

When some children reject this possibility, they usually cannot justify their answer; or if they attempt an explanation, the reasons offered serve only to confirm their realistic beliefs.

5 (4:6): "Having dreamed of Santa Claus, asserts that his dream *is made of snow.*—Can we touch our dreams?—*No.*—Why?— *Because it's made of snow.*—But the snow, we can touch it!— *When you do not have gloves, you cannot touch it.*"

15 (6:0): "Can we touch our dreams?—*No, it is not allowed. When you touch it, there are prickles and they stick to your hands.*"

17 (5:0): "Can we touch our dreams?—*No.*—Why can't we touch them?—*Because it's bad.*—How do you know?—*I have known that for a long time.*—What does it do?—*It eats you up.*"

An example of the emotional reaction aroused by the questions is observable in this last subject. These reactions are very frequent and may follow upon any question. They do not seem to be typical of any particular stage and they often jeopardize the effective continuation of the examination. For example, a little girl had to be classified in stage 0 because she started to cry at the very first question and categorically refused to answer any additional question on dreaming. Repeated attempts to resume the examination during later periods failed to change the child's attitude.

Finally, it should be stated that the realism of stage 1, particularly among the less primitive, is sometimes expressed in more subtle terms than those of the examples given above. Some children, indeed, recognize that there is a difference between the content of dreams and the content of everyday reality. They know that the dream is essentially an illusion, yet they continue to consider it an objective phenomenon, that is, external to the dreamer. One such example will bring this out:

21 (5:0): "You know what a dream is?—*Yes.*—Do you dream sometimes at night?—*Yes.*—Now, tell me, where does a dream come from?—*It comes from outside; I don't know.*—Where are the dreams made, where do they come from?—*In heaven, perhaps. I don't know.*—Do they come from inside of you, or from outside of you?—*From outside of me.*—Who makes the dreams come?—*Jesus . . . I don't know.*—Is it you or is it somebody else?—*Somebody else.*—Who?—*Jesus, perhaps.*—While you are dreaming, where is your dream, where does it go on, in what place is it? —*In front of me.*—Is it inside of you or in your room?—*In my room.*—Is it in your room for real, or is it only as if it were there? Or does it only seem to be there?—*It is as if it were in my room, but it is not there for real.*—While you are dreaming, are your eyes closed or open?—*Closed.*—Then, where is your dream?—*In my room when I am dreaming.*—When you dream that you are playing in the street, where is your dream, is it in the street or in your room?—*In the street. I cannot dream in the street because I never play there.*—Is there something in front of you, when you are dreaming?—*Yes, but they are not real people.*—[. . . .]—Why do you say that I could not see your dream?—*Because you are not asleep.*—If I were asleep?—*You would see it.*—[. . . .]—What is a dream made of?—*With nothing. It can be seen the same as I see you there.*"

For this child, the dream is surely realistic. It depends in no way upon the intervention, voluntary or not, of the sleeper: it exists in itself, it comes from the outside and takes its place in front of the sleeper. But, at the same time, it is different from everyday reality: there is something in front of the sleeper, but *they are not real people.*" To repeat a comparison already suggested by Piaget, the dream is assimilated to that privileged universe of the child which contains, among other things, fairies and ghosts. The child knows that the dream is illusive; he does not confuse it with real objects and persons. But he nevertheless remains essentially realistic, since he does not yet recognize any subjective element. In short, to account for the various phenomena of everyday reality, the child creates a second universe for himself, just as objective to him as the first, but reserved for beings who are more alien, or less accessible to him.

STAGE 2

Mitigated Realism

Between the stage of absolute realism and that of integral subjectivism, there is a transitional period in which the progressive interiorization of the dream can be witnessed. This transition usually takes the form of a continuous oscillation between the interiorization and externalization of the phenomenon. Contrary to Piaget's predictions, no unique type of confusion can be noted. According to him, the child belonging to this intermediate stage should see the dream as coming from the inside, but taking place on the outside, somewhat like what happens at the cinema: the image comes from within the apparatus, but it is projected on the outside. The results of the present study show beyond doubt that this type of confusion is far from being the only one to occur, even if it does arise more often than other types. As a matter of fact, the completely opposite conception is quite often observed. For several children, the dream takes its origin on the outside and goes on in the inside, as for instance, *"in the eyes," "in the head," "in the ear," "in the tummy,"* etc. At first glance, one might be tempted to explain the emergence of this new type of response by the structure of the questionnaire. The questions about the origin of dreams are possibly more insistent in the present examination than in Piaget's and may thus entail the risk of inducing children to elaborate rather special explanations. This hypothesis, however, does not seem likely for three main reasons. In the first place, the above-noted insistence of the questions does not in fact lead the children to attribute an external origin to the dream; it rather favors responses of an artificialistic type (e.g., God, heaven, the devil, etc.), and it has been seen that these responses are never interpreted here in terms of external origin. In the second place, this new type of reaction is not more exclusive than the one referred to by Piaget: the same questionnaire elicits a large variety of explanations, a variety which would probably not occur if the questions were not so pointedly suggestive. Finally, even on a purely theoretical basis, it is not evident that this type of response would be more artificial than the type described by Piaget: if the child, as he begins to rid himself of pure realism, becomes particularly impressed by the fact that the dream is not visible to others, and if he is not yet in a position to understand the complete subjectivity of the phenomenon, it is only natural that he should seek first to interiorize the course of the spectacle rather than its origin. At any rate, the main reason for the difference between our results and those of Piaget is probably due to the number of children examined. It may well be that Piaget has examined too few children belonging to the intermediate stage to allow for the possible emergence of all types of reactions.

This mitigated realism may manifest itself in a number of ways. Besides the two types of reaction already described, others are also observed. They may be less clearly defined, but no less indicative of the hesitancy characteristic of the child of this level. Thus, some subjects will alternately suggest an external and an internal origin, an interior and an exterior development, and so on, without, however, arriving at the exclusion of either of the two hypotheses. Others will accept the subjectiveness of the dream without hesitation, but with a residue of realism: for instance, they will uphold the possibility that others can see the dream inside the head of the dreamer, but the dream remains material in spite of its essentially personal and internal character.

30 (9:0): "While you are dreaming, where is your dream, where does it go on, in what place is it?—*In my head.*—Is it inside of you or in your room?—*Inside of me.*—If we could open your head while you are dreaming, could we see your dream?—*Yes.*—Why do you say we could see your dream?—*Because it's like a story, like a little play.*"

Still almost all the answers given by some other children, undoubtedly closer to stage 1, reveal a realistic attitude; the few subjective elements they may resort to are very precarious and become submerged in a mass of contradictory statements.

As may be noted, the protocols classified as belonging in stage 2 show a great variety and represent about all the degrees of transition between the two opposite attitudes: absolute realism and integral subjectivism. Since the meaning value of a classification depends on the homogeneity of its classes, it becomes important to divide these various protocols into subclasses typical of the main steps of this transition. At first glance, many clues seemed to be of possible use in making these discriminations; but all of them had to be eliminated successively for inefficacy. For instance, children for whom realism was still predominant were inclined to locate the dream "*in the tummy*" or "*in the heart,*" rather than "*in the head,*" "*in the eyes,*" or even "*in the imagination.*" If this indication could have been used to identify two widely divergent classes of subjects, the task would undoubtedly have been greatly simplified. But this criterion would have met with too many exceptions. The subdivision actually adopted includes three substages, but it admittedly does not comprise all the gradations that might be desired. The analysis has shown that further subdivisions were in fact useless or even superficial; indeed, different responses may manifest the same level of development and may be given by children of the same age.

SUBSTAGE 2A

The explanations offered by children in substage 2A are almost totally identical with the realistic answers of stage 1. These subjects, however, make an effort, still very faltering and awkward, to interiorize the dream, when questioned on either its origin, on its course, or on any other aspect of the phenomenon. Frequently, this attempt at interiorization is almost immediately denied by the child.

2 (4:6): "[Begins by stating that the dream comes from heaven and hell.] While you are dreaming, where is your dream, where does it go on, in what place is it?—*In my heart.*—Is it inside of you or in your room?—*In my room.*—You told me a moment ago that the dream was in your heart. Then, if we could open your heart while you are dreaming, if we could look into your heart, could we see your dream?—*No.*—Why do you say that we could not see your dream?—*Because I don't want to.*—Then, where in your heart is your dream?—*It is not in my heart, it came out there.*"

For other children, the denial is not explicit. The subjective element is no sooner expressed than it seems to be simply forgotten and is disregarded in subsequent answers.

44 (4:6): "Tell me, where does a dream come from?—*From the kitchen.*—Where are the dreams made, where do they come from?

—You close the door, then the little girl she comes in with her schoolbag.—Do the dreams come from inside of you, or from outside of you?—*From outside.*—Who makes the dreams come?—*It's ourselves: we sleep, then we dream.*—While you are dreaming, where is your dream, where does it go on, in what place is it?—*Outside.*—Is it inside of you or in your room?—*In my room.*—Is it in your room for real, or is it only as if it were there? Or does it only seem to be there?—*For real, yes.*—[. . . .]—Why do you say that I could see your dream?—*Because we sleep, then the dream opens the door, then it shuts the door, then it comes in to pay us a visit.*"

For this subject, it seems that the dream is a reality independent of the dreamer. Even though he claims to have the power of calling them forth, he persists in assimilating the dreams to personages really existing. The question may even be raised whether the child's statement *"it's ourselves, we sleep, then we dream"* truly indicates the beginnings of a belief in the personal origin of dreams. It could just as well be a simple description of events in the order of their inevitable succession (*ourselves, we sleep, then the dream comes*), or else a manifestation of the magical thinking which leads small children to claim exceptional powers for themselves. At any rate, since the data do not allow a delimitation of the exact scope of the child's remarks, it seems reasonable to assign them the more advanced meaning, and to give the child credit for it.

SUBSTAGE 2B

In substage 2B, there is a steadier balance between realism and subjectivism. It may even happen that answers tinged with realism are definitely the minority. But because the ratio of these two attitudes is almost always impossible to ascertain and inevitably involves debatable interpretations, it seems more in order to class all the protocols in the same given group, even at the risk of attenuating their essential diversity. In short, as soon as subjective elements play a definite role in the child's explanation, and as long as this explanation still indicates a confusion between the interiority and the exteriority of the dream, the protocol is classified in substage 2B. This confusion is clearly apparent whenever a subject rightly belongs to the present level.

32 (6:0): "Then, tell me, where does a dream come from?—*When you sleep.*—Where are the dreams made, where do they come from?—*In the house.*—Where in the house?—*In the bed.*—Where in the bed?—*In the eyes.*—Do the dreams come from inside of you, or outside of you?—*From outside.*—Who makes the dreams come?—*Accidents, as if a car would turn upside down.*—[....]— *It's people like ourselves.*—Why are they the ones to make the dreams come?—*They are the ones who make the accident.*— While you are dreaming, where is your dream, where does it go on, in what place is it?—*In front of ourselves.*—Is it inside of you or in your room?—*In my room.*—Is it in your room for real, or is it only as if it were there? Or does it only seem to be there?—*For real.*—While you are dreaming, are your eyes closed or open?— *Closed.*—Then, where is the dream?—*In front of me.*—Is there something in front of you, while you are dreaming?—*Yes.*—Your mother, when she is in your room, can she also see your dream?— *No.*—And I [. . .]?—*No.*—Why do you say that I could not see your dream?—*Because it's inside of me, but in front of me. I don't understand that at all. I am all mixed up!*—Then, tell me, what do we dream with?—*With the eyes.*—If we could open your eyes while you are dreaming, could we see your dream?—*No.*—Why do you say that we could not see your dream?—*It's in front. It's also inside of me. I'm all mixed up.*—Then, where is your dream? —*I don't know.*"

This example is of course exceptional for the clearness of the hesitations and doubts elicited by the questioning. Most children of this stage, however, make much stronger statements, even if these are just as contrary to the truth.

16 (7:0): "Then tell me, where does a dream come from?—*It comes from the night when it is dark.*—Where are the dreams made?—*I don't know.*—Do they come from inside of you or outside of you?—*From outside of me.*—Who makes the dreams come? —*Perhaps the wind pushes the dreams.*—[. . . .]—While you are dreaming, where is your dream, where does it go on, in what place is it?—*In my heart.*—Is it inside of you or in your room?—*Inside of me.*—If we could open your heart while you are dreaming, if we could see into your heart, could we see your dream?—*No.*— Why do you say that we could not see your dream?—*It's invisible, a dream.*—Then, where is it, in your heart, your dream?—*It's everywhere in my heart.*—[. . . .]—Then, tell me, what do we dream with?—*You think about it, it falls into your head, and it goes into your heart.*"

20 (9:0): "Then, tell me, where does a dream come from?—*We think . . . . It comes into our head.*—Where are the dreams made, where do dreams come from?—*From ourselves, on the forehead . . . . no, in the forehead. We think.*—Do they come from inside of you, or from outside of you?—*From within me.*—Who makes the dreams come?—*God. He says: let them come!*—[. . . .]—While you are dreaming, where is your dream, where does it go on, in what place is it?—*By our side.*—Is it inside of you or in your room? —*In my room.*—Is it in your room for real, or is it only as if it were there? Or does it only seem to be there?—*It's only as if.*—While you are dreaming, are your eyes closed or open?—*Closed.*—Then, where is your dream?—*It's in our room, but we think about it with our head.*—If we could open your head while you are dreaming, if we could look into your head, could we see your dream?—*No.*— Why do you say that we could not see it?—*Because . . . we see it . . . because it's invisible . . . because it's God. If He wants us to see it, we can see it.*—Then, where is it in your head, your dream?— *On the forehead.*"

THE RESULTS

Examples need not be multiplied. It can be seen clearly enough how children of substage 2B account for their dreams. The internal and subjective element is inevitably supplemented by some contribution from the outside. This realistic background may be strictly limited to the acceptance of the possibility that others may see the same dream. For some subjects, indeed, the dream arises from within (*"from the eyes," "from the head," "from the mind,"* and so on), and develops inside also (*"in the tummy," "in the head," "in the mind,"* and so on). The fact, however, that the dreamer is not the only one who can look at the spectacle reveals a residual confusion between the interiority and the exteriority of the phenomenon.

SUBSTAGE 2C

The only trace of realism remaining in all children classified in substage 2C consists in granting a certain materiality to the dream. The dream is interior; it is even invisible under normal conditions, but it could be touched or seen if the head of the dreamer could be opened without waking him up, because *"it's a paper running through the head," "it comes written sometimes," "it's made of cloth,"* etc. The child may even deny the possibility of seeing the dream inside the head, but the reason he gives is not sufficient to prove that he believes that the dream is not material.

50 (6:0): "While you are dreaming, where is your dream, where does it go on, in what place is it?—*In my head.*—Is it inside of you or in your room?—*Inside of me. It can't be in my room. If I dream of a wolf, and then it comes into my room, brrr . . . .*—If we could open your head while you are dreaming, if we could look into your head, could we see your dream?—*No.*—Why do you say that we could not see your dream?—*If Jesus sees you opening my head, He removes my dream; a dream belongs to us.*—Then, where is it

in your head, your dream?—*Near the ears, because I must hear it.*
—[. . . .]—What is a dream made of?—*With earth, and all that . . . .*"

For this child it is obvious that the dream is invisible, not because of its immateriality but because of its individuality. The remainder of the examination clearly shows that, in spite of the initial negative response, the dream is assimilated to a material, physical object: it has an exact location in the head, and it is compared to familiar objects (it is made *"with earth, and all that"*).

The opportuneness of grouping responses of this type in a special category may no doubt be questioned. Since they must be interpreted as another indubitable form of realism, why classify in substage 2C confusions bearing on the immateriality of the dream, and relegate to substage 2B those relating rather to its interiority? The main reason for this differentiation derives from the fact that the confusion of *internal* and *external* is still more primitive than that of *material* and *immaterial*. Piaget (1926) has already noted a rather marked timelag in the disappearance of these two particular forms of realism.

> . . . the distinction between internal and external . . . becomes complete at about the age of 9-10 (beginning of third stage). Finally, it is not till about 11 that this distinction between internal and external leads the child definitely to understand that the dream is not a material image, but simply a thought [p. 121].

Over and above providing more precise chronological information, the present experiment completely supports Piaget's observations since, on that point, the median age of substage 2C children (material-immaterial confusion) is 7:1 while the median age of substage 2B children (internal-external confusion) is only 5:8. Such a difference is certainly not to be dis-

THE RESULTS

regarded. It is all the more striking for being derived from a very crude statistical technique, a technique which, when applied to truncated distributions, tends to minimize existing differences.

STAGE 3

Integral Subjectivism

During the third stage, all traces of realism disappear. The origin of the dream and its course are henceforth interiorized: they are located *"in the head," "in the imagination," "in the mind," "in the eyes,"* etc. Let it be noted immediately that, for Piaget, the fact of locating the dream in the eyes would constitute a residue of realistic thinking. But it seems that it is chiefly because children note the visual quality of the dream that they locate it in the eyes. At the same time, subjects insist so much on the internal character of the phenomenon that it would be illogical to ascribe realistic beliefs to them.

40 (8:0): "While you are dreaming, where is your dream, where does it go on, in what place is it?—*In my eyes. Not near my eyes: in my eyes.*"

11 (8:0): "What do we dream with?—*With our eyes closed.*"

The subject of this stage not only interiorizes the dream, but he also states that it cannot be seen by others because *"it's my own thinking," "it's my imagination," "we build it in ourselves," "thought cannot be seen,"* etc. Even if the head of the dreamer were opened, his dream could not be seen because *"thought is invisible," "it's a spirit," "it's thinking and that has no place,"* etc. Moreover, the cause of the dream is almost always objective: *"it's because we have thought about that during the day, and it comes back to our mind during the* night," "it's because we have overeaten," "we are not lying down properly," "we are not sleeping well," etc. Finally, the dream is made "of thoughts," "of nothing," "of imagination," "of voices," "of air," "of shadows," or of any other substance that the child may think of in an attempt to express immateriality. In short, the dream is personal, interior, invisible, and immaterial.

The child's remarks are often ambiguous and may lead the examiner to suspect that they reveal residues of realistic beliefs when in fact there are none. In this matter, some confusions noted by Piaget proved to be more verbal than real. For instance, he mentions a confusion between the origin of dreams and the persons or things dreamed about. And, in fact, responses of this kind may occur.

37 (10:0): "Then tell me, where does a dream come from?—*From what you see.*"

48 (11:0): "Who makes the dreams come?—*The things we dream of.*"

In all such cases, however, the continuation of the examination can disclose the exact meaning of these expressions: things seen during the day come back to the mind during sleep and are, in this sense, the origin of the dream. Therefore, this explanation does not entail a real confusion between internal and external, but rather points to the origin of the dream by stating one of its causes. Subjects are sometimes very explicit in this ascription.

22 (11:0): "*It can be a thing you have seen or heard and which is imagined differently, but on the same topic.*"

6 (10:0): "*When during the day you see something dreadful on television, you don't like that . . . . And then, in the evening, you dream of that during the night.*"

15 (9:0): *"If, for instance, before you go to bed, you see cowboys on television, you have a nightmare. But you can dream a nice dream, if you have read good books."*

A similar pseudo confusion is frequently elicited by the questions on the location of the dream. The child does not seem to grasp the exact scope of the questions and describes the place where the events of the dream occur, or also the place where the sleeper is during the dream.

3 (9:0): *"While you are dreaming, where is your dream, where does it go on, in what place is it?—Let's say in a house, outside, on the lakes, anywhere sometimes."*

114 (11:0): "[Same question.]—*It depends on the dream you have; if you dream that you are in Africa, it is in Africa.*"

102 (12:0): "[Same question.]—*If we are at home in our bed, it's going on at home.*"

There again, answers to subsequent questions inevitably rule out the hypothesis of a true confusion. These various examples indeed illustrate clearly the danger of an isolated, and possibly too literal, interpretation of the child's remarks. In fact, the questions are not always taken in the sense intended by the examiner. It is thus important to base the diagnosis on the whole set of explanations given by a subject. Some questions, perhaps too suggestive, often elicit incorrect answers even from subjects who belong to stage 3. In this respect, special mention should be made of the third and fifth questions on the origin of dreams ("Do dreams come from inside of you, or outside of you? Is it you, or is it somebody else?"), and also of the second question on the location of dreams ("Is it inside of you or in your room?"). When the remainder of the examination does not corroborate the errors to which these questions may have given rise, it seems that such errors should be attributed to a misunderstanding of the meaning of the questions themselves, and not to confusions deriving from genuine realism.

Among children of stage 3, which is characterized by the disappearance of realism, many will occasionally still resort to precausal beliefs of another sort. For instance, numerous explanations tinged with artificialism, finalism, or moralism may be found. In fact, these other forms of primitive thinking do not appear during the third stage exclusively. The preceding stages all show evidence of a constant mixture of realistic, artificialistic, and finalistic conceptions. But until realism has completely disappeared, it does not seem essential, in the determination of stages, to grant particular importance to other forms of precausality. It is altogether normal that realism should be accompanied by various precausal beliefs, since it is the very source of these beliefs. At the third stage, however, it becomes mandatory to take note of the other manifestations of precausal thinking, in order to avoid identifying the disappearance of realism with the concurrent disappearance of any other form of precausality. The division of stage 3 into two substages aims precisely at making this distinction clear.

SUBSTAGE 3A

Substage 3A is comprised of all children who, although they say that the dream is interior, personal, and immaterial, will occasionally call upon artificialistic, finalistic, or moralistic factors. Here are some examples.

40 (9:0): "Then, tell me, where does a dream come from?—*From the dreadful things we have seen or read.*—Where are dreams made, where do they come from?—*From our thinking.*—Do they come from inside of you or from outside of you?—*From inside of me.*—Who makes the dreams come?—*God.*—Is it you or somebody else?—*Somebody else.*—Who?—*God.*—While you are

dreaming, where is your dream, where does it go on, in what place is it?—*In my head.*—Is it inside of you or in your room?—*Inside of me.*"

34 (9:0): " . . . Then, do you know why one dreams, why there are dreams?—*It's God who allows it.*"

40 (10:0): "[Same question.]—*To make a change.*"

51 (12:0): "[Same question.]—*To make us laugh.*"

35 (6:0): "[Same question.]—*Sometimes, it teaches us a lesson.*"

111 (11:0): "[Same question.]—*Because we have to have some.*"

As may be seen, finalistic remarks almost always occur at the same point in the examination. Admittedly the wording of the questions on the cause of the dream has something to do with this; yet finalism does not, on that account, become artificial. If with some children the "why" calls for an explanation in terms of finality, it is precisely because their thinking is naturally oriented toward this primitive form of causality.

SUBSTAGE 3B

Children of substage 3B give a perfect explanation of the dream, and the questioning no longer brings out any indication of precausal thinking.

26 (12:0): "Then, tell me, where does a dream come from?—*From our intelligence.*—Where are dreams made?—*In our memory.*—Do they come from inside of you, or from outside of you?—*From inside of me.*—Who makes the dreams come?—*Sleep.*—[. . . .]—While you are dreaming, where is your dream, where does it go on, in what place is it?—*Inside of me, in my thinking.*—Is it inside of you or in your room?—*Inside of me.*—If we could open your head while you are dreaming, and if we could look into your head,

could we see your dream?—*No.*—Why do you say that we could not see your dream?—*It's invisible, it's my thinking.*—Then, where in your head is your dream?—*In my thinking.*—Is there anything in front of you, while you are dreaming?—*Yes.*—What is in front of you?—*The things which are there, in my room.*—[. . . .]—Why do you say that I could not see your dream?—*It's inside of me, it's invisible.*—Then, tell me, what do we dream with?—*With our thinking.*—[. . . .]—Then, do you know why we dream, why there are dreams?—*It is caused by our digestion, our digestion is bad.*—What is a dream made of?—*With nothing, with thinking.*"

• • •

This qualitative analysis must be followed by the presentation of the quantitative data. Table 7 shows the distribution of all the protocols in the scale of stages so far described. This table is divided into two sections. The first gives the results in raw percentages. For each age level these percentages are calculated on 50 subjects, except at 4, 5, and 6 years of age where some protocols had to be eliminated for lack of sufficient information, the examiner not having been able to complete the examination satisfactorily. The data in this first section allow the computation, in years and months, of the median age of the children for each one of the stages, as well as the relative frequency of each one of these stages in the total sample. The second section of the same table translates the raw percentages into cumulative percentages, and, on the basis of these data, indicates the age of accession to each one of the stages.

The increase in the median age of the children of each stage confirms first of all the logical significance of the classification: those answers ascribed to the first stages mainly on the basis of theoretical criteria are given in fact by the youngest children, and are thus shown to be truly primitive. The regularly ascending gradation of these median ages also supports the postulate of stage transitivity for the group as a whole, and thereby justifies the cumulation of percentages. It is on the

Table 7

Distribution of subjects by age and developmental
stage in the questionnaire on dream

Age	N	Raw percentages							Cumulative percentages					
		0	1	2A	2B	2C	3A	3B	1	2A	2B	2C	3A	3B
12:0	50	0	0	0	4	2	22	72	100	100	100	96	94	72
11:0	50	0	0	0	2	4	46	48	100	100	100	98	94	48
10:0	50	0	0	0	0	2	32	66	100	100	100	100	98	66
9:0	50	2	2	0	16	4	38	38	98	96	96	80	76	38
8:0	50	0	0	2	6	10	50	32	100	100	98	92	82	32
7:0	50	4	2	6	8	12	46	22	96	94	88	80	68	22
6:0	49	10	10	4	20	14	35	6	89	79	75	55	41	6
5:0	46	24	24	17	17	4	4	9	75	51	34	17	13	9
4:6	50	46	26	14	12	2	0	0	54	28	14	2	0	0
4:0	49	55	20	2	22	0	0	0	44	24	22	0	0	0
Total		141	84	45	107	54	273	293						
Median age		4:5	4:8	4:11	5:8	7:1	8:7	10:1						

Age of accession   4:4 5:0 5:5 6:0 6:5 9:7

basis of this cumulation that the age of accession to the several stages could be determined. As may be noted, stage 3 is
reached at the age of 6:5. The total disappearance of realistic
beliefs occurs, then, at a much earlier age than Piaget's observations would have led us to predict: according to him, integral subjectivism should appear only when the child has
reached nine or ten years of age. One must not forget, however, that the ages suggested by Piaget are avowedly approximate: he probably confined himself to computing the mean
age of the children belonging to the last stage. Obviously, this
mean age cannot be compared to the age of accession to a

stage, since the two figures do not have the same meaning at all; it corresponds rather to the median ages calculated in the present experiment (8:7 for stage 3A, and 10:1 for stage 3B). These figures are much closer to those of Piaget, and the remaining disparity may be explained by differences in the samples. Be that as it may, it is not the mean age, nor is it the median age, but the age of accession to successive stages that provides direct information on the evolution of infantile realism and that figure must be used as a norm for subsequent diagnoses. In the present sample, the realism that characterizes the explanation of dreams is first perceptible shortly after the age of four (stage 1), and then recedes rather rapidly, to disappear completely about the age of six and a half (stage 3A). The difference observable between the ages of accession to stages 3A and 3B (6:5 and 9:7) already points to the much later disappearance of forms of precausality other than realism. The analysis of the other questionnaires will no doubt support these facts.

The distribution frequencies reveal, on the other hand, a significant disproportion in the relative number of subjects located at each one of the stages. Levels characterized by some form of realism (stages 1 to 2C inclusively) always contain rather few subjects, while the others (stages 3A and 3B) comprise a much greater number. This disproportion, however, does not seem sufficient to raise doubts about the authenticity of infantile realism. This phenomenon may be quite simply explained, when it is noted that the third stage is already reached at the age of 6:5, while the examination carries on up to the age of twelve. Under these conditions, it is altogether normal to find the greatest number of children in the third stage. The proportion of subjects normally located at that level can be estimated at about 60 per cent, since, among the 500 subjects of the total sample, 300 are between seven and twelve years of age. The 56.6 per cent proportion noted in

Table 8

Sex differences on the questionnaire on dream

Age	Sex	N	0	1	2A	2B	2C	3A	3B	X²	df	
12:0	G	25	0	0	0	0	1	5	19	0.39	1	P>.01
	B	25	0	0	0	2	0	6	17			
11:0	G	25	0	0	0	0	2	10	13	0.32	1	P>.01
	B	25	0	0	0	1	0	13	11			
10:0	G	26	0	0	0	0	1	12	13	6.17*	1	P<.01
	B	24	0	0	0	0	0	4	20			
9:0	G	25	1	0	0	3	2	9	10	0.12	2	P>.01
	B	25	0	1	0	5	0	10	9			
8:0	G	25	0	0	1	1	4	12	7	1.30	2	P>.01
	B	25	0	0	0	2	1	13	9			
7:0	G	25	0	0	1	2	4	13	5	2.56	3	P>.01
	B	25	2	1	2	2	2	10	6			
6:0	G	24	2	2	1	6	7	4	2	7.85	2	P>.01
	B	25	3	3	1	4	0	13	1			
5:0	G	24	7	3	5	4	2	1	2	3.77	3	P>.01
	B	22	4	8	3	4	0	1	2			
4:6	G	25	8	8	3	5	1	0	0	3.98	2	P>.01
	B	25	15	5	4	1	0	0	0			
4:0	G	24	12	6	0	6	0	0	0	0.75	2	P>.01
	B	25	15	4	1	5	0	0	0			
Total	G	248	30	19	11	27	24	66	71			
	B	246	39	22	11	26	3	70	75			
						Over-all X²				27.21	19	P>.01

* When a correction is made for continuity, this X² drops to 4.78 and is no longer significant.

the present findings is, therefore, far from excessive. Some critics might perhaps find in this explanation a new reason to contest the authenticity of realistic beliefs: if these beliefs disappear at such an early age, is this not precisely because they never constituted the core of infantile thinking, or even because they never really existed? This argument cannot be upheld against the analysis of the present results. Whenever the youngest children (4:0 and 4:6) succeed in understanding the questions and in communicating their thinking, their remarks unfailingly include realistic elements and, at any rate, none of these subjects could be classified in the third stage. It may also be added that, in the total sample, a proportion of 29 per cent of the subjects are located at stages at least partially realistic (stages 1 to 2C). One would have ample justifications for adding to this proportion the large majority of children of stage 0. Their realistic beliefs are easily recognizable, even if the examination does not provide an opportunity for these to be expressed formally. Anyone who has witnessed the fright that seizes some children at the very opening of the examination, and their consequent obstinate refusal to answer further questions, can understand to what extent these children confuse dream and reality. It is indeed regrettable that the present technique could not be used, with a minimum of efficiency, for the examination of children who have not yet reached at least the age of four or five.

Table 8 presents a comparison of boys and girls for each separate age, and for all ages taken together. None of these differences is significant at the .01 level.

CHAPTER IX

The Concept of Life

The classification of answers to the questionnaire on life raises specific difficulties. It is difficult to understand why, in the large number of similar investigations, no mention is ever made of these problems. They may arise from different sources, but they are all related to the differentiation of the main phases of the evolution of animistic beliefs. In the present study, the existence of these beliefs cannot be questioned. The number of children who attribute life to one or to several inanimate objects is indeed so large that it is impossible not to recognize that very special form of thinking which Piaget calls animistic. In fact, only 31.5 per cent of the children of the complete sample can correctly classify the objects included in the questionnaire. Of course, this percentage alone provides no information on the genetic aspect of animistic beliefs. Only the analysis of the criteria of discrimination resorted to by each individual child makes it possible to differentiate the main phases of this evolution.

First, it must be acknowledged that Piaget's scale of stages has proved to be incomplete in several respects. It is therefore a matter of surprise that some investigators, Dennis and Russell for instance, used Piaget's scheme unmodified without encountering, apparently at least, any major obstacles. The framework set by Piaget's descriptions is much too restrictive to include all of the children's responses. According to him, the criterion for the differentiation of the living from the nonliving would vary quite markedly from one stage to the next and would therefore be easy to identify. Life, defined at first by activity or usefulness in general, would later be reserved to mobile objects and would, finally, during the third phase only, be limited to objects whose movement is conceived as autonomous. The presence of these criteria in the child's thinking is undeniable, since almost all of the protocols contain this kind of explanations. However, the application of these criteria by the child is not as systematic as Piaget's descriptions would lead one to believe. The same protocol generally includes criteria of various sorts and of various levels. One particular child, for instance, refers to movement in general to attribute life to an *automobile* or to the *sun*, but a few minutes later he will invoke the absence of autonomous movement to refuse life to a *bicycle* or a *pencil*. Does this mean that the child conceives of the movement of the sun and the automobile as autonomous, and merely forgets to mention it at the precise moment that these questions are put to him? Or should one rather conclude that the criterion which he is applying at this precise moment assimilates life globally to the movement of objects, whatever be the nature of this movement? It is impossible to decide between these two hypotheses. Because the assessment of responses should not entail unnecessary inferences as to the child's tacit intentions, the examiner is bound to conclude that protocols of this description involve at least two different criteria.

This lack of systematization is still further demonstrated by the fact that the more primitive criteria, classified in the first stage by Piaget, are frequently combined with the reputedly more advanced criteria. Thus, some subjects will appeal to the activity or the usefulness of, for example, the *sun*, in order to attribute life to it (e.g., *"because it gives light," "because it shines,"* and so on), while a few moments later these same subjects will rely upon the movement of objects, often even upon the autonomous character of this movement, to say these objects are alive or not alive. The extreme difficulty met in attempting to discriminate Piaget's stage 1 (life identified with the activity of objects) from stage 2 (life identified with movement) must indeed be emphasized. The activity of an object is almost always described in terms of movement; or, reciprocally, the movement of an object is confused with its main activity or its usefulness. Accordingly, verbal expressions such as *"the pencil writes," "the lamp lights up," "the bell rings," "the wind blows,"* may just as validly refer to the movement as to the activity or the usefulness of these objects. Of course, the meaning of certain remarks is not always that ambiguous. For instance, the child who considers the *bell* as alive *"because it tells us to go to church,"* the *watch, "because it gives the time,"* or the *automobile, "because it carries people"* is no doubt alluding to the usefulness of these various objects; but, because these reasons are never the only ones invoked by a given subject, it would seem completely unfounded to base a special stage on this type of explanations. The analysis of the protocols even reveals that these references to the usefulness of objects, far from being typical of the most primitive stages, as Piaget claims, are very frequently associated with the most mature concepts.

The data reported below (see Table 9, p. 138) actually show that among 161 subjects who rely on autonomous movement for their classification, 107 also mention usefulness or activity in order either to refuse or to attribute life to certain objects. It is admittedly possible, but not very likely, that there is a residue of primitive animistic thinking in all these children. It seems more reasonable to consider these various responses, not as true criteria of differentiation between animate and inanimate, but rather as simple definitions or pure descriptions of the objects mentioned. The child resorts to this kind of answers when he does not take the trouble to seek the real explanation, or when he does not succeed in finding it, although he remains convinced that his classification is the correct one.

114 (12:0): " . . . Is the sun alive?—*Yes.*—Why do you say it is alive?—*It moves about, everywhere.*—The table?—*No.*—Why? —*It does not go by itself.*—An automobile?—*No.*—Why?—*It has to have someone to make it go.*—A cat?—*Yes.*—Why?—*It sees, it hears, it comes over when you call it.*—A cloud?—*No.*—Why?— *It's water, and water is not alive.*—A lamp?—*No.*—Why?—*It needs electricity. It has to be connected to work.*—A watch?—*No. Why?—It has to be wound up. It is a thing that had to be made; God did not make it.*—A bird?—*Yes.*—Why?—*It can see, it's an animal, it can walk, it can fly.*—A bell?—*No.*—Why?—*You need someone to make it ring.*—The wind?—*Yes.*—Why?—*It makes us cool.*—An airplane?—*No.*—Why?—*You need someone to make it work.*—A fly?—*Yes.*—Why?—*It can walk, it can fly.*—The fire?— *No.*—Why?—*If you want to have fire, it must be made with something, a match, and light it up.*—A flower?—*Yes.*—Why?—*It can grow, it does not stay there.*—The rain?—*No.*—Why?—*It's water, it's clouds, they fall in spite of themselves.*"

It is quite clear that, for this child, the criterion for discrimination is autonomous movement. To the question on the wind, he gives an explanation which refers obviously to usefulness; but the protocol as a whole strongly suggests the possibility that the first answer by which he attributes life to the wind is really based upon autonomous movement even though, when asked to justify his answer, he merely gives a simple definition of the wind which is purely functional like all infantile definitions. At any rate, the results of the present study do not warrant the retaining of stage 1 of Piaget's scale. On the one hand, the distinction between activity and movement is really too hard to make and, on the other hand, usefulness does not seem to help in distinguishing animate from inaminate, since the child never calls upon usefulness alone and since it is found coupled indifferently with all the other criteria indicating the evolution of the concept of life.

While usefulness or activity cannot be regarded as true differentiating criteria, there is another type of explanation which, although more or less disregarded by Piaget in his system of stages, occurs so frequently that it is hardly possible to ignore it completely. For many children, indeed, life is the possession of certain attributes observable in man or animal. Thus, to be alive, one must be able to *"speak," "eat," "see," "breathe," "have a body and a soul," "have an intelligence,"* etc. These anthropomorphic or zoomorphic criteria do not inevitably lead to the total disappearance of animism: the *wind*, for instance, will be declared living *"because it breathes,"* the fire, *"because while burning it happens to eat things up,"* etc. In many cases, however, the subject thus succeeds in establishing correct distinctions, without ever having to rely on the habitual criterion of autonomous movement. These children usually invoke movement in order to attribute life to animals; but they never state precisely that this movement is autonomous and resort rather to anthropomorphic traits when refusing life to inanimate but mobile objects. In brief, it seems as if the child knew perfectly well that only animals and plants are living; but, because he does not know, or does not immediately find the exact differentiating criterion, he simply makes comparisons between what he knows to be living and what is nonliving, in order to enhance such features as are found only in living beings.

104 (11:0): "You know what it is to be alive?—*Yes.*—What does it mean?—*Not being dead; one can move.*—Give me the name, tell

me some thing which is alive?—*A monkey, an animal.*—Is a mountain alive?—*No.*—Why?—*Because it stays there.*—The sun?—*No.* —Why?—*It has no intelligence.*—The table?—*No.*—Why?—*It does not move, it does not speak.*—An automobile?—*No.*—Why? —*It does not speak, it does not hear, it does not see.*—A cat?—*Yes.* —Why?—*It has an intelligence.*—A cloud?—*No.*—Why?—*It has no intelligence.*—A lamp?—*No.*—Why?—*It has no intelligence.*— A watch?—*No.*—Why?—*It has no intelligence.*—A bird?—*Yes.*— Why?—*It flies.*—A bell?—*No.*—Why?—*It has no intelligence.* —The wind?—*No.*—Why?—*Because it's invisible.*—An airplane? —*No.*—Why?—*It has no intelligence.*—A fly?—*Yes.*—Why?—*It can fly.*—The fire?—*No.*—Why?—*It has no intelligence.*—A flower?—*Yes.*—Why?—*It grows.*—The rain?—*No.*—Why?—*It has no intelligence.*—A tree?—*Yes.*—Why?—*It grows.*—A snake?—*Yes.* —Why?—*It moves, it crawls.*"

Responses of this kind are open to two possible interpretations. Either the child uses these anthropomorphic notions as a criterion because in the past he has learned that only animals and plants are alive and has never sought to understand what makes them essentially different from inanimate objects; or else, he uses a criterion he does not succeed in explaining easily, and his explanations of the anthropomorphic type serve merely as a screen to justify his first statements, but are not a determining factor in his classification.

This second interpretation seems to be quite probable when, in confirmation, it is noted that some subjects would rather change their explanations in the course of the examination than attribute life to some inanimate objects possessing that trait which had been used until then to deny life.

37 (11:0): "You know what it is to be alive?—*Yes.*—What does it mean?—*I cannot say it.*—Give me the name, tell me some thing which is alive?—*A hen.*—Is a mountain alive?—*No.*—Why?—*It's a thing, it cannot walk, it cannot move.*—The sun?—*No.*—Why?—

*It can move, but it has no soul . . . . Yet, a hen does not have a soul;
it's because it's a thing.*—The table?—*No.*—Why?—*It cannot
walk.*—An automobile?—*No.*—Why?—*It can move, but it does
not have a heart; instead of a heart, it's a motor.*"

The function of these anthropomorphic notions is thus rather
difficult to specify. At any rate, whether they serve as a real
criterion or mere justifications, they save the child from the
intellectual effort required for the discovery of the true principle of classification, while allowing him to free himself from
any animistic belief. For this reason, despite the perhaps
superficial character of these explanations, it is necessary to
take them into account in the description of the beliefs related
to the concept of life.

Piaget (1926) noted the occurrence of these anthropomorphic answers in some children, but he regarded them as
strictly individual and accessory.

> The child will add to its spontaneous ideas various adventitious
> definitions (to live is to speak, or to be warm, or to have blood,
> etc.). But all the children who gave these secondary definitions
> were also able to give the usual answers, all being simply juxta-
> posed together, so that it was possible to neglect these various
> secondary notions, whose completely individual character clear-
> ly showed them to be the result of chance conversations over-
> heard, etc. [p. 195].

These criteria are no doubt really accessory. But the reasons
proposed by Piaget to regard them as such do not seem to be
binding. At least, they are not corroborated by the present
experiment. Indeed, even if anthropomorphic criteria are generally coupled with explanations based on movement, there
are some children who rigorously restrict themselves to the
first. Table 9 presents a tabulation of the various criteria of
differentiation used by all the children in the experiment. This

Table 9

Criteria of differentiation between living
and nonliving objects

Criteria[1]	Chronological age										Total
	12:0	11:0	10:0	9:0	8:0	7:0	6:0	5:0	4:6	4:0	
M and AM	5	2	2	6	0	1	0	0	1	0	17
M, AM and An	5	7	2	7	4	7	1	0	1	0	34
AM and An	0	0	0	2	1	0	0	0	0	0	3
AM, M and Ac	9	6	7	4	2	2	5	2	2	0	39
AM, M, An and Ac	12	16	15	9	5	2	4	4	1	0	68
M and An	3	4	6	8	5	6	5	3	3	1	44
M and Ac	2	4	4	1	4	3	3	4	4	2	31
M, An and Ac	11	9	9	7	20	19	14	7	6	3	105
M	0	0	1	2	0	2	0	0	1	0	6
An	0	1	2	2	4	3	5	1	0	1	19
An and Ac	1	1	2	1	2	1	2	1	1	0	12
NIC	2	0	0	1	3	4	11	28	30	43	122
Total	50	50	50	50	50	50	50	50	50	50	500

[1] M = General movement (not specified) Ac = Activity
AM = Autonomous movement NIC = No identifiable
An = Anthropomorphism concept

very gross tabulation does not take into account the relative
frequency of these criteria in each protocol. Moreover, it deals
merely with the analysis of the reason appealed to by the subjects and completely disregards whether the various objects
are declared to be alive or not. Yet, it is to be noted that 19
children abide exclusively by anthropomorphic reasons and
never give what Piaget calls "usual answers." This figure may
seem negligible, but it should be observed that very few children restrict themselves to the use of a single criterion: only

25 subjects resort systematically to one and the same type of explanation. It could perhaps be alleged that these 19 children use only anthropomorphic criteria because the examiner does not insist enough in his quest for the real reasons. But the fact is that even in those cases in which the child has been subjected to a longer and more patient questionnaire, his attitude did not change. On the other hand, the occurrence of anthropomorphic notions is so frequent that they could hardly be assigned a purely individual or accessory value: all told, 285 children had recourse to these notions during the examination. This frequency itself constitutes ample proof of the necessity of finding a place for anthropomorphism in the classification of the various beliefs related to life. Care will be taken, however, not to grant this criterion more importance than the general movement of objects, since anthropomorphism in itself cannot be regarded as a valid criterion, except when it assumes the form of attributes truly proper to the living, that is, biological attributes such as the capacity *"to be born," "to eat," "to drink," "to die,"* and the like. The child's attention is not, in fact, focused on these essential traits. He is attracted instead by accidental or secondary features such as the ability *"to speak," "to see," "to play," "to have a face,"* and so on. While he may occasionally mention some specifically biological traits, he surely does not grasp their exact meaning, since these traits are generally part of an enumeration and are not given any particular importance.

9 (9:0): "Is a mountain alive?—*No.*—Why?—*Because it does not drink, it does not play.*"

35 (10:0): "Is an airplane alive?—*No.*—Why?—*Because it cannot eat, work.*"

In short, these anthropomorphic notions are imperfect chiefly because they do not allow a valid discrimination between the living and the nonliving. They almost always lead whoever uses them as criteria to errors of classification and may be compared, in this respect, to the criterion of general movement, which does not any more effectively insure the validity of discriminations. It may, moreover, be noted that these two types of errors occur among children of the same given age. The question remains, however, why some children succeed, on the basis of these anthropomorphic notions, in classifying without error all the objects listed in the questionnaire. The most simple and logical explanation seems to derive from the fact that these notions do not actually play the role of a true criterion; the child resorts to them merely for the immediate justification of his answers. He assumes, at the start, because he has already learned or understood the fact, that only animals and plants are alive, and discovers in them, especially in man, enough differentiating traits to justify his assertions without having to go through a real effort of understanding. This is indeed the reason why the child will constantly change his explanations whenever the notions previously called upon do not apply to a new object. After having refused life, for instance, to the *mountain*, the *sun*, the *wind*, because these objects "*do not have legs*," he will rather resort to the absence of "*hands*" or "*a mouth*" to say that the table is an inanimate object. If anthropomorphism were to him a genuine criterion, the child would not feel the necessity of thus progressively modifying the reasons he invokes to support his answers; he would instead make mistakes by assigning life to all such inanimate objects which share the attributes previously resorted to. Ultimately, in these cases, the anthropomorphic notions play the same role as the explanations based on the usefulness of objects: they amount to mere remarks to which the child resorts when he is convinced that his classification is the correct one, but does not care, or lacks the capacity, to discover the real explanation.

Because it makes allowance for all these observations, the developmental scale finally adopted here differs noticeably from Piaget's. It includes four main stages. Stage 0 contains children for whom the words "living" and "life" represent no definite concept. The three following stages describe the main steps marking the progressive distinction between animate and inanimate or, better, the gradual disappearance of animistic beliefs.

STAGE 0

Incomprehension or Refusal

Stage 0 comprises the subjects who obviously do not understand the meaning of the questions. Some children admit spontaneously that they do not know what it is all about and simply refuse to be examined; other children answer at random without ever giving any valid reason for their affirmations or denials.

24 (4:6): "You know what it is to be alive? What does it mean?—*I don't know.*—Is a mountain alive?—*No.*—Why do you say it is not alive?—*Because it is sand.*—The sun?—*Yes.*—Why?—*It's warm when the sun is there.*—The table?—*Yes.*—Why?—*Because it's alive.*—An automobile?—*No.*—Why?—*Because it's not alive.*—A cat?—*Yes.*—Why?—*It says 'meeow.'*—A cloud?—*No.*—Why?—*It's a sky, a cloud.*"

15 (6:0): "You know what it is to be alive, to live?—*No.*—What does it mean, do you think?—*It means we have fallen into a ditch.*—You, are you alive?—*No.*—Give me the name of some thing which is alive?—*Heaven . . . . I don't know what it means.*—Is a mountain alive?—*Yes.*—Why?—*I don't know.*—The sun?—*Yes.*—

Why?—*I don't know.*—The table?—*No.*—Why?—*Because it's not alive.*—An automobile?—*No.*—Why?—[. . . .]—A cat?—*Yes.*—Why?—*A little boy told me.*"

As in the questionnaire on dreams, it is possible to observe here certain confusions arising from word assonance. One subject, for instance, will confuse the word *vivant* (alive) with the boy's name "Yvan," or simply with *vent* (wind), and thus will readily speak of the "*cold,*" of "*wings to fly,*" of "*trees making wind by shaking their leaves,*" etc. Another will mistake the expression *être en vie* (to be alive) for *avoir envie* (to have a longing for), and will freely indulge in increasingly fantastic associations. The absence of a genuine concept is also manifested by constant contradictions. Reasons proposed are even at times very similar to those met with at superior stages; but the fact that the child appeals without distinction to the same reason to attribute or to deny life clearly indicates that his explanations are not genuine. Instead of being crystallized in a concept, they rather constitute mere descriptions or free associations.

13 (6:0): "You know what it is to be alive?—*Yes.*—What does it mean?—*To be born.*—Give me the name, tell me some thing which is alive.—*Animals.*—A mountain?—*No.*—Why?—*I know it.*—The sun?—*No.*—Why?—*Because I know it.*—The table?—*No.*—Why? —*I know it.*—An automobile?—*No.*—Why?—*It runs.*—A cat?— *Yes.*—Why?—*We often see some cats.*—A cloud?—*Yes.*—Why? —*Because I say so.*—A lamp?—*No.*—Why?—*Because it's not alive.*—A watch?—*No.*—Why?—*Because it runs.*—A bird?—*Yes.* —Why?—*Because it flies in the air.*—A bell?—*No.*—Why?—*Because I know it.*—The wind?—*No.*—Why?—*Because it's something cold and it does not run.*—An airplane?—*No.*—Why?— *Because it flies in the air, like birds.*—A fly?—*Yes.*—Why?—*Because it flies in the air.*"

The child's contradictions should not cause surprise: they are normal for him. Being still unaware of the principles of logic, the young child in his thinking naturally resorts to juxtaposition. By the operation of this mechanism, all the elements related to a given concept are, so to speak, agglutinated without any hierarchy in such a way that the child's attention will be centered successively on the various and often contradictory aspects of the reality under his immediate consideration. He will thus declare the *automobile* to be alive *"because it runs,"* while, a few minutes later, he will refuse life to the same automobile *"because it does not breathe, it does not eat, it has no soul,"* and the like. Since these contradictions are typical of infantile prelogical thinking, is one justified in relegating to stage 0, that is, to the level of subjects who manifest an obvious lack of understanding of the questions, the children who contradict themselves by using the same reasons without distinction to explain both life and nonlife? In answer to this question, let it be recalled that this last type of contradiction is not entirely comparable to that deriving from the mechanism of juxtaposition. Juxtaposition usually leads to a contradiction in the sequence of judgments, but the affirmations rest each time upon consistent grounds: movement, for instance, is always a sign of life, and the absence of anthropomorphic traits is always a sign of nonlife. Now, as can be seen in the protocol given above, this consistency is exactly what is lacking in children classified in stage 0: on the one hand, the *"yes's"* or the *"no's,"* and, on the other, the reasons invoked in each of these cases are completely independent from each other. Moreover, we meet enough subjects who always give indiscriminately the same answer (always *"yes"* or always *"no"*) to all items of the questionnaire. In short, the children of this stage do not seem to attach any particular importance to their answers; they are led by their fancy, and their explanations most often arise from pure description.

STAGE 1

Animistic Thinking Based upon Usefulness, Anthropomorphism, or Movement

The stage 1 subjects commit errors of the animistic type by attributing life to one or many inanimate objects. These errors derive from the fact that the criteria they use are inadequate (usefulness), imperfect (anthropomorphism), or simply incomplete (movement). More frequently a combination of two, and sometimes even of three, of these criteria can be observed.

11 (10:0): "You know what it means to be alive?—*Yes.*—What does it mean?—*It means that we are alive, that our soul is with our body.*—Give me the name of some thing which is alive.—*A cat, a dog, a person, a bear, a crocodile, a parrot, a bird.*—Is a mountain alive?—*Well . . . yes, I mean . . . it's alive: it holds itself together.* —Why do you say it is alive?—*Because it stands up.*—The sun?— *Yes.*—Why?—*Because it gives light.*—The table?—*Yes.*—Why? —Because it stands up.*—An automobile?—*Yes.*—Why?—*Because it stands up and then it runs.*—A cat?—*Yes.*—Why?—*Because you can see: it walks, and then it mews.*—A cloud?—*No.*—Why?—*Because it does not stand up, it does not run, it does not speak.*—A lamp?—*No . . . yes . . . no.*—Yes or no?—*No.*—Why?—*It does not speak, it does not walk, it does not see.*—A watch?—*No.*—Why?— *It does not walk, then it does not speak.*—A bird?—*Yes.*—Why?— *Because it sings, and then it flies.*—A bell?—*No.*—Why?—*Because it does not see, it does not walk.*—The wind?—*Yes . . . let's say yes.* —Why?—*Because it gives us air, I don't know.*—An airplane?— *No.*—Why?—*Because it does not talk.*—A fly?—*Yes.*—Why?— *Because it flies.*—The fire?—[Hesitates] . . . *Yes.*—Why?—*Because it burns, and then it comes up all of a sudden.*—A flower?—*Yes.*— Why?—*Because it grows then . . . that's all.*—The rain?—*Yes.*— Why?—*Because it falls . . . . *"

10 (7:0): "You know what it is to be alive?—*Yes.*—What does it mean?—*That we are not dead.*—Give me the name, tell me some

thing which is alive?—*A cow, people, dogs, cats, rabbits.*—A mountain?—*No.*—Why?—*It does not move.*—The sun?—*Yes.*—Why?—*It moves about.*—The table?—*No.*—Why?—*It does not move.*—An automobile?—*No.*—Why?—*It does not move.*—A cat? —*Yes.*—Why?—*It moves.*—A cloud?—*Yes.*—Why?—*It moves.*— [. . . .]—The wind?—*Yes.*—Why?—*It moves.*—An airplane.— *Yes.*—Why?—*Because it moves.*—The rain?—*Yes.*—Why?—*Because it moves.*—A tree?—*No.*—Why?—*Because it does not move.* —A snake?—*Yes.*—Why?—*Because it moves.*—A bicycle?—*Yes.* —Why?—*Because it moves.*"

52 (4:6): "You know what it is to be alive?—*No.*—What does it mean?—*I don't know.*—Give me the name, tell me some thing which is alive.—*My turtle.*—Is a mountain alive?—*No.*—Why?— *It does not have a mouth.*—The sun?—*Yes.*—Why?—*It has a mouth.*—The table?—*No.*—Why?—*It does not have a mouth.*— An automobile?—*Yes.*—Why?—*It has wheels.*—A cat?—*Yes.*— Why?—*It has mouths.*—A cloud?—*Yes.*—Why?—*It has mouths since it rains.*—[. . . .]—The wind?—*Yes.*—Why?—*It has mouths; it blows.*"

As may be noted, in spite of the imperfection, and sometimes of the diversity, of the criteria invoked, the child's thinking is always consistent. He never resorts to the same reason to attribute or to refuse life. As to the number of errors, it varies widely from one subject to another. There are many children who endow all or almost all of the objects listed in the questionnaire with life. On the other hand, many children make only one or two mistakes. If there were a definite relationship between the number of errors and the age of the child, it would no doubt be advantageous to subdivide the subjects of stage 1 into two or several substages, and to classify only the more animistic subjects in the most primitive stages. But, as indicated in Table 10, this relationship is far from obvious: the children of each age are distributed about equally in re-

Table 10

Distribution of stage 1 subjects by age and number of errors
(nonliving objects claimed to be alive)

Age	N	Number of errors (raw data)				
		1	2	3-5	6-9	10-14
12:0	8	2	0	2	1	3
11:0	9	1	2	2	1	3
10:0	11	5	2	0	2	2
9:0	12	1	3	4	2	2
8:0	18	2	4	3	4	5
7:0	21	3	5	5	4	4
6:0	20	3	3	5	5	4
5:0	13	1	0	3	2	7
4:6	16	0	0	6	3	7
4:0	7	2	0	0	4	1
Total	135	20	19	30	28	38

spect to the number of errors. Under these conditions, any division seems altogether arbitrary. The same observations may also be made about the possible relationship between the frequency of errors and the type of criterion resorted to: but as children generally offer two or three different types of explanation, no particular tendency can be isolated.

Finally, another kind of error that occurs quite frequently among stage 1 subjects should be noted. It is the denial of life to animate objects, such as plants, and even, at times, certain animals. These errors may not be an indication of animistic thinking, but they surely show how primitive is the concept of life held by these children. These errors are the direct consequence of the use of an imperfect criterion: it is because life is identified with movement, for instance, that some objects *"planted in the ground,"* and, in this sense immobile, are considered to be inanimate; it is also because the living must have *"legs"* or *"feet"* that life is refused to the *fish* or to the *snake*. These, no doubt, must be regarded as striking examples of the consistency noted above.

STAGE 2

Autonomous Movement with Some
Residual Animistic Thinking

The essential advance of subjects in this stage over those of the first stage is the discovery of autonomous movement. From then on, these subjects distinguish between mobile objects which receive their impetus from an external source and those which move by themselves. Even though life is reserved to this last category, two main reasons still prevent the complete disappearance of animism. In the first place, the child persists for a long time in deluding himself about the real source of the movement of objects. The more removed these objects are from his experience or his direct knowledge, the more persistent these illusions: accordingly, animism will recede much more rapidly in his answers on mechanical objects (e.g., *bicycle, automobile*) than in those on natural phenomena (e.g., *sun, wind,* and so on). In the second place, the discovery of autonomous movement does not definitively displace the inadequate or imperfect criteria of the first stage. In fact, the most frequent occurrence is that the child relies upon autonomy to justify some of his responses, but for the other responses still resorts frequently to usefulness of objects, to their possessing anthropomorphic traits, or to their general movement. All subjects of this stage, however, at least make a mention of autonomous movement.

47 (9:0): "You know what it is to be alive?—*Yes.*—What does it mean?—*One is born.*—Give me the name of some thing which is alive.—*People.*—A mountain?—*No.*—Why?—*It does not move, it cannot eat.*—The sun?—*Yes.*—Why?—*It does not eat, but it turns around.*—The table?—*No.*—Why?—*It cannot eat.*—An automobile?—*No.*—Why?—*We have to make it run ourselves.*—A cat?—*Yes.*—Why?—*It can eat.*—A cloud?—*Yes.*—Why?—*Because they bump together and the rain falls.*—A lamp?—*No.*—Why?—*It doesn't light up by itself.*—A watch [examiner points at electric clock on the wall]?—*No.*—Why?—*It can go around but it's because it is connected.*"

40 (11:0): " . . . The sun?—*Yes.*—Why?—*It's like ourselves; it lies down; in the morning it wakes up [c'est comme nous autres; il s'en va se coucher; le matin il se réveille].*—The table?—*No.*—Why?— It's only wood.*—An automobile?—*No.*—Why?—*It's tin and iron.* —[. . . .]—An airplane?—*No.*—Why?—*It's only wood, then a motor makes it fly.*—A fly?—*Yes.*—Why?—*It flies.*—The fire?— *No.*—Why?—*You have to light it up with matches.*"

30 (10:0): "What does it mean to be alive?—*It means that you can move about, play, that you can do all kinds of things.*—Give me the name of some thing which is alive.—*You.*—Is a mountain alive?— *Yes.*—Why?—*Because it has grown by itself.*—The sun?—*Yes.*— Why?—*Because it gives light.*—The table?—*No.*—Why?—*Because the tree which was used to make the table is dead.*—[. . . .] —A cloud?—*Yes.*—Why?—*Because it sends water on the earth.*— The wind?—*Yes.*—Why?—*Because it pushes things.*—The fire?— *No.*—Why?—*Because it cannot light up by itself.*"

All the children of stage 2 make errors and attribute life to some inanimate objects. This is indeed the feature which distinguishes children of this stage from those of the next stage who, while using the same criteria of classification, will no longer show any trace of animism. As to the possible relationship between the number of errors and the child's age, the data are erratic and do not warrant any attempt at a differentiation (Table 11). On the other hand, the child's lack of a system is here again an impediment to the identification of any sort of relationship between the number of errors and the type of criterion resorted to.

Table 11

Distribution of stage 2 subjects by age and number of errors (nonliving objects claimed to be alive)

Age	N	Number of errors (raw data)				
		1	2	3	4	5-12
12:0	18	2	4	4	5	3
11:0	12	2	3	2	1	4
10:0	12	3	1	1	1	6
9:0	12	4	2	1	3	2
8:0	7	1	1	4	0	1
7:0	5	3	0	2	0	0
6:0	6	1	1	3	0	1
5:0	4	0	1	0	1	2
4:6	3	1	0	2	0	0
4:0	1	0	0	0	1	0
Total	80	17	13	19	12	19

Hence, the second stage is essentially a transition stage. At one time or another during the examination, all subjects make mention of the correct principle of classification, namely, autonomous movement. However, they all persist in attributing life to inanimate objects either because they are mistaken about the real source of movement, or because they still rely upon imperfect or inadequate criteria.

STAGE 3

Total Disappearance of Animistic Thinking

The third stage corresponds to the fourth level of Piaget's scale. It comprises all the subjects who never grant life to inanimate objects, at least to those listed in the questionnaire. Life is reserved to animals and plants, or to animals only. Explanations may refer to autonomous or general movement, to anthropomorphism, or to usefulness, indiscriminately.

111 (12:0): "You know what it is to be alive?—*Yes.*—What does it mean?—*We are not dead. Our blood keeps running, we are not separated from our soul.*—Give me the name of some thing which is alive?—*Human persons, animals, vegetables, fruits.*—A mountain?—*No.*—Why?—*It's like the carpet on the floor.*—The sun?—*No.*—Why?—*It's like a light.*—The table?—*No.*—Why?—*It's made of wood.*—An automobile?—*No.*—Why?—*It's made of metal.*—A cat?—*Yes.*—Why?—*It walks, it mews.*—A cloud?—*No.*—Why?—*It's water, vapor.*—A lamp?—*No.*—Why?—*It is used to hold a light; it's like a decoration.*—A watch?—*No.*—Why?—*It runs with electricity.*—[....]—The fire?—*No.*—Why?—*We make it ourselves; it does not make itself.*—A flower?—*Yes.*—Why?—*It grows, it's vegetal.*"

6 (9:0): " . . . The sun?—*No.*—Why?—*The sun, it gives light to the earth, while an animal, it runs, and then, as for us, we speak.*—The table?—*No.*—Why?—*It does not move.*—An automobile?—*No.*—Why?—*It's not a person, nor an animal, then it's made of metal.*—A cat?—*Yes.*—Why?—*It moves, it mews.*—A cloud?—*No.*—Why?—*It's not an animal, nor a person, it doesn't speak; it moves, but it doesn't run.*—A lamp?—*No.*—Why?—*Because it doesn't move or speak.*—A watch?—*No.*—Why?—*It doesn't speak.*—A bird?—*Yes.*—Why?—*It moves, it walks in the air, it flies.*—A bell?—*No.*—Why?—*It's made of iron, it doesn't speak.*—The wind?—*No.*—Why?—*It talks to us; it doesn't move.*—An airplane?

—*No.—Why?—It's made of iron.—A fly?—Yes.—Why?—It moves, it flies in the air, it stings.—The fire?—No.—Why?—It doesn't speak; it doesn't run.—A flower?—No.—Why?—It doesn't talk.— The rain?—No.—Why?—It's water; it doesn't talk, it doesn't run, it doesn't move.—A tree?—Yes.—Why?—It grows, it has foliage .... The flower also is alive; the plant has a kind of life, because it grows."*

16 (9:0): *" . . . A mountain?—No.—Why?—It doesn't walk, it always remains at the same place.—The sun?—No.—Why?—It cannot move, it remains always at the same place.—The table?—No. —Why?—It cannot displace itself.—An automobile?—No.—Why? —It needs a motor to make it run.—A cat?—Yes.—Why?—It can walk.—A cloud?—No.—Why?—It cannot displace itself.—A lamp?—No.—Why?—It cannot walk by itself.—A watch?—No.— Why?—It cannot displace itself.—A bird?—Yes.—Why?—It can fly.—A bell?—No.—Why?—It needs a man to ring it.—[....]— The fire?—No.—Why?—It does not displace itself as it wishes."*

Most often stage 3 children still refuse life to plants. They do so as much for reasons of autonomy (e.g., *"it does not move by itself, it's the wind which makes them move," "it does not grow by itself, they have to be planted"*; and so on) as for anthropomorphic reasons (e.g., *"it does not have a soul, an intelligence, a will"; "it does not have any eyes, any feet"*; and the like). In fact, among the 155 subjects of this stage, only 53 regard the *flower* and the *tree* as being alive. On the other hand, some children grant life to the mountain; but, then, according to all indications, instead of thinking of the mountain as such, they rather make allusion to the covering trees or vegetation (e.g., *"it is living because it has roots"*). In spite of appearances, these answers are evidently not animistic at all. Some exceptional subjects (11 in all) also deny life to one or the other of the animals listed in the questionnaire. In almost every case, these are animals which the child meets less frequently (e.g., *snake*), or which he habitually associates with death (e.g., the *fly*, which, as a matter of fact, brings the child to speak occasionally of fly swatters). Some surprise may perhaps arise at finding in the last stage subjects who limit living beings to such an exaggeratedly restricted domain. But it must be recalled that the scale of stages does not seek to shed light on the accuracy of the infantile concept of life, but rather on the evolution and the extension of animistic beliefs. The recognition of life, especially of plant life, depends much more upon school learning than upon the natural, personal development of thought.

Stage 3 also includes subjects who, in answering the last five questions, regard some inanimate objects as more "alive" than others, even though they refrained, in the course of the examination proper, from attributing life to any of these.

48 (9:0): "Is there one of these two which is more alive than the other: the rain or the fire?—*The rain.*—Why?—*Because it puts out all kinds of things and it makes the plants grow.*—The wind or a bicycle?—*The bicycle.*—Why?—*Because it runs on wheels and it's a little more alive than the wind.*"

15 (10:0): " . . . the rain or the fire?—*Yes, the rain.*—Why?—*Because the rain can put out the fire, but the fire cannot put out the rain.*—The wind or a bicycle?—*Yes, the wind.*—Why?—*The wind, when there is a storm, it never stops; a bicycle, it needs some one to make it work.*"

These responses still seem to be tainted with animism. It would be unwise, however, to take these various assertions literally: they are probably due to the excessively suggestive form of the questions. These questions, in their present form, hint at the possible existence of various levels within life itself and easily lead the subject to introduce refinements of which he might never have thought by himself. The artificial character of these responses is indeed manifested by the speciousness of the reasons called upon for their justification. Just after having first claimed that the *rain* is more alive than the *fire*, the child will sometimes hasten to answer that the *rain* is not alive, should the examiner take the trouble to question him anew on the *rain* only. One can clearly see that the word *alive* does not have the same meaning for the child in both cases. In short, this part of the examination does not meet its objective, and it is preferable to disregard it when the time comes to assess the protocols.

• • •

Finally, it remains to be verified whether the statistical analysis corroborates the main elements of this assessment of subjects into four main stages. An inspection of Table 12 immediately raises a problem on the transitivity of stages. It may be noted that the median age of the stage 3 subjects is slightly lower than that of the stage 2 subjects. Two interpretations are possible. The first one consists in the simple assumption that these two stages do not correspond to two different phases in the evolution of the concept of life. They should therefore be reassembled into one single stage, despite the fact that stage 3 children no longer make the animistic errors into which stage 2 children occasionally still fall. The evolution of the concept of life, at least in children from four to twelve years of age, would be indicated by a succession of three phases only, ranging from the total absence of a well-defined concept of life (stage 0) to the emergence of an increasingly systematic, and decreasingly animistic, concept (stage 1 and a fusion of stages 2 and 3).

The second interpretation rather considers this lack of discrimination between the median ages of stages 2 and 3 to be due to the very limitations of the sample. At ages eleven and twelve, not enough children have reached stage 3 for the computation of the median age of that stage to be considered

Table 12

Distribution of subjects by age and developmental stage
in the questionnaire on life

| | | Stages | | | | | | |
| | | 0 | 1 | 2 | 3 | 1 | 2 | 3 |
Age	N	Raw percentages				Cumulative percentages		
12:0	50	4	16	36	44	96	80	44
11:0	50	0	18	24	58	100	82	58
10:0	50	0	22	24	54	100	78	54
9:0	49	2	25	25	49	99	74	49
8:0	48	6	37	15	42	94	57	42
7:0	49	8	43	10	39	92	49	39
6:0	48	23	42	12	23	77	35	23
5:0	50	60	26	8	6	40	14	6
4:6	50	62	32	6	0	38	6	0
4:0	50	84	14	2	0	16	2	0
Total		249	275	162	315			
Median age		4:7	7:1	9:8	9:6			
Age of accession						5:3	7:4	9:7

valid. When there are less than 75 per cent of the twelve-year-old children included in the last stage, it is not possible to rely on the median age computed for that stage by the usual technique. It will no doubt be recalled that the influence of this factor has already been noted in the second part of chapter VII (Methods of Analysis). In the present case, because the sample is arbitrarily cut off at the age of twelve, it becomes impossible to determine the total distribution of children reaching stage 3, and the median age of this third level is artificially brought nearer to the median age of the second level. It is logical to assume that if the sample included children of thirteen and more, a larger and larger number of subjects would reach stage 3, and consequently the median age of the children of this stage would markedly increase. This is a hypothesis which, no doubt, needs to be tested, but which is surely legitimate on the basis of the observations made on the very evolution of previous stages. There is no reason to doubt that the persistence of animistic notions which still color the concept of life of stage 2 children, in spite of the fact that they have already reached the criterion of autonomous movement, would not in the end totally disappear with an increase in chronological age. The percentage drop in stage 3, observed at age twelve, is by no means a sufficient reason to question the reality of a natural progression, which could indeed be so validly anticipated on examination of the remainder of the distribution. This drop is not limited to the questionnaire on life; it may be found in practically all the other tests undergone by the present sample. Until a valid explanation has been found for this general phenomenon, it is preferable to assume that the sample of twelve-year-old children is not truly representative of the normal population and contains too many weak elements.

For all these reasons, the second interpretation has been retained. Stages 2 and 3 are deemed to be different and, with due reservations, transitivity is assumed. Table 12 gives the median age of the children of each stage: 4:7 for stage 0; 7:1 for stage 1; 9:8 for stage 2; and 9:6 for stage 3. It should be noted that the number of subjects does not reach a total of 50 for all ages. Between six and nine years of age, some subjects (6 in all) are eliminated on account of the ambiguity of their answers: all the objects listed in the questionnaire are said not to be alive, including animals and plants. Since it is not possible to know whether these answers manifest a total lack of understanding of the questions or an excessive limitation of the concept of life, it is preferable not to classify these proto-

Table 13

Sex differences on the questionnaire on life

Age	Sex	N	Stage 0	1	2	3	X^2	df	
12:0	G	25	0	6	11	8	2.92	2	P>.01
	B	25	2	2	7	14			
11:0	G	25	0	4	8	13	1.78	2	P>.01
	B	25	0	5	4	16			
10:0	G	26	0	8	8	10	5.35	2	P>.01
	B	24	0	3	4	17			
9:0	G	24	0	9	6	9	3.44	2	P>.01
	B	25	1	3	6	15			
8:0	G	24	2	12	3	7	4.28	2	P>.01
	B	24	1	6	4	13			
7:0	G	25	2	11	1	11	0.02	1	P>.01
	B	24	2	10	4	8			
6:0	G	22	5	10	1	6	0.29	2	P>.01
	B	26	6	10	5	5			
5:0	G	25	16	6	2	1	0.33	1	P>.01
	B	25	14	7	2	2			
4:6	G	25	18	5	2	0	2.12	1	P>.01
	B	25	13	11	1	0			
4:0	G	25	21	3	1	0	0.00	1	P>.01
	B	25	21	4	0	0			
Total	G	246	64	74	43	65			
	B	248	60	61	37	90			
					Over-all X^2		20.53	16	P>.01

cols. The computation of the age of accession to each one of the stages reveals, on the other hand, a more rapid evolution than that foreseen by Piaget. Stage 1 is reached at 5:3 years of age, stage 2 at 7:4, and stage 3 at 9:7. Piaget sets at eleven or twelve years of age the accession to the last stage or, in other words, the complete disappearance of animism. Once again, this disparity may be explained by the character of the samples and by the nature of the techniques used in the computation of these ages.

The separate tabulation of the results of boys and girls (Table 13) shows no significant difference.

These general results leave no possible doubt on the existence of animistic thinking among children: as many as 43.7 per cent of the subjects attribute life to some inanimate object. This percentage even reaches 58.1, if one excludes from the sample (since there is no reason to do otherwise) those children who were considered to be unclassifiable and those of stage 0. This figure is so much more impressive because it rises above that of all percentages obtained in the individual analysis of the objects listed in the questionnaire. The results of this analysis are shown in Table 14. They indicate, for instance, that even though the *sun* is the object most often regarded as alive, it is claimed to be so by only 42.7 per cent of the children. Then follow, in order of animism frequency, most of the meteors, slightly ambiguous mechanical objects, and, finally, the most obviously inanimate objects. It must be noted that these percentages are calculated for subjects of stages 1 to 3 only. At the lower ages, the subjects are very few: at the age of four, for instance, there are only 8. At these levels, therefore, percentages are less reliable and should be interpreted with caution. In observing, for instance, that 63 per cent of the four-year-old children say that the sun is alive, it should be borne in mind that this percentage is based only upon the number of those children who could be classified in the last three stages, and not upon the total number of four-year-old children. Despite the difficulties of interpretation involved, this translation into percentages is nevertheless neces-

Table 14

Percentages of animistic errors for each age level
and for each inanimate object listed
in the questionnaire on life

Age	4:0	4:6	5:0	6:0	7:0	8:0	9:0	10:0	11:0	12:0	
N	8	19	20	37	45	45	48	50	50	48	
Object											Over-all %
Sun (2)[1]	63	68	65	46	38	42	37	42	30	42	43
Wind (9)	75	37	65	38	36	33	27	24	32	37	35
Cloud (5)	50	42	60	38	24	27	25	20	20	27	29
Rain (12)	63	42	55	27	18	27	21	22	14	19	25
Automobile (4)	50	79	70	22	22	20	15	18	16	15	25
Fire (11)	63	47	35	30	16	22	15	20	18	25	23
Airplane (10)	50	74	20	30	29	29	12	14	14	15	23
Bicycle (13)	38	47	55	30	22	24	12	10	8	10	20
Watch (7)	38	53	50	19	22	16	10	12	14	12	19
Bell (8)	25	100	45	11	11	22	10	12	8	10	19
Mountain (1)	50	37	40	14	11	4	2	12	10	21	14
Lamp (6)	63	37	40	11	11	9	4	8	8	8	13
Pencil (14)	25	32	40	19	11	16	6	4	6	6	12
Table (3)	0	21	15	8	7	0	0	6	2	4	5

[1] The figure in parentheses indicates the relative order of presentation of the item in the questionnaire.

sary if comparisons between ages are to be made possible. In this connection, it should be recalled that this is precisely the kind of individual item analysis that the investigators most critical of Piaget almost always resort to. A study of the present results shows how artificial this method is: it inevitably results in the masking of the real dimensions of a phenomenon such as animism. Be that as it may, this individual item analysis at least permits the elaboration of a scale which confirms the usual observations on the relative tenacity of animistic beliefs: the child attributes life most frequently and for a longer period of time to those objects which are most removed from his direct experience.

CHAPTER X

The Origin of Night

The data yielded by this questionnaire corroborate the existence of a third form of precausal thinking in the child. Piaget gave it the name of artificialism because it consists in postulating the intervention of a maker at the origin of all things. At first glance, however, a rather baffling difference is noted between the artificialism described by Piaget and that manifested by the Montreal children. The artificialism observed in the present sample is less elaborate: admissions of artificialism hardly ever take the indirect and roundabout forms reported by Piaget. His Geneva children, for instance, would explain the night by the formation of clouds coming from the smoke of chimneys, and finally by the intervention of the men who kindle chimney fires. Montreal children are more inclined to accept the direct intervention of a human agent, and seldom resort to intermediate causes. It could be argued that the content of the questionnaire does not allow for the expression of these particular tendencies and that the questioning, for lack of insistence, does not incite the child to give the precise details of his system of explanation. Yet, the impression arising from the analysis of all the protocols runs absolutely counter to this hypothesis: the questions and subquestions are so insistent that the child finally repeats himself for want of being able to find new elements of explanation.

If the artificialism noted in the present study seems to be less elaborate than that referred to by Piaget, the reason is rather that it assumes forms which are less primitive or, at least apparently, more far-fetched. It is more far-fetched in the sense that, instead of resorting to man as a maker, it almost always calls upon the intervention of divine power to explain the formation of the night. Out of 256 explanations of an artificialistic type, 230 attribute such quasi-magical powers to God. This recourse to God, whom the child has been taught to regard as omnipotent, saves him from calling upon intermediate agents or operations. If God takes it upon Himself to make clouds, or to cause the disappearance of the sun, He will do it directly, through His sole power, or by a personal and immediate action. On the basis of the child's own words, one would almost be led to believe that his explanation is supernatural rather than artificialistic. However, this is merely an illusion. In spite of His evident, absolute, and special powers, God is conceived of, by the youngest children most particularly, after the fashion of a human being using human means: *"He pushes the clouds with His hands,"* for instance, or *"He brings the sun to sleep in His home,"* and the like. In short, despite its more far-fetched and seemingly more mature character, this divine artificialism nevertheless remains comparable to that based upon human industry. Besides, such a conception is more convenient for the child; the discovery of the limits of human ability will not shake his artificialistic convictions, but will quite simply widen the breach dividing the respective fields of operation of man and of God.

How can this phenomenon be explained? Why have children such a general tendency to place God at the origin of a phenomenon like night? Two particular circumstances seem to elicit this type of answer: the religious teaching the child has received and the very nature of the topic of the questionnaire. The first factor is evident: at a very early age, the child is taught to look upon God as an omnipotent Being and as the Creator of all things. From this belief to the idea of His intervention in the daily course of events, there is but one step which the child readily takes. The decisive influence of this factor is corroborated by an obvious fact: it is especially at the age at which the child usually receives his first religious instructions that this type of artificialism is preponderant. Moreover, this phenomenon appears not only in answers to the questionnaire on the origin of night, but also to those on dream and on the movement of clouds. Even though not designed for that purpose, these two last questionnaires very frequently give rise to explanations of an artificialistic type. In these tests also, it is at the age of the child's first religious instruction that divine artificialism is most strikingly mani-

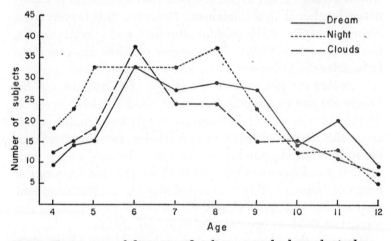

FIG. 1. Frequency of divine artificialism at each chronological age level and in each one of the three questionnaires eliciting explanations of an artificialistic type: *concept of dream, origin of night,* and *movement of clouds.*

THE RESULTS

fest. Figure 1 illustrates these various observations for each one of the questionnaires. All these findings could create some doubt on the spontaneous character of infantile artificialism. Indeed, if these beliefs find their expression mostly through the notions the child has acquired on divinity, how is it possible to prove that they are not the mere repetition of adult teachings? On the simple basis of a questionnaire specifically designed to explore the child's conceptions about the origin of things, it is hardly possible to discriminate exactly, within so complex a field, spontaneous from acquired elements. Hence, the interest of recalling, in this matter, Piaget's conclusions (1926) based upon a mass of observations much broader and more diversified.

> . . . religious instruction has influenced only a section of the children under our observation and even among those whose artificialism is thus qualified it is limited to intensifying a tendency towards artificialism already pre-existing in the child and not created by it [p. 269].

In support of his interpretation, Piaget adduces two arguments. In the first place, the fact that the child may convert his religious teaching into excessive artificialism implies that his mind is already conditioned to select, among experiential data, those which best agree with this form of thinking. Secondly, the existence of artificialistic beliefs among the youngest children attests that these beliefs are independent of any formal religious teaching, since they come first and thus prove their primitive and spontaneous character. The results of the present study corroborate this second argument at least, since, out of 26 explanations based upon a purely human artificialism, 19 are given by the subjects of four and four and a half years of age, that is, by children still too young to have received formal religious instruction.

The second factor likely to explain the frequency of divine artificialism derives from the very object of the questionnaire. When induced to talk about the night, the child is easily led to certain associations between the sky, heaven, and God, since heaven is the place where, from the very beginning, he has learned to locate God. This is another phenomenon observed by Piaget (1926) in the course of his examinations on the origin of celestial bodies.

> . . . where the sun and the moon and the stars are concerned a strong influence may be at work since the planets are much nearer in association to a God living in Heaven than are the material objects located on the earth [p. 269].

To reduce the influence of this factor to its minimum, the child should rather have been questioned on the origin of certain terrestrial objects such as lakes, rivers, mountains, and so on, which are nearer to man and less likely to arouse reflections related to God. The reason why we nevertheless chose the origin of the night is that these other topics are not as accessible to the experience of city children. It should, moreover, be pointed out, to be exact, that the difference noted between the artificialism described by Piaget and that manifested by the Montreal children is not as important as it may seem at first. Piaget's descriptions tend to stress this difference, because he insists almost exclusively on the human elements present in infantile artificialism. Yet the examples he produces to illustrate his questionnaire show plainly the important place of divine elements in this artificialism, for they are present in at least one third of these examples. His interpretation seems therefore to refer, not so much to the analysis of infantile ideas on the specific problem of the origin of night, but rather to the more general analysis of beliefs related to the origin of a multitude of objects.

Piaget's scale of stages also includes the following distinction, which cannot possibly be preserved in the present classification. Among all the explanations of night founded on the coming on of clouds, he discriminates between those which regard these clouds as forming the substance of night (stage 2), and those which rather consider them as some sort of screen merely keeping out daylight (stage 3). Yet, it is almost impossible to establish with assurance and objectivity the true position of the children in relation to these two interpretations. In about twenty subjects only were answers explicit enough (e.g., *"it is black air coming from everywhere"*) to express unequivocally the idea of night as a substance. For so few, a special category would not have been justified. Even in the examples reported by Piaget, it is not always easy to disentangle the real meaning of the child's explanation. For instance, Piaget classifies in stage 2 the subject who feels that the clouds must be black in order to make the night. Such an interpretation is, at the very least, debatable. That white clouds cannot make the night is not necessarily due to the fact that the darkness of the night is substantially made of black clouds; but it may be more simply that their opacity is not such as to mask daylight, somewhat as if the blinds of a window were too pale to hide the light completely. It may perhaps also be because the child, struck by the fact that all clouds at night seem dark, seeks to express as best he can the impossibility of finding white clouds at night.

In the end, the analysis of the protocols warrants, as with the two previous questionnaires, the identification of four general stages. Children who show an evident lack of understanding are, as usual, classified in stage 0. The three other stages describe the evolution of artificialistic beliefs: absolute artificialism, artificialism interspersed with physical explanations, and absolute physicalism. Stages 1 and 3 each include two substages.

STAGE 0

Incomprehension or Refusal

The stage 0 children do not answer the questions at all. They remain completely speechless or occasionally break this silence only to give way to all kinds of associations elicited by the words of the examiner, but without really answering the questions.

46 (5:0): "You know what the night is?—*No.*—Tell me, what is night?—*I don't know.*—Why is it dark at night?—*The beggars, and then the bandits are outside.*—Where does the dark come from at night? What makes it night?—*I don't know.*—Can we make the night in this room? If I pull the blinds down, is it going to be dark? —*Yes.*—Then, how is it, where does the dark in the room come from?—*I don't know, and then I don't want to play at that any more.*"

40 (4:0): "You know what the night is?—*Yes.*—Tell me, what is night?—*It's bad men.*"

25 (5:0): "You know what the night is?—[. . . .]—Tell me, what is night?—*The sun.*—Why is it dark at night?—*There is too much sun.*—Where does the dark come from at night? What makes it night?—*It comes in the back and in front.*"

The belief that night is filled with strange beings or animals is not specific to stage 0 children. On the contrary, these emotional descriptions are very frequent; but most of the subjects add explanations which allow them to be included in one of the ulterior stages. It should, however, be noted that stage 0 contains only eleven subjects; this is sure evidence of the familiarity the phenomenon of night has for children. Be it as it may, subjects who do not really respond to the questionnaire must, in spite of their small number, be grouped in a special category.

STAGE 1

Absolute Artificialism

Stage 1 subjects usually begin by explaining the night in a finalistic manner: *"the night is made for sleeping,"* it becomes dark *"so we may go to sleep,"* or *"to let us know that it is time to go to bed,"* etc. A few children hold strictly to these interpretations, remaining unshaken by the examiner's remarks on the possibility of sleeping during the day. In most cases, however, the insistence of the questions will elicit a more explicit artificialistic explanation in the form of recourse to the action of God, or again, but much more rarely, to the intervention of terrestrial agents. This artificialism is of a radical type: night is manufactured or controlled directly by this agent, and never through the intervention of astrological, physical, or meteorological agents, or even of pseudo-meteorological substances such as smoke, dark air, and so on. If the child believes that the maker of the night uses materials or instruments, he will speak of *"black chalk,"* for instance, *"ink," "electric lights to shut off," "window shades to lower,"* and the like. The very large majority of subjects, however, place God Himself at the origin of night and for this reason, no doubt, do not even find it necessary to call in material elements; the omnipotence of the divine will or word and the efficacy of certain means, practically related to magic or legerdemain, are amply sufficient to explain the emergence of night.

Subjects may refer to the moon and the stars, the nightly presence of which they have had the opportunity to observe. When answering questions on the cause of day (the last items in the questionnaire), they will even go as far as to speak of the sun; but for all these stage 1 children, celestial bodies play no active role in the formation of night. The moon and the stars emerge simultaneously with the night; they come with the night, but are not the cause of it. Also, the sun shines during the day, but its role is limited to the embellishment of certain days: some days are sunny, others are not.

3 (7:0): "You know what the night is?—*Yes.*—Tell me, what is night?—*It's for sleeping, then it becomes dark, then there are stars, and then the moon.*—Why is it dark at night?—*Because it's the evening.*—Why is it dark when it is evening?—*Because it's no longer the day.*—Why is it dark, when it is no longer the day?—*Because the day is over.*—Why is it dark, when the day is over?—*Because we must sleep.*—Where does the dark come from at night? —*From the sky.*—What makes it night?—*God.*—How does He make it?—*He takes His hands.*—And then?—*He takes something, then it becomes dark.*—What thing does He take?—*A black thing.* —What thing?—*A blanket.*—What does He do with it?—*He says something, then the blanket disappears and then it becomes black.* —What becomes black?—*The sky.*"

21 (8:0): " . . . Can we make the night in this room? If I pull the blinds down, is it going to be dark?—*No, because outside it will not be dark.*—But, in the room, it will be dark?—*Yes, it will be dark.*—Then, how is it, where does the dark in the room come from?—*It comes from the blinds, because someone has pulled down the blinds.*—And the dark outside, what is it?—*It's night.*— When it is light, why is it light?—*Because it's not the evening, it's the morning.*—What makes it day?—*The sun shines.*—Yes, but what makes it day?—*It's God.*"

This last subject may possibly have understood "*Qu'est-ce qu'il fait, le jour?*" ("What does it do in the daytime?") instead of "*Qu'est-ce qui fait le jour?*" ("What makes it day?"), and then his answer "*il fait soleil*" ("*the sun shines*") has a natural explanation. But this answer does not lead him to revise his first conceptions; as soon as the exact meaning of the question is grasped, he reverts to artificialistic interpretations, the explanatory value of which seems to him irrefutable.

Two main tendencies may be distinguished among the subjects of stage 1. They correspond to two substages, the first comprising exclusively finalistic interpretations (substage 1A), and the second interpretations (substage 1B) both artificialistic and finalistic, or exclusively artificialistic.

SUBSTAGE 1A: FINALISTIC INTERPRETATIONS

The subjects of substage 1A do not yet state their interpretations in a precise artificialistic form: they merely explain the night on the basis of its finality, or its usefulness to man.

40 (5:0): "You know what the night is? Tell me, what is night?— *It's when we sleep.*—Why is it dark at night?—*It means that we keep lying down all the time.*—Where does the dark come from at night? What makes it night?—[Silence]—Do you sleep sometimes during the day?—*Yes.*—Is it dark when you sleep during the day? —*No.*—Then, why is it dark at night?—*Because it's time to go to bed.*—Why is it dark only at night?—*Because it's time to go to bed.* —Does it happen sometimes that it is night and you are not sleeping? When you stay up late at night, is it dark outside?—*Yes.*— Then, how is it that it is dark and that you do not sleep?—*Because sometimes I stay up later.*—Can we make the night in this room? If I pull the blinds down, is it going to be dark?—*Yes.*—Then, how is it, where does the dark in the room come from?—*It's because the blinds are closed.*—And the dark outside, what is it?—*It's bad; some bad men walk by, during the evening.*—When it is light, why is it light?—*Because it's time to get up.*—What makes it day?— [Silence]."

It may not seem to the point to reserve one definite stage to these exclusively finalistic interpretations in a scale dealing with the evolution of artificialism. But all artificialistic beliefs derive precisely from this finalism. The child begins by seeking the *why* of things before questioning himself about the *how*. Since the cause of every thing is always interpreted in relation to man, the child will also attribute its origin to man.

This interpretation of Piaget's, which considers infantile artificialism as growing out of finalism, is completely corroborated by the present results: subjects who hold exclusively to finalism (substage 1A) are younger than those who appeal to artificialistic elements (substage 1B and stage 2). Indeed, children of later stages will almost unfailingly invoke reasons of usefulness before establishing relationships of an artificialistic type.

SUBSTAGE 1B: FINALISTIC AND ARTIFICIALISTIC, OR EXCLUSIVELY
ARTIFICIALISTIC INTERPRETATIONS

The most explicit artificialistic beliefs become manifest in stage 1B; but they are still intermingled, in most subjects, with finalistic remarks.

13 (4:0): "You know what the night is? Tell me, what is night?—*It's in my room. You cannot go outside at night.*—Why is it dark at night?—*Because if you don't sleep, Santa Claus doesn't give you any toys.*—Then why is it dark at night?—*Because we sleep.*—Where does the dark come from at night? What makes it night?—*Well, bandits, they make something; that comes from . . . mother pulls the blinds down, then it's very dark.*—Do you sleep sometimes during the day?—*Yes.*—Is it dark when you sleep during the day?—*Yes.*—It's dark everywhere?—*Yes.*—Then why is it dark at night?—*Because we sleep, and then because mother puts the light out.*—Does it happen sometimes that it is night and you are not sleeping?—*Yes.*—When you stay up late at night, is it dark outside?—*Yes.*—Then, how is it that it is dark and that you do not sleep?—*Well, mother puts the light out because daddy, he is sleeping.*—Can we make the night in this room? If I [. . .]?—*Yes.*—Then how is it, where does the dark in the room come from?—*Well, it's . . . Where? . . . . Well, we pull the blinds, then it's dark.*—When it is light, why is it light?—*Because mother sometimes, she washes the dishes, then she puts the light on.*—Yes, but outside, why is it light?—*Well, mother puts the light on, then it goes that far.*—

What makes it day?—*It's . . . I don't recall. Well, it's mother who puts the light on, and this makes the day.*"

35 (6:0): "You know what the night is? Tell me, what is the night? —*It's when it's dark.*—Why is it dark at night?—*To go to bed.*— Where does the dark come from at night? What makes it night?— *God.*—How does God do it?—*God calls the dark, it's to put us to sleep.*—Do you sleep sometimes during the day? Can we sleep during the day?—*Yes.*—Is it dark when we sleep during the day? —*No.*—Then, why is it dark at night?—*For sleeping.*—Are there times when it is night and you do not sleep?—*Yes.*—When you stay up late at night, is it dark outside?—*Yes.*—Then, how is it that it is dark when you do not sleep?—*I don't know. It's because we are supposed to sleep.*—Is it possible to make this room dark? If I [. . .]?—*Yes.*—How is it then? Where does the dark in the room come from?—*It's because the windows have been shut out; the dark comes from the blind.*—And the dark outside, what is it? —*It's the sky.*—When it is light, why is it light?—*Because the dark has gone.*—What makes it day?—*God; He says to the dark: go away.*"

The essential characteristics of absolute artificialism specific to the first stage are easily identified in these children. No further examples need be given since, with the exception of very few subjects who maintain strictly artificialistic explanations without any apparent finalism, the protocols are markedly homogeneous.

STAGE 2

Semiartificialistic and Semiphysical Interpretations

In stage 2, artificialism assumes a more disguised form: the fabricating agent is still necessary, but henceforth uses natural, physical elements (e.g., clouds, fog, sun, and so on), or, more rarely, artificial material (e.g., the smoke from trains or from houses). The child will also often add animistic elements to his explanation: the sun goes down (*se couche*) and causes the night, because "*he too must take a rest*"; the clouds wander about in the sky and come to hide the sun, "*because they want to do it*"; etc.

Two important differences between this and Piaget's classification are to be noted at this point. First of all, the disappearance of the sun becomes an important explanatory factor not only at the last stage of the evolution but already at the beginning of this intermediate level. Secondly, animism is coupled with artificialism, or even pure physicalism, often enough to raise doubts about Piaget's interpretation on the incompatibility of these various types of beliefs. According to him, when the child outgrows the period of mythological artificialism (stage 1) and reaches the period of technical artificialism (the present stage 2), or that of pure physicalism (stage 3), the advent of these more mature modes of explanation should mark the disappearance of animistic beliefs which, from then on, have become useless. Now, among the subjects examined here, as many as 43 are patent exceptions to that rule. This number admittedly constitutes a minimum, since many children adopted the popular expression "*le soleil s'en va se coucher*" ("*the sun goes down*") which makes it impossible for the examiner to determine whether the expression still conceals traces of animism. These facts are not really so difficult to understand. It seems only natural that stars, clouds, smoke, and the like, even though made by man or God, should be endowed with some kind of consciousness or life so that they may obey the will of their maker. The child finds no other way to explain the docility of natural elements. Animistic thinking, on the other hand, is so tenacious that it survives even after the disappearance of the artificialism resorted to by the child in his explanation of night. As a matter of fact, the analysis of the questionnaire on life has shown that the sun and the clouds are among the objects most frequently and most lastingly regarded as living. It is not, then, surprising that to explain the night the child may rely exclusively on the disappearance of the sun or the arrival of clouds, while still granting them life or consciousness.

Thus stage 2 comprises all the children whose artificialism is interspersed with physical elements. These interpretations are almost always coupled with finalism, and sometimes even with animism.

5 (6:0): "You know what the night is?—*Yes.*—Tell me, what is night?—[Silence]—Why is it dark at night?—*It's time to go to bed.* —Where does the dark come from at night? What makes it night? —*When there is no sun; the sun, it rolls like a ball, then it goes very far.*—[....]—Then, why is it dark at night?—*It's because it's time to go to bed.*—Why is it dark only at night?—*It's to go to bed.*— [....]—Explain to me how it is that it is dark when there is no more sun.—*The sun goes far away; he is tired; God has taken away the sun, then He made it fall like a ball.*—Where does the sun go, when it is night?—*It comes here sometimes, it goes at my little cousin's who lives far away.*—Why does the sky become dark at night?—*This is why, the sun is gone.*—[....]—Then, how is it, where does the dark in the room come from?—*The sun will not be there.*—And the dark outside, what is it?—*I don't remember. Then the clouds always stay white, then the sun also.*—When it is light, why is it light?—[Silence.]—What makes it day?—*When the sun comes about, he makes the day, it's time to . . . lunch.*"

16 (7:0): "You know what the night is? Tell me, what is night?— *It's when it's dark.*—Why is it dark?—*Because the sun is not there. It's trains which make black smoke.*—Where does the dark come from at night? What makes it night?—*It's the sky which has become dark.*—Where does it come from, this smoke? What makes this smoke?—*You put coal in, it burns and this makes smoke and it goes up in the sky.*—How do the trains make this smoke?—*It's because they go by very, very fast.*—[....]—Explain to me how it

is that it is dark when there is no more sun?—*Because the sun is not there. It cannot give any more light. It's the moon which is there.*—Where does the sun go, when it is night?—*Down under us, there are also people.*—Why does the sky become dark at night? —*Because the smoke goes down.*—[....]—What makes it day?— *It's when you work, and the children go to school."*

49 (9:0): " ... Tell me, what is night?—*It's dark.*—Why is it dark at night?—*The clouds make it dark.*—Where does the dark come from at night ... ?—*From the sky.*—Where do these clouds come from?—*From the sky.*—How does the sky make these clouds, with what does it make them?—*It's good Jesus. He makes them and hangs them in the sky. He makes them alone, with nothing.*— [....]—Are the clouds of the night white or black:—*They're white.*—[....]—When it's light, why is it light?—*It's good Jesus. He makes it light. He says: light! Then, it's light."*

40 (8:0): " ... Tell me, what is night?—*When we sleep.*—Why is it dark at night?—*To sleep.*—Where does the dark come from at night?—*The dark, it comes from the sky. It's God who wants it.*— [....]—Then, why is it dark at night?—*Don't know. It's because God wants it.*—Why is it dark only at night?—*Because the sun goes away.*—[....]—Explain to me how it is that it is dark when there is no more sun.—*Because the sun lights up; then, when it's gone there is nothing to light up, except the moon a little bit.*— Where does the sun go at night?—*It goes down in the clouds [il se couche dans les nuages].*—[....]—Then, why is it not dark like during the night, when it rains?—*Because the sun is there in the air, even if you don't see it: it's the water which hides the sun.*— Then, why is it dark only at night?—*Because the sun is down [est couché]."*

These various examples effectively illustrate the more mature artificialism of stage 2 children. This artificialism gradually yields to physical explanations which use natural elements such as the clouds, or even artificial ones such as the smoke. But the action of these elements is far from being perfectly understood and considered as objective by the child. In some aspects, this action is comparable to the intervention of human beings, and it is through this anthropomorphism that the child's animism is revealed.

It is also instructive to note how the various types of explanation are intermingled in the child's mind. As clearly shown by the second example quoted above, some subjects may, at a given moment, mention the physical elements, but they immediately neglect these in favor of artificialistic explanations, obviously more satisfactory. For the third subject, on the contrary, the various elements are much better integrated and compose a single system to which physicalism and artificialism contribute in nearly equal parts. For the last subject, finally, this balance is again broken, but now in favor of physicalism. This shows clearly the characteristic function of an intermediate stage, which is to group together almost all the possible steps between two opposite conceptions. However, individual differences in verbal fluency are so great that it becomes an impossible task to assess, without bias, the relative importance of the various components of a child's protocol. It is therefore necessary to resort to a less refined classification which undoubtedly makes up in objectivity what it may have lost in subtlety.

STAGE 3

Absolute Physicalism

The third stage is characterized by the disappearance of artificialistic notions. Henceforth the darkness of night is explained by the action of strictly physical and natural elements: disappearance of the sun, formation of clouds through evaporation from the seas, movement of winds, thickening of fog, and the like. The system the child chooses to adopt does not, as may readily be foreseen, always conform with reality. Even explanations given at school are seldom completely reflected in the child's answers. Most children develop a personal theory in which the details, in particular, seem to spring from the imagination. But, whatever its value, the system elaborated is limited to the intervention of physical elements: night is no longer the result of some fabrication; it is essentially a natural phenomenon.

The disappearance of artificialism, however, does not entail the simultaneous disappearance of the other forms of precausality. The finalistic ties between night and sleep prove to be particularly enduring: of the 183 subjects of stage 3, 77 still rely in part on finalistic reasons. Moreover, some 20 of these 77 subjects openly use animistic terms—hence the necessity of distinguishing two substages.

SUBSTAGE 3A: PHYSICALISM STILL TAINTED WITH FINALISM OR ANIMISM

For the children of substage 3A, the origin of night is natural, but the explanation is saturated with finalistic beliefs relating night to sleep, and day to work. Moreover, the celestial bodies or the meteors responsible for the forming of the night are sometimes explicitly considered to be alive.

21 (9:0): "... Why is it dark at night?—*Because we've had a completely sleepless day, and then at night we must rest.*—Where does the dark come from at night? What makes it night?—*I was about to say the clouds, but it's not that.*—[....]—Then why is it dark at night?—*Because it's not the day.*—Why is it dark only at night?—*For resting, because we had a sleepless day.*—[....]—You have spoken, a moment ago, of the clouds. Where do the clouds come from, what makes the clouds?—*The wind;* [then, in a very low voice] *no, it's not that.*—Then how does the wind make the clouds? How does it make them?—*With all the fog of the wind, this makes the clouds.*—Why do they come only at night, these clouds?—*It's*

because during the day they rest, and at night they get up.—Can
white clouds make the night?—*No. Ah! it's true!*—Why do you say
that . . . ?—*Because the night is dark and the clouds must be black.*
—[. . . .]—Then it is black clouds which take the place of white
ones, or white clouds which turn black?—*The white clouds become black.*—[. . . .]—Then how is it, where does the dark in the
room come from?—*It's because the light illuminates and we shut
out the light, we block it.*—And the dark outside, what is it?—*It's
the light . . . the sun goes away.*—Explain to me how it is that it is
dark when the sun is no longer there.—*The sun goes down [va se
coucher] and there is no more light.*—Where does the sun go at
night?—*It goes down behind the sky [il se couche derrière le firma-
ment].*—Why does the sky become dark at night?—*Because the
sun is gone.*"

14 (10:0): " . . . Why is it dark at night?—*To go to bed. To tell us
when to go to bed, or when to come inside.*—Where does the dark
at night come from? What makes it night?—*It's dark because the
sun goes away.*—Explain to me how it is that it is dark when the
sun is no longer there.—*It's the sun which lights up the earth.*—
Where does the sun go at night?—*It goes on the other side: it lights
up half of the earth.*—[. . . .]—Then, why is it not dark as during
the night, when it rains?—*Because the clouds are not black, they
are white; it lights up a little bit.*"

These examples clearly illustrate how, with the help of the
examiner's questions, children end up by defining quite precisely notions which were at first very vague. This initial confusion can probably be attributed to their unfamiliarity with
the problem proposed and is observable at all levels. But children of the present stage are characterized as being satisfied
with strictly astrological or meteorological solutions. As for
finalistic beliefs, they are extremely tenacious. After having
generated artificialism, they still survive for some time. Piaget
takes this as a proof of the fact that, instead of disappearing all
at once, human or theological artificialism undergoes a mere

transformation whereby all attributes hitherto reserved to man or God are now ascribed to natural phenomena.

SUBSTAGE 3B: PHYSICALISM FREED FROM ANY PRECAUSALITY

In substage 3B, the interpretation sheds all remnants of pre-causal thinking. Darkness comes from the disappearance of the sun which now hides *"behind the clouds"* or *"behind the mountains,"* or goes *"to illuminate other countries,"* or disappears *"to the west," "to the east," "to the south,"* or *"to the north,"* or *"does not move but the earth turns on itself,"* and the like. Some answers still remain ambiguous (e.g., *"the sun goes down"* [*va se coucher*], *"the sun hides behind the clouds,"* and so on); but, because they belong to adult colloquial vocabulary, it is not possible to regard them as sure evidence of animistic thinking.

23 (12:0): "... Tell me, what is the night?—*It's when the sun goes down. It's dark.*—Why is it dark at night?—*Because the sun is down and it's the sun which projects light during the day.*—Where does the dark come from at night? What makes it night?—*It comes from nowhere, it's the color of the sky. In the daytime, it's the sun which makes it blue, and when the sun is gone it becomes dark.*— [....]—Where does the sun go at night?—*Behind the clouds.*— Where to?—*To the east, I think.*—What clouds?—*Any of them.*— [....]—Then why is it not dark like at night when it rains?—*It's only because it's hidden by the clouds.*—Then why is it dark only at night?—*Because at night, it is not there, it is behind the moon.*"

48 (12:0): "... Why is it dark at night?—*Because the earth turns on itself, then this produces the day and the night.*—Where does the dark come from at night? What makes it night?—*It comes from the absence of the sun.*—Explain to me how it is that it is dark when the sun is no longer there?—*It's the sun which produces light, and so if the sun is absent, we cannot have this light.*—Where does the sun go at night?—*The sun is on the other side of the earth. It's not the sun which goes, it's the earth which turns.*"

In this scale describing the child's beliefs concerning the origin of night, the distribution (Table 15) of the subjects within the stages supports the postulate of transitivity: the seriation of median ages is perfectly regular. The age of accession to the various stages shows how general and enduring the child's artificialistic beliefs can be. As early as at the age of four, 64 per cent of the children already belong to substage 1B at least, that is, to the first stage of genuine artificialism. Stage 1A, it will be recalled, comprises purely finalistic interpretations. Already well established at the age of four, artificialism does not disappear in the average child until the age of about nine

Table 15

Distribution of subjects by age and developmental stage
in the questionnaire on night

		Stages										
		0	1A	1B	2	3A	3B	1A	1B	2	3A	3B
Age	N	Raw percentages						Cumulative percentages				
12:0	50	0	2	0	10	26	62	100	98	98	88	62
11:0	50	0	2	2	24	20	52	100	98	96	72	52
10:0	50	0	0	4	20	30	46	100	100	96	76	46
9:0	50	0	8	10	38	20	24	100	92	82	44	24
8:0	50	0	0	24	54	14	8	100	100	76	22	8
7:0	50	0	4	28	42	16	10	100	96	68	26	10
6:0	50	0	10	36	36	12	6	100	90	54	18	6
5:0	50	10	14	50	20	4	2	90	76	26	6	2
4:6	50	2	26	54	10	6	2	98	72	18	8	2
4:0	50	10	26	42	16	6	0	90	64	22	6	0
Total		22	92	250	270	154	212					
Median age		4:6	4:8	5:1	7:8	9:5	10:8					
Age of accession								—	—	6:2	8:10	10:10

Table 16

Sex differences on the questionnaire on night

Age	Sex	N	0	1A	1B	2	3A	3B	X²	df	
12:0	G	25	0	1	0	2	8	14	0.76	1	P>.01
	B	25	0	0	0	3	5	17			
11:0	G	25	0	1	0	7	7	10	3.26	2	P>.01
	B	25	0	0	1	5	3	16			
10:0	G	26	0	0	2	7	7	10	3.38	2	P>.01
	B	24	0	0	0	3	8	13			
9:0	G	25	0	2	3	11	5	4	2.78	3	P>.01
	B	25	0	2	2	8	5	8			
8:0	G	25	0	0	10	12	3	0	7.96	2	P>.01
	B	25	0	0	2	15	4	4			
7:0	G	25	0	2	9	9	2	3	3.38	2	P>.01
	B	25	0	0	5	12	6	2			
6:0	G	24	0	3	7	8	4	2	1.53	2	P>.01
	B	26	0	2	11	10	2	1			
5:0	G	25	2	3	14	5	0	1	0.50	2	P>.01
	B	25	3	4	12	4	2	0			
4:6	G	25	1	9	11	3	0	1	2.40	2	P>.01
	B	25	0	5	15	2	3	0			
4:0	G	25	4	5	10	5	1	0	0.14	2	P>.01
	B	25	1	8	11	3	2	0			
Total	G	250	7	26	66	69	37	45			
	B	250	4	21	59	65	40	61			

Over-all X² 26.09 20 P>.01

when stage 3 is reached. In the course of this long period, artificialism will have undergone some modifications. The most evident change occurs around the age of six; at that age, accession to stage 2 marks the decline of the preference for artificialistic reasons in favor of a progressive interest in natural explanations. Thus artificialism seems to evolve much more slowly than realistic and animistic beliefs. It should be recalled that the realism associated with the concept of dream is manifested clearly at the age of four and a half only, and disappears as early as six and a half or so; the stages of the concept of life, on the other hand, are distributed between the ages of five to nine. It seems that the two factors discussed previously can account for these facts. Religious instruction, at a very early age, provides matter for the artificialistic tendencies of the child's thinking. As this influence becomes increasingly important during the first school years, it imposes ready-made solutions that the child is not yet in a position to appraise. Further, since the phenomenon of night is particularly well known to children, the youngest among them can express beliefs which would escape observation, were it not that conditions are well adapted to their ability to understand and communicate.

It should finally be pointed out that the differences between boys and girls (Table 16) are never significant at the .01 level.

CHAPTER XI

The Movement of Clouds

The purpose of the questionnaire on the movement of clouds was to throw light on the child's dynamistic thinking. It must be admitted that the choice of this topic did not prove very fortunate. Contrary to all expectations, it gives rise to almost every known form of precausal thinking. Dynamism as such, whenever it can be identified, is enmeshed in too intricate a mass of various beliefs to be assessed in isolation. Far more explanations are actually oriented in the direction of artificialism than in that of dynamism: God, men, or celestial bodies are usually said to be at the origin of the movement of clouds. Dynamism is rarely explicit and is always dependent on other forms of precausal thinking. It occurs only when the artificialistic action is not exerted directly upon the clouds, but rather through a control at a distance. Clouds are then endowed with the required power of moving about by themselves in order to submit to external commands.

There are two ways of explaining this rare occurrence of dynamism. Either dynamistic beliefs do not constitute a particular form of precausality and are essentially the same as animistic thinking; or they exist as such, but the questionnaire on the movement of clouds is unsuitable for bringing them out. The present data do not allow a definitive choice between these two hypotheses. Only a more extensive study of animism and dynamism could uncover the limits of their respective roles in the child's mind. As a matter of fact, Piaget himself had to assemble very diversified observations before he was able to conclude that dynamism in the child exists. Observations derived from his questionnaire on the movement of clouds would certainly not have warranted so general a conclusion. In fact, his results on this particular problem do not differ fundamentally from those yielded by the present investigation. But these considerations should certainly have been taken into account before we made a selection of questionnaires most likely to reveal the child's dynamistic beliefs.

Even though the inadequacy of the present data excludes the possibility of making a definite choice between the two hypotheses formulated above, certain arguments seem to favor the second. Thus, for instance, the idea of an autonomous force or a magical power inherent in clouds is clearly indicated in a few protocols. Granted that this belief is not explicitly formulated frequently enough to provide any information as to the course of its evolution, it is nevertheless the only explanation resorted to by many of the children. Moreover, those children who adopt a different type of explanation often use this magical power as an additional and necessary element of interpretation.

47 (7:0): " . . . What makes the clouds move?—*Nobody.*—Then, how do they move?—*They move all alone.*—How do the clouds go about moving all alone?—*They go forward.*—How?—*All alone.*— Are the clouds moving all alone, or is there something to make them move?—*There is nothing to make them move.*—Do the clouds know they are going forward?—[Smiles] *No.*—Why do you say they do not know?—*Well, they are not people.*"

40 (10:0): " . . . What makes the clouds move?—*God.*—How does God go about making them move?—*He makes something like miracles. He pushes them.*—Are the clouds moving by themselves, or is there something to make them move?—*By themselves, sometimes, but not always.*—[. . . .]—Why do you say they can go where they want?—*Because they can find their way by themselves, and God helps them.*"

In the second place, these dynamistic beliefs will be observed again in greatly increased intensity in the child's interpretation of the floating or sinking of objects, as will be seen in the next questionnaire. It is this last argument which more than the other speaks in favor of the second hypothesis. If, indeed, the scarcity of dynamistic explanations elicited by the questionnaire on clouds were taken to mean that this form of precausal thinking is not really present in the child, how could it be so vividly evident in another questionnaire bearing on another phenomenon? In view of these facts, it seems more legitimate to conclude that the examination on clouds, on account of its very structure or of its content, does not provide for an effective exploration of dynamistic notions. This questionnaire does in fact lead the child to adopt a quite different mode of reasoning and elicits artificialistic explanations, which generally dispense with any recourse to dynamism: either the clouds are moved through God's direct action (e.g., "*He pushes them,*" "*He drags them,*" and so on), or else the divine power is effective in itself and can be exerted from a distance (e.g., "*it's God who makes them move with His will*").

The question remains why the examination on the movement of clouds so generally gives rise to artificialistic solutions and, preferably, to solutions based upon God's intervention. Many hypotheses are possible. The very wording of the questions may actually lead children to seek an external cause to the movement of clouds. Instead of asking "*What makes the clouds move?*" ("*Qu'est-ce qui les fait avancer, les nuages?"*), it would no doubt have been better to ask a still more neutral question, (e.g., *"How is it that clouds move?"* (*"Comment il se fait qu'ils avancent, les nuages?"*). The present wording is likely to be misunderstood by many who could possibly give it the following meaning: *"Who makes the clouds move?"* (*"Qui est-ce qui les fait avancer, les nuages?"*). The prevalence of artificialistic responses may also be explained in part by the examiner's lack of insistence which results in accepting only the most superficial and the easiest solutions. It is also possible that the child may have a natural affinity for this form of thinking, and that this affinity may be all the closer for being sustained by religious instruction. Finally, as it is also true of the origin of night, the phenomenon investigated in the present questionnaire is likewise related to the sky, and is thus naturally associated with those beings whom the child is accustomed to locate in heaven. On this latter point and as an example of this confusion, it is interesting to quote the amusing remark of an eight-year-old subject, who asked the examiner: *"Is it catechism or geography, we are now doing?"*

In any case, there is no need whatever to know the relative significance of these several factors in order to determine the characteristic levels of the evolution of beliefs bearing on the movement of clouds. Even though these levels do not measure dynamistic thinking, as intended, they are still worth considering because they always provide additional evidence of the actual existence of all the forms of precausality observed in the three previous questionnaires. The protocols are classified into four main stages, among which only three of Piaget's five are to be found. Explanations corresponding to Piaget's first and fourth stages are much too thinly scattered to constitute independent levels: the magical connection of the movement of clouds with that of man (e.g., *"it's us, when we are walking, we make the clouds move"*) is mentioned by 12 children only, and the mechanism of air reflux (i.e., the wind which makes the clouds move originates from the clouds themselves) appears only fifteen times at most.

STAGE 0

Incomprehension or Refusal

In stage 0, the usual features are to be observed again: refusal to answer the questions; refusal to acknowledge the movement of clouds; obvious lack of understanding of questions; inability to find personal solutions; and, consequently, total acceptance of the examiner's suggestions. Some explanations belong to pure imagination and cannot be assimilated to real beliefs.

18 (4:0): " ... What makes the clouds move?—*Me.*—How is that? —*I make it move with my hands.*"

46 (4:0): " ... What makes the clouds move?—*Serge, my six-year-old brother.*"

27 (5:0): " ... What makes the clouds move?—*God.*—How does God go about making the clouds move?—*He throws a paper.*— Can the clouds move by themselves, or is there something to make them move?—*There is something, a paper.*"

Except for some purely verbal confusions (the word *nuage* [cloud] taken for *sauvage* [savage] or *image* [image]), most children start talking about all kinds of things so that it becomes impossible to identify the starting point of their various lucubrations. Thus, to account for the movement of clouds, there will be references to *"microbes," "children with fireworks," "house and church," "police and firemen," "factories which are tied behind,"* etc.

At first glance, some explanations may be compared with those given at later stages, but the details added by these stage 0 subjects betray a total lack of understanding.

44 (4:0): " ... What makes the clouds move?—*The machines.*— How do the machines go about making the clouds move?—*It's because they want, they make them crush the man.*—Do the clouds move by themselves, or is there something to make them move?— *There are wheels* [manifestly speaks of an automobile].—[....]— Why do you say they know?—*Because the man, he wants to break the car, then . . . the slippers are under the car.*"

41 (4:6): " ... What makes the clouds move?—*The Blessed Virgin.* —How does the Blessed Virgin go about making them move?— *She is dressed.*—[....]—Why do you say that they know?—*Because the Blessed Virgin wants them to lunch.*—[....]—But why do they move, the clouds?—*Because they think that a Blessed Virgin walks alone.*"

Another type of explanation which is very frequent among the younger children merits special notice. It consists in imagining that the clouds are moving *"because they have feet."* Answers of this kind come from a superficial association with the word *"marcher"* (to move, which also means to *walk*) and manifest a complete ignorance on the part of the subject.

23 (5:0): " ... What makes them move?—*The moons.*—How do the moons go about making the clouds move?—*They walk.*—Who? —*The moons.*—[....]—Why do you say that they know?—*Because they have feet.*—[....]—Why can they go where they want? —*Because . . . .*—Because of what?—*Because they have feet.*— But why do the clouds move?—*You don't know why?*—No.—*It's because they have feet.*—Then, what does this do?—*It's because they are unable to walk if they don't have feet.*—Why do the clouds sometimes move fast and sometimes move slowly?—*Because, if somebody scares them, they run fast.*"

In some cases, it is not the addition of inconsequential details, but rather the total absence of explanatory remarks which justifies the classification in stage 0. These children are indeed satisfied with mentioning "*God,*" "*the moon,*" "*thunder,*" "*rain,*" or even the "*wind,*" and so on, in answer to the first question on the cause of the movement of clouds, but they are afterwards incapable of justifying, even in a rudimentary way, the meaning of this first answer. This inability can no doubt be explained by the lack of real notions on the subject, and the occasional spontaneous remarks are pure associations elicited by the examiner's questions. To bring the child to speak about the clouds is almost always tantamount to inducing him to display his knowledge of meteorological phenomena or of celestial bodies, topics he naturally likes to talk about. However, there is a great danger of mistaking simple remarks for real explanations. It seems preferable, even at the risk of being too rigorous in the assessment of the protocols, not to classify children in higher stages unless they prove capable of developing a system of explanation consistent with the phenomenon to be accounted for. The system does not have to conform with reality; it suffices that the various elements chosen by the child be verisimilar and be expressly applied to the explanation of the phenomenon. When these minimal requirements are lacking, the protocols are classified in stage 0 and are thus considered equivalent to interpretations based upon pure imagination, fabulation, or ignorance.

STAGE 1

Human or Divine Action

In stage 1, the explanation of the movement of clouds gives rise to all the modes of precausality already described. However, realism and artificialism constitute the basis of all the various elaborations and are thus typical of this first level. The other types of precausal relations are frequently grafted upon this initial structure, but in an irregular and sporadic fashion.

Realism is manifested through beliefs of a magical type: it is we who, by walking, make the clouds move. Divine artificialism permeates most answers and constitutes the most general characteristic of this stage. Animism is sometimes coupled with the foregoing explanations and serves mainly to account for the submission of clouds to divine commands or to human signals. A fourth type of precausal thinking, dynamism, is shown here for the first time and also completes the interpretations just mentioned: the child appeals to dynamism to provide the clouds with the power to move by themselves, and thus to fulfill their function. Lastly, finalism is used occasionally to emphasize the fact that clouds have to move.

29 (7:0): " . . . What makes the clouds move?—*God.*—How does God go about making the clouds move?—*God gets inside, then makes them move like a car.*—Do the clouds move by themselves, or is there something to make them move?—*They move by themselves.*—Do the clouds know that they are moving?—*Yes.*—Do they know that it is God who makes them move?—*Yes.*—Why do you say that they know?—*Because it's heavy inside, then they know it.*—[. . . .]—Can the clouds go where they want?—*No.*— Why can't they go where they want?—*Because it's God who drives and brings them where He wants.*—But why do the clouds move? —*To follow us when we walk, to know where we are going.*—Why do the clouds sometimes move fast and sometimes move slowly?— *Because when we go fast, God makes them go fast; then when we don't go fast, God makes them go slowly.*—Yourself, can you make the clouds move?—*Yes.*—When I walk and you stand still, do the clouds move?—*Yes.*—And at night, when everybody is asleep, do the clouds move?—*No.*—Why don't they move?—*Because, during the night, people will not move. People must move for the clouds to move.*—[. . . .]—Do the clouds move when you stand still?— *No.*—Why don't they move?—*Because if we stand still, God sees*

that we're stopping, then He stops the clouds also.—Can the wind make the clouds move?—*No.*—Why can't the wind make the clouds move?—*Because the trees are not high enough."*

The last remark made by this subject should be noted. Surprising as it may seem, it manifests a conception particularly widespread among children, and already noted by Piaget: the wind comes from trees, or more generally, from all the objects whose movement is in reality caused by the wind.

23 (4:0): ". . . Can the wind make the clouds move?—*Yes.*—How does the wind go about making the clouds move?—*Because it shakes hard.*—Where does the wind come from?—*Well, it comes from the trees."*

12 (6:0): ". . . How does the wind go about making the clouds move?—*It brings it with its branches."*

108 (11:0): ". . . Give me the name of some thing which can make some wind.—*A tree."*

Unfortunately, the data do not permit a more detailed study of these beliefs on the origin of the wind. Too many children refused to admit the participation of the wind in the movement of clouds and, consequently, were not given the last part of the examination.

The example quoted above, 29 (7:0), is noteworthy for the richness of its content: all modes of precausality are simultaneously and explicitly displayed. Such protocols are very rare. The systems most often resorted to do not include more than two or three types of relationships variously combined, while leaving a clearly preponderant place to explanations of an artificialistic type. This artificialism is moreover restricted to the intervention of a God who is quite often humanized, and whose action may take all forms from physical contact to remote control.

48 (7:0): " . . . What makes the clouds move?—*God.*—How does He go about . . . ?—*He pushes them with his hands.*"

43 (4:6): " . . . What makes the clouds move?—*The same thread which makes the sun move. It's God who holds the thread.*"

9 (4:0): " . . . Do the clouds move by themselves, or is there something which makes them move?—*There is something to make them move. The Child Jesus pushes a button, then they move, the clouds.*—Why do the clouds sometimes move fast and sometimes move slowly?—*Because Jesus pushes another button, and then He makes them move fast.*"

18 (6:0): " . . . What makes the clouds move?—*It's God.*—How does He go about . . . ?—*He just has to say: 'I want the clouds to move,' and they move.*"

8 (7:0): " . . . How does God go about . . . ?—*God makes them move by himself, with nothing, nothing.*"

To summarize, in stage 1, the movement of clouds is explained by causes foreign to both meteorology and physics. The artificialistic or magical techniques fully satisfy the children's intelligence. They do not themselves think of attributing a role, no matter how trifling, to phenomena contiguous in time or space such as *celestial bodies, rain, wind,* and the like. They never even mention these agents, and it is only at the examiner's suggestion that some subjects will accept the role of the wind. But this concession is in no way a genuine conviction since, at the first opening, most subjects revert to their primitive system.

9 (5:0): " . . . What makes the clouds move?—*They move by themselves when we walk.*—[. . . .]—Can the wind make the clouds

move?—*Yes.*—How does the wind go about making the clouds move?—*I don't know. When the wind is strong, the clouds move fast.*—[. . . .]—Why do the clouds sometimes move fast and sometimes move slowly?—*Because, when we run, they move fast; then when we do not run, they don't move fast."*

Even though reverting to his initial belief, the child has nevertheless accepted the examiner's suggestion. Is this the indication of a slightly superior intellectual level, due to greater permeability to external influences? This hypothesis is not supported by the present results, because there are no observable differences in age between children who accept the suggestion about the wind and those who do not. It is therefore not possible to assume that there is a difference in level between the two groups and to classify them into substages.

STAGE 2

Autonomous Movement, or Action of Other Celestial Bodies

In the second stage, magical beliefs have completely disappeared. God's action is also much less frequent and above all much less exclusive. The child no longer considers that this action alone is sufficient to explain the movement of clouds: he always adds the necessary cooperation of an intermediary agent, chosen among celestial bodies, or among atmospheric phenomena, with the exception of winds.

21 (7:0): " . . . What makes the clouds move?—*The sky.*—How does the sky go about making them move?—*It's God who makes that go.*—Then, what do the clouds move with? What makes them move?—*The stars.*—How do the stars go about making the clouds

move?—*The stars slide on the sky, it makes the sky go forward, it makes the clouds move.*"

However, interpretations of this kind, based partly upon divine intervention, are exceptional in the second stage. The topics most frequently introduced are of two types. The first of these seeks the cause of the movement of clouds in cosmology or meteorology; but because he is still incapable of positing the wind as the origin of this movement, the child will resort in turn to the sun, the earth, the moon, the stars, the sky, the rain, and so on. Briefly, because he thinks in a syncretic way, he is led to postulate causal relationships between phenomena which are simply contiguous in space or time.

26 (8:0): " . . . What makes the clouds move?—*It's the earth, the earth which turns.*—How does the earth go about making the clouds move?—*The earth turns, then the sky turns with it, then the clouds turn.*—[. . . .]—Do the clouds move by themselves, or is there something to make them move?—*It's the earth.*—[. . . .] —Why do the clouds sometimes move fast and sometimes move slowly?—*The earth turns fast sometimes, then sometimes slowly.*"

49 (8:0): " . . . What makes the clouds move?—*The sun.*—How does the sun go about making the clouds move?—*With its light. At night it's the moon which makes them move.*—[. . . .]—But why do the clouds move?—*Because the sun makes them move.*— Why do the clouds sometimes move fast and sometimes move slowly?—*It's the sun which makes them move fast sometimes, and sometimes slowly.*"

29 (8:0): " . . . What makes the clouds move?—*The sky.*—How does the sky go about making the clouds move?—*It moves, then it brings them . . . it's not anything which makes the clouds move . . .* [long meditation] . . . *When it has to rain, they go everywhere.* —What makes them go everywhere?—*The sky.*—How does the sky go about . . . ?—*It hitches them to itself . . . the sky moves by itself.*"

The topics of the second type rest upon an apparently integral dynamism; the clouds move by themselves, without being openly influenced or directed by any external agent. In stage 1, the few manifestations of dynamism were but accessory: the clouds could move by themselves in order the better to comply with the orders of man or God. In the second stage, on the contrary, the clouds are no longer directly submitted to somebody's will, and they move about on their own power.

22 (5:0): " . . . What makes the clouds move?—*They move along by themselves, all alone.*—How do the clouds go about moving along by themselves?—*I don't know.*—[. . . .]—Do they know that they move along?—*No, they don't have eyes.*—[. . . .]—Why can they go where they want?—*Because they like that.*—But why do the clouds move?—*Because they are lonesome.*—Why do they sometimes move fast and sometimes slowly?—*When it rains hard, they go fast; when it doesn't rain, they don't go fast.*"

38 (11:0): " . . . What makes the clouds move?—*Nature.*—What in nature?—*They move by themselves.*—How do they go about moving by themselves?—*It's because it's like a ball of water, it gives water.*—[. . . .]—Why can't they go where they want?— *Because sometimes it's too big, and they burst and they cannot go any further when they are open.*—But why do the clouds move?— *To go to some other places.*—Why do the clouds sometimes go fast and sometimes slowly?—*When they are heavier, they move more slowly.*"

Finalistic or animistic remarks are often added to all these explanations. Upon the examiner's suggestions, the child may also resort to the wind in his interpretations. The presence or absence of either one of these elements does not seem, however, to reflect any perceptible difference in developmental level, and the statistics do not warrant any subdivision based on these factors. The essential features of this level are thus the total disappearance of magical realism and divine artificialism as exclusive causes of the movement of clouds, and the introduction of physical factors which are, however, still inadequate. These physical factors are generally quite sufficient to explain the phenomenon: but in the child's system, it may happen, although not very often, that they must still be supplemented by God's action to be effective.

A cursory analysis of this intermediate stage seems to indicate that it is not continuous with adjacent stages. For the first time, in fact, the intermediate level is not characterized by the child's oscillation between two opposite conceptions. What is visible, on the contrary, is that new beliefs have come to replace those of the preceding level, and these new beliefs seem to have nothing in common with those which will prevail at the next level. It becomes difficult, under these conditions, to explain the linking of these stages and, especially, to determine the psychological significance of this intermediate level. On closer examination of the protocols, however, it is possible to see that this discontinuity is but apparent. Under the guise of physicalism, the child's explanations still conceal relationships of the artificialistic type. It is sufficient to observe how the child conceives the manner in which heavenly bodies act upon each other to become convinced that this action is in no way assimilated to physical or chemical influences, but rather to human gestures.

8 (8:0): " . . . What makes the clouds move?—*The sun.*—How does it go about . . . ?—*It blows on them.*"

23 (8:0): "[Same question.]—*Vapor.*—How does it go about . . . ? —*By pushing them.*"

49 (7:0): "[Same question.]—*The moon.*—How does it go about . . . . ?—*It drags them.*"

35 (10:0): "[Same question.]—*The sun. When the sun is hidden, and it wants to show itself, it pushes them.*"

21 (4:0): "[Same question.]—*The sun. It hides in the clouds; it steers the wheel.*"

The anthropomorphism of all these responses shows unequivocally the persistence of stage 1 artificialistic beliefs: with only slight differences, the same procedures remain effective. Celestial bodies are substituted for man or God; in this sense, it may be said that, though the technician is no longer the same, the technique used does not change. In short, instead of disappearing, stage 1 artificialism is merely transformed. It is associated with more natural physical concepts, but it still remains operative. Thus here again, in spite of appearances, the usual feature of intermediate levels is shown in a mixture of varying ratios of two opposite conceptions.

The protocols are not always so clearly related to artificialism. Whenever the child declines to give precisions on the action of sun or earth, or whenever he pronounces in favor of the autonomous movement of the clouds, the examiner might be tempted to interpret this response in terms of absolute physicalism. Yet, how can an effective action of celestial bodies on clouds be imagined without resorting, at least implicitly, to artificial and even magical procedures? How, for example, can the sun cause the clouds to move forward without being itself considered as an omnipotent being who, like God, imposes his will on the clouds, chases them, draws them along with Him, and so on? Further, even autonomous movements of clouds follow certain rules which express an almost inevitably anthropomorphic finalism: clouds move to water gardens in all countries, or to produce the night by hiding the sun. Thus, it is still man's will which subordinates the movements of clouds to its own purposes, even though this subjection is not made explicit in the child's answers.

STAGE 3

Action of the Wind (or Movement Regarded as Illusive)

The stage 3 child finds the correct explanation by himself: he spontaneously designates the wind as the cause of the movement of clouds, and almost always holds to mechanical or physical principles.

3 (10:0): " . . . What makes the clouds move?—*The wind.*— Where does the wind come from?—*From nowhere, it's always there.*—Can the clouds make wind?—*No.*—[. . . .]—Give me the name of some thing which can make wind?—*A fan.*—Why do the clouds sometimes move fast and sometimes slowly?—*Because sometimes the wind pushes them hard, then some other times not hard.*—Can the clouds go where they want?—*No.*—Why do you say that they cannot go where they want?—*Because if the wind blows on one side, they must go that way.*"

Also classified in stage 3 are the few subjects for whom the movement of clouds is not real but illusive. This interpretation, even though incorrect, is not without meaning and is completely based upon objective physical criteria. Because they already know that the apparent movement of the sun is illusive, many children undoubtedly apply the same explanation to the movement of clouds.

25 (8:0): " . . . What makes the clouds move?—*They don't move. We are the ones who move. The clouds always remain at the same place; then when we walk, they seem to move, but it's not true.*"

However, the fact that children come to discover the role of the wind in the movement of clouds, or to consider this movement illusive, does not necessarily imply that all primitive beliefs have vanished completely. Elements of precausal thinking will still continue for some time and permeate their explanatory systems. In order to mark with greater precision the moment of accession to pure physicalism, it is necessary to distinguish two substages.

SUBSTAGE 3A: CORRECT EXPLANATIONS, BUT STILL TAINTED WITH PRECAUSALITY

Substage 3A comprises the protocols characterized by some residual forms of precausality. The most enduring beliefs are perhaps the artificialistic and finalistic notions of previous levels, but they are too often combined with manifestations of animistic and dynamistic thinking to be considered as typical of this substage.

15 (6:0): " . . . What makes the clouds move?—*It's God with the wind. He has a large mouth and He blows.*"

28 (10:0): "[Same question.]—*The wind.*—Where does the wind come from?—*From a big man, like the one in our first grade book.*"

13 (8:0): "[Same question.]—*They move by themselves, the clouds! It's because it's like smoke; then smoke, it goes up by itself in the sky.*—Why do the clouds sometimes move fast and sometimes move slowly?—*Because when they go fast, it's because the wind blows on them.*—[. . . .]—Where does the wind come from? —*From nowhere.*"

104 (12:0): " . . . What makes the clouds move?—*Isn't it the earth which turns?*—How does the earth go about making the clouds move?—*The clouds stay there and the earth turns and they seem to move.*—[. . . .]—But why do the clouds move?—*To rain almost everywhere, not always at the same place.*"

3 (10:0): " . . . Why do you say that they can go where they want? —*Because they move. If the cloud doesn't want to go in the direction of the wind, the cloud will stop so that it won't go.*"

These few examples effectively illustrate how recourse to

physical causes is often associated with concepts that are still essentially primitive. The appeal to artificialism is particularly clear. Instead of acting directly upon the clouds, God hereafter uses an intermediate agent: He Himself makes the wind which takes upon itself the task of moving clouds. It may sometimes be asked whether these protocols do not rather belong to the second stage, wherein it is precisely these semi-artificialistic and semiphysical explanations that predominate. Two complementary reasons seem, however, to speak against this proposal. In the first place, the artificialism of the previous stages bears directly upon the movement of clouds, while that of substage 3A concerns the origin of the wind. It would indeed be illogical to neglect these latter manifestations of artificialism; but it would be equally so to assimilate them without further ado to the former since the questionnaire is specifically concerned with the child's ideas on the movement of clouds, and not on the origin of the wind. It is, moreover, a very likely supposition that, among the forms of artificialism, the slowest in disappearing are those related to the explanation of the origin of things. Should this hypothesis be correct, the fact of resorting to an intermediate physical cause, even if artificialistic in its own origin, would manifest a progress in the evolution of thinking. The second reason, which is purely statistical, confirms the preceding observation, for the median age of stage 3A children is almost two years more than that of the children of the preceding level. Such a considerable difference in age cannot be ascribed to chance and strongly suggests that there are in effect two genuine levels of development.

SUBSTAGE 3B: CORRECT EXPLANATIONS FREED FROM ANY
PRECAUSAL THINKING

In substage 3B, the movement of clouds is explained exclusively by the wind or as the result of an illusion, and no trace of primitive beliefs is observed. The child's notions on the origin of the wind are not always exact, but they no longer depend upon gross artificialism: the wind usually comes from the sky, from a disturbance of the air, from the rotation of the earth, from the trees, the oceans, or even the clouds themselves. This last type of explanation is rather infrequent, however, and seems generally to derive from questions that are too suggestive, as is aptly illustrated in the following examples.

36 (12:0): " . . . Where does the wind come from?—*I have never asked myself that question. I am puzzled.*—When moving, can the clouds make wind?—*It's the wind which makes them move, they cannot make wind. It's like a mass of air . . . that can make some wind, yes.*—When there is no wind, can the clouds move by themselves?—*I don't think so. They would stay in the same place. I would be surprised.*—Where does the wind come from?—*It comes from the clouds, a little, one could say. When the wind carries the clouds, the clouds happen to produce some other wind also.*"

37 (12:0): " . . . Where does the wind come from?—*From the sky.*—Can the clouds make wind?—*No.*—While moving, can the clouds make wind?—*Yes. The wind, it would come from the clouds, then!*—When there is no wind, can the clouds move by themselves?—*No.*—Where does the wind come from?—*From the clouds.*"

It may be finally noted that one of the questions is often misunderstood by children and may elicit pseudo-animistic answers; for many children the expression, "*to go where they want,*" is taken to mean, "*to go anywhere,*" and thus gives rise to affirmative answers.

26 (12:0): " . . . Can the clouds go where they want?—*Yes.*—Why do you say that they can go where they want?—*Because the wind places them anywhere.*"

48 (11:0): " . . . Can the clouds go where they want?—*Yes.*—Why . . . ?—*Because, over all the earth, there are clouds; it can rain anywhere.*"

Table 17

Distribution of subjects by age and developmental stage in the questionnaire on the movement of clouds

		Stages								
		0	1	2	3A	3B	1	2	3A	3B
Age	N	Raw percentages					Cumulative percentages			
12:0	49	0	14	4	39	43	100	86	82	43
11:0	50	0	20	8	26	46	100	80	72	46
10:0	49	0	24	6	37	33	100	76	70	33
9:0	50	0	28	18	34	20	100	72	54	20
8:0	50	6	38	18	28	10	94	56	38	10
7:0	50	0	46	22	22	10	100	54	32	10
6:0	50	8	76	4	10	2	92	26	22	2
5:0	50	40	36	10	12	2	60	24	14	2
4:6	50	58	36	2	4	0	42	6	4	0
4:0	50	64	26	10	0	0	36	10	0	0
Total		176	344	102	212	166				
Median age		4:5	6:6	7:8	9:5	10:8				
Age of accession							4:8	7:3	8:10	—

• • •

Table 17 shows the classification of subjects in the stage scale just analyzed. Except for two age levels, where two subjects were eliminated on account of errors on the part of the examiner, all percentages are calculated on the basis of 50 subjects. The gradation of median ages is perfectly regular and therefore the cumulation of percentages is justified. The age

Table 18

Sex differences on the questionnaire
on the movement of clouds

Age	Sex	N	Stage 0	1	2	3A	3B	X^2	df	
12:0	G	24	0	5	2	9	8	4.00	2	P>.01
	B	25	0	2	0	10	13			
11:0	G	25	0	4	4	8	9	2.06	2	P>.01
	B	25	0	6	0	5	14			
10:0	G	25	0	9	1	5	10	6.20	2	P>.01
	B	24	0	3	2	13	6			
9:0	G	25	0	9	5	5	6	4.54	3	P>.01
	B	25	0	5	4	12	4			
8:0	G	25	2	12	4	6	1	3.08	2	P>.01
	B	25	1	7	5	8	4			
7:0	G	25	0	14	6	4	1	3.12	2	P>.01
	B	25	0	9	5	7	4			
6:0	G	24	4	19	0	0	1	4.81	1	P>.01
	B	26	0	19	2	5	0			
5:0	G	25	9	11	3	2	0	1.18	2	P>.01
	B	25	11	7	2	4	1			
4:6	G	25	13	9	1	2	0	1.13	1	P>.01
	B	25	16	9	0	0	0			
4:0	G	25	19	6	0	0	0	3.13	1	P>.01
	B	25	13	7	5	0	0			
Total	G	248	47	98	26	41	36			
	B	250	41	74	25	64	46			
			Over-all X^2					33.25	18	P>.01

of accession to the various levels is set at 4:8 years for stage 1, 7:3 years for stage 2, and 8:10 years for stage 3. However, stage 3B is not quite reached at the age of 12. In fact, at that last level, a slight decline in the increase of percentages is observed, as occurs almost inevitably whenever accession to a stage is somewhat tardy.

A comparison of the number of subjects located at each one of the stages shows two particular facts. First, stage 0 contains more subjects than the corresponding stage in the questionnaire on the origin of night (see Table 15, p. 179). This first observation may no doubt be explained by the fact that the movement of clouds is a phenomenon less accessible to the child's experience. It must be pointed out that all the subjects belong to an urban population: different results might possibly have been obtained from children living in a rural milieu, which is less mechanized and much more favorable to the observation of natural phenomena. The second fact to be noted is the quite considerable difference between the proportions observed in stages 1 and 2: stage 1 alone contains 34.4 per cent of the subjects of the total sample, and stage 2 only 10.2 per cent. This disproportion comes as a confirmation of the previous remarks on the prevalence of divine artificialism in the children's precausal thinking and, more precisely, on the role of religious instruction in the persistence of these beliefs. It is indeed at the age of six, that is, at the time when religious instruction becomes more uniform and more intensive, that a sudden increase in the frequency of these responses is observed.

Finally, once more, the comparison of the results for boys and girls (Table 18) yields no significant differences.

CHAPTER XII

The Floating and Sinking of Objects

On two occasions in his study on the development of intelligence, Piaget makes use of the problem of the floating of objects. His first experiment (1927) is centered upon the child's understanding of various physical laws and aims to verify the existence of a primitive type of precausal thinking: the floating and sinking of objects is explained at first in terms of dynamistic or vitalistic forces which are gradually dissimulated under the guise of physicalism until they are definitely replaced by static physical notions. His second experiment (Inhelder and Piaget, 1955) has a totally different purpose. Its object is rather to throw some light on the reasoning processes of young children. At this point, Piaget disregards the content of their conceptions in order to consider exclusively the form, logical or prelogical, of the thinking mechanisms involved in a simple classification of floating and nonfloating objects. Even though the stages identified in this second experiment are formulated from a totally different point of view, they nevertheless can be integrated with the previous data for their schematization and completion.

The questionnaire used in the present study was elaborated exclusively from observations drawn from Piaget's first experiment. And yet the stage scale to which it leads is much nearer to that provided by Piaget's second investigation: it lays more stress on the precision of the thinking processes than on the presence or absence of dynamism. In fact, manifestations of dynamism proved to be so numerous, and at times so ambiguous, that it would have been impossible to establish a valid distinction on the basis of this sole factor. Out of 433 subjects capable of giving an answer to the most crucial questions, 274 used dynamistic terms either directly (e.g., *"the marble sinks because the water is not strong enough"*) or indirectly (e.g., *"the boat floats because it is heavy, because it moves,"* etc.).

Even though Piaget sees in all such expressions sure indications of dynamistic thinking, it is not easy to differentiate, especially in certain answers, purely metaphorical language from true precausal thinking. The fact that many adults speak spontaneously of the force of the water or of moving objects does not mean that they are not thinking in purely static terms. The ambiguity prevails, whether dynamism is formulated directly or masked under physicalistic terms. When, for example, a child says that an object floats because it is heavy, he may be assimilating weight with strength; but he may also be resorting to some form of syncretic thinking whereby he is inferring the existence of a causal relationship between two properties of a given object. In the latter hypothesis, recourse to the weight of objects would not imply dynamism any more than recourse to color, shape, substance, and the like. No doubt some children spontaneously link the weight, the shape, or even the substance of bodies with the notion of strength; for instance, they will say that *"the boat is heavy enough to hold itself above the water,"* that *"it is not heavy enough, it does not have the strength to go into the water,"* that *"it is wide enough to keep from sinking,*" that *"heavy means strong,*" and the like. The present data, incomplete as they are, would not support the conclusion that all subjects who invoke physical factors in their explanations hold such dynamistic beliefs. Under its present form, the questionnaire does not inquire deeply enough into the meaning of the child's answer. The questions bearing on the comparison between two equal volumes of water and wood, in particular, did not yield any significant results and could not be considered in the assessment of the protocols. The fact is that a child may come across the correct answer to these questions by pure chance; but generally, when urged to give further explanations, he will simply repeat his initial answer (e.g., *"because water is heavier than wood,*" or *"because wood is lighter than water"*).

The flaws in the questionnaire, however, do not invalidate the general results of the experiment. It must be granted that the stages to be described do not, as expected, deal specifically with the evolution of dynamistic thinking as such; but they provide direct information on the developmental levels of the child's logical reasoning processes, and they also emphasize the influence exerted by precausal beliefs within these processes. In addition to a stage 0, in which the instances of lack of understanding are grouped, the scale includes three main stages, the last two of which are divided into two substages.

STAGE 0

Incomprehension

The use of concrete material to be manipulated during the examination has obvious repercussions on the children's behavior. Interest in the examination is visibly increased and the attention is easier to maintain. In fact, in this experiment, children no longer refuse to answer. This closer cooperation, however, does not ensure an improvement in understanding. Many subjects are still incapable of dealing with the essential problems of the questionnaire and must therefore be classified in stage 0. Signs of lack of understanding are numerous.

First, the predictions are usually made at random, or they do not seem to proceed from any valid principle. The stage 0 child is almost always identified by the following behavior: simple acquiescence in the examiner's most recent suggestion, systematic alternation or, most often, uniformity of prediction (all objects presented will either float or sink). If the examiner repeats his question, the child often changes his first prediction even before he is allowed to check it by depositing the object on water.

Further, the stage 0 child almost never justifies his predictions and has no greater success in explaining his empirical verifications. The most frequent answers are: *"I don't know,"* *"because it's like that," "because I know it," "because mother told me,"* and the like. Some expressions are at times singularly close to explanations that properly belong to later stages; but these are almost always to be taken as simple commentaries and should not be equated with real reasons.

29 (6:0): "... The nail, will it go to the bottom or will it remain on the water?—*It will remain on the water.*—Why do you think ... ? —*Because it's like a boat.*—[Experiment.] Why does it go to the bottom, do you think?—*It's a small nail.*"

30 (4:6): "[Miniature boat.]—*It will remain on the water.*—Explain to me, why you think ... ?—*Boats remain on the water.*— [Large marble.]—*It will go to the bottom.*—Why ... ?—*It's a ball.*"

27 (4:6): "[Miniature boat.]—*It will go to the bottom.*—Explain to me, why ... ?—*Because it's a boat.*—[Experiment.] Why does it

remain on the water?—*Because it's a boat.*—[....]—[Small marble.]—*It will go to the bottom.*—Why...?—*Because it's a marble.*"

6 (4:6): "[Miniature boat.]—*It will go to the bottom.*—Explain to me, why... ?—*Because it's true.*—[Experiment.] Why does it remain on the water?—[Silence.]—[Large marble.]—*It will go to the bottom.*—Why... ?—*Because I want.*"

20 (4:6): "[Miniature boat.]—*It will go to the bottom.*—Explain to me, why... ?—*I like that.*—[Experiment.] Why does it remain on the water?—*I don't want to.*"

7 (4:0): "[Miniature boat.]—*It will float.*—Explain to me, why...? —*A boat floats because it goes too fast.*—[Large marble.]—*That will sink.*—Why... ?—*A marble doesn't float, you know.*—[....] —[Nail and wooden peg.] How is it that the small nail went to the bottom and that the stick remains on the water?—*Because a nail goes to the bottom, then not wood, because wood floats.*"

When the child uses such expressions as *"it is a small nail," "it's a ball," "it's a marble," "it's made of wood,"* and the like, he does not necessarily refer to the volume, the shape, or even the substance of objects; if he does, nothing indicates that these expressions go beyond the level of pure description. For instance, seeing that a wooden peg floats and that a nail sinks, what can be simpler for the child than to note: *"a nail, this goes to the bottom, but not wood, because wood floats."* A remark of this kind is a simple reading of the empirical facts and does not in itself imply any intellectual inquiry. Indeed, the scarcity and the inconsistency of such remarks are evidence of their purely descriptive character. Prompted as they are by a few objects only, they never bear consistently on the same aspects of reality; they seem thus to be far more a manifestation of the child's interest in the immediately perceptible qualities of objects than of his capacity for applying systematic principles, no matter how primitive.

STAGE 1

Precausal Explanations (Finalism, Animism, Dynamism, etc.)

In stage 1, the explanations do not go beyond the precausal level. Only finalistic, animistic, or purely dynamistic reasons account for the floating of bodies. Finalism takes the form of a kind of fatality, or moral necessity: the boat *"is made to float," "it must go on the water," "if it didn't float, people would drown,"* and the like; on the other hand, the large marble sinks *"because it's not a thing made to go on the water,"* or simply because *"it must."* As for animism, it takes the usual form: an object floats because *"it doesn't want to go to the bottom," "it's afraid of sinking," "it prefers to float," "it doesn't want to get wet,"* and the like. One subject even goes so far as to imagine the presence, within each object, of a being responsible for its behavior in the water.

31 (4:0): "[Miniature boat.]—*It will go to the bottom.*—Explain to me, why ... ?—*Because it will turn over like this.*—[Experiment.] Why does it not go to the bottom?—*Can I make it go down to the bottom?*—Try it and you will see.—*It comes up again!*—Why does it not stay at the bottom?—*Because the man who is under this* [under the roof] *doesn't want to go down.*—[Large marble.]—*It will go to the bottom.*—Why ... ?—*Because the boat is here.*—Yes, but also, why do you think ... ?—*Because it's a ball.*—[Wooden bead.]—*It will go to the bottom.*—Why ... ?—*Because there is a boat.*—Then, why do you think ... ?—*Because it doesn't want.*— Why does it remain on the water?—*Because there is a man who is right here in the hole, then he doesn't want to take it to the bottom. He doesn't like that, he doesn't want to be drowned.*—[....] —[Nail.]—*It will go to the bottom.*—Why ... ?—*Because there are two marbles down there, and then a bead, then a boat over on top.*—Yes, but why do you think ... ?—*Because there is a man here* [in the nail] *and he likes to go to the bottom.*—[....]—[Nail and wooden peg.] How is it that the small nail went to the bottom

and the stick remains on the water?—*Because there is a man in the small stick and he is mad, he'd rather not let himself be taken to the bottom, and the man in the nail, him, he'd rather go down."*

This interpretation recalls, in certain ways, the one which explains the floating of boats by the presence of a pilot, and it may be by this simple analogy that the child has come to imagine such a system. The principle which brings the child to appeal to the conductor's function is nevertheless a dynamistic one: the boat remains on the surface because of the movement initiated by the pilot. Dynamism may further explain the sinking, just as easily as the floating, of objects. Thus, according to some subjects, the marble sinks *"because it gives itself a push,"* or can reach the very bottom because *"it is stronger than the large boat."* On the other hand, according to other subjects, the marble sinks *"because it is tired"* and, therefore, does not have the strength to remain on the surface. These purely precausal associations constitute the essential characteristic of stage 1 explanations. Occasionally, the child will refer to the weight, the volume, the shape, or the substance of the objects. As in stage 0, however, these remarks have a merely descriptive meaning, as can be determined here again by their scarcity and inconsistency.

The quality of the predictions of stage 1 subjects does not show much progress forward from stage 0. The most primitive mechanisms (simple alternation, uniform predictions, etc.) are again observed, but their intensity has decreased. Since most subjects are apparently guided by the whims of imagination only, it is impossible to identify the criterion they use for classification. Indeed certain explanations are based on sheer fantasy: *"the large marble floats because it is red, and the small marble sinks because it is black"*; or else, *"the marble went to the bottom because the boat did not want to let it stay on the water,"* and the like. And yet once his prediction has been

THE RESULTS

made, the child may be so sure of his judgment that even when the empirical test runs counter to it, he sticks to his initial interpretation.

43 (4:6): "[Miniature boat.]—*It will go to the bottom.*—Explain to me, why ... ?—*It must sink.*—[Experiment.] Why does it remain on the water, why does it not go to the bottom?—*If you would wait, it would go to the bottom.*"

17 (5:0): "[Miniature boat.]—*It will move, then after, it will go to the bottom.*—Explain to me ... ?—*I don't know very well.*—[Experiment.] Why does it remain on the water?—[The child tries to push the boat down.] *Because it didn't want to drop.*—Then, why does it remain on the water?—*Because it didn't want* [still trying to push it down].—[Large marble.]—*It will go to the bottom.*—Why ... ?—*If I throw it, it will go.* ... *Suppose it remains on the water!*—You are not sure?—*No.*—Then, what is most certain?—*It will remain on top.*—[Experiment.] Why does it go to the bottom, do you think?—*Because I threw it too hard.*—If you would throw it more slowly, it could remain on the water?—*Yes.*"

The last sections of the questionnaire yield no additional information. The problem of the floating of plasticine is never solved at this level. The child either refuses to try anything, or else he molds the plasticine in various shapes without ever thinking of hollowing it out. An interesting, though rather infrequent, performance consists in modeling the plasticine into the shape of living beings that are capable of floating (e.g., that of a fish, or of a man). This solution may perhaps be explained by animistic beliefs which are particularly widespread at this level. Not only does the child fail to make the plasticine float, but he also fails to explain the examiner's success, except by pseudo proofs, which are once more only simple descriptions (e.g., "*it's because you have made it hollow*," "*it's because it looks like a boat*," "*it's made like a hat*," "*it's bigger and it prevents it from sinking*," and the like).

STAGE 2

Physical Explanations, But Tainted with Illogical Reasons (Contradictions or Misconceptions)

Stage 2 explanations are based on physical principles which are very uneven in quality but quite clear in purpose. These principles are no longer mere descriptions but genuine justifications; from this point on, they guide the predictions instead of just being used after the experiment to describe the phenomena observed. The factors called upon are the volume, the weight, the substance, or the shape of objects, as well as the quantity of water in the receptacle. But underlying all these physical, and seemingly quite mechanical, notions are persisting dynamistic beliefs: large objects float more easily than small objects because *"they have a greater holding power over the water"*; or, inversely, the smallest succeed in floating because *"the water does not have enough room to take hold of them."* Analogous beliefs are revealed in explanations that appeal to the shape of objects, their substance, or the quantity of water. In short, the child imagines a kind of combat between confronting elements, a combat which ends with the victory of the stronger or the more cunning.

Frequent as they are, these clear expressions of dynamism do not constitute the distinctive character of stage 2 subjects. Together with the other precausal beliefs, mainly finalism and animism, they are but intermingled with the principles of objective causality derived from the physical properties of the objects themselves. The essential characteristic of children of this level is that the systems they elaborate utilize physical principles in either a wrong or a contradictory way: the answers are either systematically false (e.g., everything heavy floats and everything light sinks), or else they simply contradict each other (e.g., some objects float because they are light, others sink, also because they are light). These inconsistencies may bear indifferently upon each of the physical properties of the elements involved in the experiment: the weight of the objects, their volume, their shape, their substance, the quantity of water in the receptacle, the quantity of air in each of the elements, and the like. Among older children, however, the reasoning on the easiest problems is faultless and becomes illogical only in the third section of the questionnaire, when they have to compare the large boat with the small marble. To separate such children from those who cannot solve even the first problems, stage 2 is divided into two substages.

SUBSTAGE 2A

In substage 2A, illogical thinking is manifested as early as the first or the second part of the questionnaire, that is, even before the proposal of the especially captious comparison between the large boat and the small marble. The child's explanations may be fully coherent, but they are systematically false in respect to reality or to the most elementary physical laws (e.g., anything heavy, big, full, thick, etc., will float, and anything light, small, hollow, thin, etc., will sink). These incorrect answers may apply to any of the objects, but they are generally limited to only a few, and the reasoning then becomes encumbered with numerous contradictions (e.g., the lightness of objects sometimes explains their floating and sometimes their sinking). In a way, these contradictory remarks are akin to those typical of stage 0 children in the questionnaire on life. In both tests, the same reasons are called upon to explain contrary facts; in the present questionnaire, however, the contradictions are no longer derived from a simple description of the facts, but indicate the continued presence of very enduring dynamistic conceptions.

45 (7:0): "[Miniature boat.]—*It will go to the bottom.*—[. . . .]— *Because it's heavy and it can go down.*—[Experiment.] Why does

it remain on the water?—*Because it's heavy.*—[Large marble.]—
It will remain on the water.—[. . . .]—*Because it's heavy.*—[Experi-
ment.] Why does it go to the bottom, do you think?—*Because it's
not heavy.*—[Wooden bead.]—*It will go to the bottom.*—[. . . .]—
Because it's not heavy.—[Experiment.] Why does it remain on the
water?—*Because it's heavy.*—[Small marble.]—*To the bottom.*—
[. . . .]—*Because it's not heavy.*—[Nail.]—*To the bottom.*—[. . . .]
—*Because it's not heavy.*—[. . . .]—[Nail and wooden peg.]—*The
small nail, it is less heavy than the small stick.*—[Small marble and
wooden bead.]—*Because the bead is heavier than the small marble.*—Have you ever seen a large boat? Then, tell me, why do the
large boats remain on the water.—*Because people go in them, and
they must not go to the bottom of the water; otherwise, people
would not be able to come out.*—[. . . .]—Then, why does a large
boat stay on the water, and a marble goes to the bottom?—*It's because the small marble, it's not heavy while, the boat, it's heavy."*

30 (7:0): "[Miniature boat.]—*It will remain on the water.*—[. . . .]
—*Because it's made of wood.*—Why, when it is made of wood,
does it remain on the water?—*I don't know.*—[Large marble.]—
It will go to the bottom.—[. . . .]—*Because it is heavy, heavier than
the boat.*—[Wooden bead.]—*It will remain on the water.*—[. . . .]
—*Because it's made of wood.*—[Small marble.]—*It will go to the
bottom.*—[. . . .]—*The small marble is made with the same thing
as the large marble.*—[Nail.]—*It will go to the bottom.*—[. . . .]—
It's not heavy enough.—[Wooden peg.]—*It will go to the bottom.*
—[. . . .]—*It's not heavy enough.*—[Experiment.] Why does it remain on the water?—*I don't know.*—[Nail and peg.]—*I don't
know. Because wood is heavier than steel.*—[Small marble and
wooden bead.]—*The small marble is less heavy than the wooden
bead.*—[. . . .]—Then, tell me, why do large boats remain on the
water?—*If there are people on the boat, they would drown.*—
[. . . .]—Then, why does a big boat remain on the water, and a marble goes to the bottom?—*The marble is not strong enough to remain on the water."*

42 (7:0): "[Miniature boat.]—*It will sink.*—[. . . .]—*Because it is
small.*—[Experiment.] Why does it remain on the water?—*Because*

there is a lot of water.—[Large marble.]—*It will go to the bottom.* —[. . . .]—*Because it's small.*—[Wooden bead.]—*It will sink.*— [. . . .]—*It is not like a boat.*—[Experiment.] Why does it remain on the water?—*Because it is big.*—[Small marble.]—*It will go to the bottom.*—[. . . .]—*Because it is small.*—[Nail.]— *It will go to the bottom.*—[. . . .]—*Because it is small.*—[Wooden peg.]—*It will remain on the water.* . . . *No, it will go to the bottom.*—[. . . .]—*Because it is small.*—[Experiment.] Why does it remain on the water? —*It is tall enough.*—[Nail and wooden peg.]—*The stick is a little bigger than the nail.*—[Small marble and wooden bead.]—*The small marble is smaller than the bead.*—[. . . .]—Then, why does a large boat remain on the water, and a marble goes to the bottom? —*Because the boat is bigger.*"

33 (6:0): "[Miniature boat.]—*It will remain on the water.*—[. . . .] —*It has something under it and that pins to the water, and that remains on the water.*—[Large marble.]—*To the bottom.*—[. . . .] —*Because it's hard.*—[Wooden bead.]—*To the bottom.*—[. . . .]— *Because it's hard. It goes to the bottom because water is not hard.* —[Experiment.] Why does it remain on the water?—*Because it's made of wood.*—Why, when it's made of wood, does it remain on the water?—*Because it's not hard.*—[Small marble.]—*To the bottom.*—[. . . .]—*Because it's like the other marble.*—[Nail.]—*To the bottom.*—[. . . .]—*It's made of iron, it's a nail.*—[Wooden peg.] —*It will go to the bottom.*—[. . . .]—*It's wood.*—[Experiment.] Why does it remain on the water?—*Wood, it is not hard, it remains on the water.*—[Nail and wooden peg.]—*The small stick is made of wood and wood floats. Wood is not hard.*—[Small marble and wooden bead.]—*It's wood like the stick. Wood is not hard.*—Then, tell me, why do the large boats remain on the water?—*Because they are made of wood. It's big.*—[. . . .]—Then, why does a large boat remain on the water and a marble goes to the bottom?—*The small marble is not heavy. The boat is big.*"

8 (10:0): "[Miniature boat.]—*It will remain on the water.*— [. . . .]—*Because it's wood. When it's wood, it floats.*—[Large marble.]—*It will go to the bottom.*—[. . . .]—*Because there is like*

air inside. When there is air, it doesn't float.—[Wooden bead.]*—It will sink.—*[. . . .]*—Because there is a hole of air inside. When there is air, it sinks.—*[. . . .]*—*[Small marble and wooden bead.]*— Because it's heavy, there is air in the marble. It's like the stick, it's light, there is air going through the stick; there is air going through the hole in the bead.—*[. . . .]*—*Then, why does a big boat remain on the water, and a marble goes to the bottom?—*A marble, there is air inside. A marble, that doesn't have a motor.—*[. . . .]*—*Then why does the boat remain on the water?—*There is no air inside. There is some, but it doesn't stay shut in like in a marble.*"

It can be seen that dynamism, even though not always explicit, seems to underlie each one of the child's explanations. Almost all the expressions used are more or less roundabout ways of speaking of the weight of objects, and this weight is often conceived as a force. When a child of this level says that an object is hard, he does not think in terms of density at all, but in terms of weight. His explanation of the floating or sinking of objects in terms of the material they are made of (e.g., wood, steel, glass, etc.) is not a mere description of the visible appearance of these several objects; it is rather an early reference to the still very vague notion of specific weight. Finally, to appeal to the size of objects to explain floating or sinking is again an ultimate reference to their weight, but this time to absolute weight. The sole consideration of the number of children who spontaneously make these connections among substance, size, hardness, and weight (e.g., *"wood is heavy, it floats"*; *"when it is hard, it cannot float, it is too heavy"*; *"it is much too big to float, it must not be too heavy,"* etc.) is sufficient to prove the validity of this interpretation.

The concept of specific weight itself seems more advanced than that of absolute weight. The former implies the beginnings of abstract thinking or, in other words, a certain detachment from the purely perceptible; thus, because weight depends primarily upon the substance of things, large objects

THE RESULTS

are not necessarily considered to be heavier than small ones. However, it cannot be said with certainty whether for the child these two notions are so very different from one another. His concept of specific weight has probably no relative meaning at all, contrary to what is normally found in adults. Having learned through experience that some materials are light and others heavy, he uses these findings as unrestricted absolutes. Every wooden object is light, no matter what its size, "*because wood is not heavy*"; every metallic object, though small, is considered to be heavy, "*because iron is heavy*." Briefly, the child who uses substance as an explanation of floating or sinking is perhaps appealing to the specific weight of the objects, but he does this without understanding its exact implications.

The last sections of the questionnaire again offer no particular interest and, at substage 2A, merely corroborate the previous data. The problem of the floating of plasticine still remains unsolved, and the child tries to explain the phenomenon by the factors mentioned.

SUBSTAGE 2B

In comparison with the preceding stage, substage 2B is characterized by the fact that illogical answers do not hereafter appear until the third section of the questionnaire is reached. Up to that point, explanations are coherent and correspond to the facts: objects float if they are light or small, and they sink if they are heavy and large. The comparison between the large boat and the small marble, however, confronts the child with a new and unexpected difficulty entailing the inconsistency specific to stage 2.

35 (6:0): "[Miniature boat.]—*It will go to the bottom.*—[. . . .]— *Because there is a thing under it.*—[Experiment.] Why does it remain on the water?—*I don't know.*—[Large marble.]—*It will go to*

the bottom.—[. . . .]—*Because it is big.*—[Wooden bead.]—*It will remain on the water.*—[. . . .]—*Because it is not big like the other one.*—[Small marble.]—*It will remain on the water.*—[. . . .]—*Because it is small like the bead.*—[Experiment.] Why does it go to the bottom, do you think?—*Because it is a little bigger than the bead.*—[Nail.]—*It will go to the bottom.*—[. . . .]—*Because it is bigger than the large marble.*—[Wooden peg.]—*It will go to the bottom.*—[. . . .]—*Because it is big like the nail.*—[Experiment.] Why does it remain on the water?—*Because it is made of wood, then the nail is made of steel.*—[Nail and peg.]—*Because the stick is made of wood, then the nail is made of steel.*—[Small marble and wooden bead.]—*Because the marble is a little bigger.*—Then, tell me, why do large boats remain on the water?—*Because they are heavy. Then they have a thing under, like the small boat, so they won't go to the bottom.*"

30 (8:0): "[Miniature boat.]—*It will remain on the water.*—[. . . .]—*Because wood floats.*—[Large marble.]—*It will go to the bottom.*—[. . . .]—*Because it is heavy.*—[Wooden bead.]—*It will remain on the water.*—[. . . .]—*It is not heavy, then it has a hole.*—[Small marble.]—*It will go to the bottom.*—[. . . .]—*It is heavy like the large one.*—[Nail.]—*It will go to the bottom.*—[. . . .]—*Because it is heavy.*—[Wooden peg.]—*It will remain on the water.* —[. . . .]—*Because it is not heavy.*—[Nail and peg.]—*The small nail is heavier than the stick.*—[Small marble and wooden bead.]— *The bead is made of wood, this floats.*—Then, tell me, why do large boats remain on the water?—*Because it's wood. The wood underneath protects it and makes the rest of it float.*—[. . . .]— Why does a large boat remain on the water and a marble goes to the bottom?—*The sea makes it float.*—Then, why can't the sea make the small marble float?—*Because the marble is small.*"

It is not hard to understand the perplexity of these children. As long as weight is not yet conceived as relative, the child considers merely absolute weight and classifies the objects into two categories only: the heavy and the light. Floating is henceforth linked with lightness; but, when faced with an example that conflicts with this rule, the child finds nothing better than to reverse his judgment in order to return, explicitly or not, to the dynamistic notion of weight.

Confronted with the contradiction in their answers, some subjects prefer not to offer any solution and escape with a noncommittal *"I don't know."* Others fall back into the most primitive finalistic or animistic forms of precausal thinking: for instance, the large boat floats *"because it has to," "to prevent people from drowning," "because it wants to,"* and the like. Others again merely render the data of observation in terms of dynamism: *"water is strong enough to hold it," "the boat is powerful enough to hold itself over the water,"* and so on. Finally, some secondary factors are called upon, such as the movement of the water or of the boat, the waves of the lake, the wind, the motor in the boat or the pilot, and so on. These are all explanations in which Piaget does not hesitate to recognize a common dynamistic element. Yet, here once more, it cannot be ascertained whether the child is not satisfied with linking, in an altogether syncretic way, events that are usually associated in his perceptions. Otherwise, how can one explain that he accords about equal importance to such details as, for example, the keel, the mast, or the anchor of the boat, details which have a natural connection with neither the movement nor the strength, nor the resistance of the boat on the water? Indeed, the child often realizes the precariousness of his argument and ends up by admitting his inability to solve the problem.

43 (10:0): "[Until the third section, weight explains the floating or sinking of objects.] Then, tell me, why do large boats remain on the water?—*It's because of the motor.*—If they had no motor, would they go to the bottom of the water?—*No.*—Explain to me why they would remain on the water.—*Because they cannot sink, because . . .* —[. . . .]—Then, why does a large boat remain on the water, and a marble goes to the bottom?—*A marble like this goes to the bot-*

*tom because it is heavy. A large boat floats, then . . . this is what I
don't know why."*

The wariness shown by these subjects in their attempts to
avoid contradiction is certainly admirable. But the explanations they offer instead indicate that they have not reached a
different level of mental development; on the very contrary,
they obviously indicate that the child's reasonings lead naturally to contradiction. The child of course tries to escape from
this impasse, but he has no available means to do so. It is also
significant that these emergency solutions appear at the same
age as contradictory solutions.

The methods the child most generally resorts to in his attempt to make plasticine float prove that he bases his reasoning upon the weight of objects, but only upon the absolute
weight. Most children choose to reduce the initial dimensions
of the plasticine ball by removing larger and larger pieces and
then, with the utmost precaution, try to make very small parti-
cles float. Others will mold the plasticine into various shapes,
trying in particular to render it as thin as possible because, as
they say, *"it is less heavy like that."* This expression which
itself is highly ambiguous may lead the observer to believe
that the child refers to relative weight. Yet, in almost all these
attempts, the child gives the impression that he still thinks in
terms of absolute weight and still believes that any change in
shape alters the weight of objects. Unfortunately, the present
data do not allow any certainty in this matter; special questions bearing on the conservation of weight would have had
to be prepared. It is, however, significant that no child at this
level ever makes an explicit allusion to the relativity of weight.
Moreover, data yielded by the same subjects, in a parallel
study dealing specifically with the conservation of weight,
seem to indicate effectively that the child of this stage ex-
presses himself in terms of absolute weight. In any case, at the

risk of misinterpreting the meaning of some answers, it seems advisable not to credit the child with the concept of relative weight until he uses it more explicitly. And so even explanations based upon vague notions of density (e.g., *"it is thinner,"* *"the weight is all in one place," "it is less compact," "it is hollow," "there is air in it,"* etc.) are herein classified with those appealing less explicitly to physical concepts (e.g., *"it has the shape of a boat," "you made it hollow," "the sides do not allow the water to fill in," "like this it is not heavy any more,"* etc.). The imperfection of the questionnaire is such that the introduction of these distinctions would involve the risk of classifying all subjects as incapable of understanding these ideas for not expressing them spontaneously.

STAGE 3

Physical and Always Coherent Explanations

Stage 3 solutions are fully coherent. Predictions are almost always perfect and the rare errors arise mainly from a lack of information, or from misapplication of principles that in themselves are valid. For instance, because the wooden bead has a hole, water will penetrate and sink it; or else, the thinness of the nail decreases its weight and may make it float. Expressions of dynamism very frequently still accompany purely physical reasons, but the other forms of precausality, notably animism, are much rarer. The comparison between the boat and the marble frequently gives rise to inadequate solutions; but, at least, the subjects no longer retreat behind easy admissions of ignorance, and they resist being forced to contradict the system they have hitherto elaborated.

The physical principles most commonly resorted to at this level are the shape of objects, their weight, or the total quantity of water in the receptacle. Whenever the child brings in weight, he now thinks in terms of absolute weight or of the specific weight of bodies. Only two subjects succeeded in formulating the correct relationship between the weight of an object and its volume (or the weight of the volume of water it displaces). In the other solutions, when the child sees a relationship, it is between the weight of the several objects and that of the total volume of water in the receptacle, or, even more frequently, between the respective weights of the two objects compared (e.g., *"the nail is heavier than the stick,"* *"the marble is heavier than the small boat,"* etc.). This latter procedure in particular shows that, for the child, the concept of weight has an absolute meaning.

SUBSTAGE 3A

Except for minimal differences, substage 3A contains solutions of the same type as in substage 2B: the same categories of reasons, the same procedures in the search of ways to make the plasticine float, and the same explanations in face of the examiner's success. There are somewhat more references to density, that is, to the presence of air or of a vacuum in the objects. This difference, however, is not sufficient to characterize the substage 3A subjects. The essential sign of accession to this stage is the cessation of contradictions or of illogical reasons.

36 (10:0): "[Miniature boat.]—*It will remain on the water.*— [. . . .]—*Because it's made like that.*—[Large marble.]—*It will go to the bottom.*—[. . . .]—*Because it's heavy.*—[. . . .]—[Wooden bead.]—*It will remain on the water.*—[. . . .]—*Because it's round, then it's not heavy.*—[Small marble.]—*It will go to the bottom.*— [. . . .]—*Because it's made of glass.*—[Nail and wooden peg.]—*Because the stick is made of wood, then the nail is made of steel.*— [Small marble and wooden bead.]—*Because the small one is made of glass, then the big one is made of wood.*—Then tell me why large boats remain on the water?—*Because it's made like that* [describes

through gestures the shape of a boat.]—[....]—Then, why does a large boat remain on the water, and a marble goes to the bottom? —*Because it's not made alike. A boat is made like this* [gesture].— [....]—Which is heavier, the small glass filled with water or the small glass filled with wood?—*The one with water.*—Why, do you think ... ?—*Because water, it's heavier than wood.*—[Plasticine.] —*It will go to the bottom.*—[....]—Try to fix it so it will remain on the water, so it will float.—*I cannot do it.*—You see, now it floats. What makes it float now?—*It's because it is hollow; then when it's in a ball, there is no hollow.*"

27 (10:0): " ... Then, tell me, why do large boats remain on the water?—*Because it has a floater.*—[....]—Then, why does a large boat remain on the water, and a marble goes to the bottom?—*Because the large boat has things under it which prevent it from sinking.*—[....]—You see, now it floats [the plasticine]. What makes it float?—*It's made like a boat.*—Why does a ball go to the bottom and that, now, remains on the water?—*The ball doesn't hold on the water because it is too heavy. There, it's less heavy.*"

39 (10:0): " ... Then, tell me, why do large boats remain on the water?—*Because there is much water. When there is much, water supports it.*—[....]—Then, why does a large boat remain on the water and a marble goes to the bottom?—*Because the large boat is made to remain on the water; it is made flat.*—[....]—In a large lake, would the marble still go to the bottom?—*No.*—[....]—*Because there is quite enough water.*—Explain to me why this floats [the plasticine], when it's like this. What makes it float?—*Nothing; it's the water which makes it float.*—Why did the ball go to the bottom a moment ago, while this, now, remains on the water?— *Because, as a ball, water goes over it. Also, with sides, water cannot go over it.*"

41 (10:0): " ... Then, tell me, why do large boats remain on the water?—*Because it's wood.*—[....]—Then why does a large boat remain on the water and a marble goes to the bottom?—*Because it's glass, and a boat, it's made of wood and, if it's a submarine, it*

will go into the water.—[. . . .]—Then, why does the boat remain on the water?—*Because it's wood, and air and water are heavy and they support it, and the boat cannot sink.*—[. . . .]—You see, it floats [the plasticine], now. What makes it float, now?—*It's because there* [the middle] *it's empty.*—Why does a ball go to the bottom, and this, now, remains on the water?—*A ball, it was all covered and there was some inside of it, while this, it's empty.*"

Thus almost all comparisons are made between the objects themselves: *"the marble is heavier than the bead," "the marble is not made like a boat,"* and so on. If it so happens that water is chosen as a term of comparison, care must be taken not to conclude immediately that the child has an exact understanding of the principle of floating. When he does not give a detailed explanation, the child probably refers to the full quantity of water in the receptacle and, under these conditions, the expression *"heavier than water"* still conceals dynamistic notions, or at least imperfect physical concepts.

Only two substage 3A subjects succeeded in making the plasticine float by molding it into a hollow shape. Some ten other subjects attempted solutions which could have been effective, had they been carried on to completion. All the other children adopted the technique of the previous stages, which consists in decreasing the quantity of plasticine by modeling the ball into various flat shapes, or by giving it the form of objects that can float. Children whose criterion of classification is the substance of objects (e.g., *"made of wood, it floats"*; *"made of metal, it sinks"*; *"made of plasticine, it sinks,"* etc). usually refuse to make any attempt at all to make the plasticine float; they are convinced that it is an impossibility *"because plasticine always sinks."* And then, to explain the examiner's success, they invoke either a change in weight, or a change in shape. The change in weight itself would, according to some, depend upon a change in density (e.g., *"as a ball, it's all together"*; *"in the ball, there is no air"*; *"in the glass, there is a vacuum"; "you made it thinner,"* etc.). Those children who resort to a mere change in shape have to rely upon pure description only to explain their answer (e.g., *"you have scooped it out," "it's like a boat," "it's like a bowl,"* etc.); but, judging by the age of such subjects, this second type of solution is no less mature than the first.

SUBSTAGE 3B
Substage 3B is reserved for the subjects who formulate the exact principle of the floating of bodies, at least once during the examination.

1 (10:0): *" . . . A boat is not heavy for its size, and a marble, it's heavy and small.—[. . . .]—The marble is small and weighs much. The boat weighs less for its size."*

37 (10:0): *" . . . Because a large boat displaces much water, then the small marble does not displace enough water for its weight.— [. . . .]—Because the large boat displaces much water, then this water is heavier than the boat."*

It is impossible to specify the exact characteristics of this substage because, among all the subjects, only two succeeded in reaching it. Both of them began by adopting the typical solution of previous stages, which consists in comparing the absolute weight of objects (e.g., *"the nail is heavier than the stick," "the small marble is heavier than the large bead,"* etc.). In both cases, also, it was the comparison between the large boat and the small marble which led them to formulate the exact principle of relative weight. Finally, one of the two succeeded in making the plasticine float and, as an explanation of this, he declared that the transformation of the plasticine modified its density, and consequently its weight. The other child explained that the change in shape produced a larger displacement of water, which was then sufficient to hold the mass of plasticine.

The fact that only two subjects reached this level may depend upon various factors. First, it is quite possible that, to become accessible to the child's intelligence, the physical principle of the floating of bodies requires a training which is usually given at a later age. The phenomenon may also be partly explained by the examination process, which does not always allow the subjects to formulate their conceptions with sufficient precision. Finally, it may be expecting too much to require the correct formulation of the physical principle involved. The data in Table 19 further show that substage 3A contains more subjects than the other stages in the scale. It is not impossible that some of these subjects should rather be classified in substage 3B; this, for instance, would apply to children who allude to density (e.g., *"it is empty," "it is not all together,"* etc.), to a variation in weight (e.g., *"it weighs less than a ball"*), or to the presence of air within the object (e.g., *"it's the air which can get into the hollow"*). However, the ambiguity of these various explanations, especially when they assume the form of simple descriptions (e.g., *"you have hollowed it out," "you have emptied it," "you made it thinner,"* etc.), makes the assessment of their exact scope almost impossible. On the other hand, the proportion of subjects classified in substage 3A (30.4 per cent) is far from excessive. On the basis of assuming a tardy accession to substage 3B, these figures would quite naturally have to be expected, since substage 3A is normally reached at about ten years of age and should consequently include approximately 30 per cent of the sample.

At any rate, the present data preclude any conclusions on the generality and even the existence of substage 3B. It has been taken here as different from the preceding stage, mainly in anticipation of the eventual examination of older subjects. It would undoubtedly be possible, at least provisionally, to end the scale with stage 3A and, accordingly, add to it the two stage 3B children without noticeably modifying the analysis of the results.

Table 19

Distribution of subjects by age and developmental stage
in the questionnaire on floating and sinking

		Stages										
		0	1	2A	2B	3A	3B	1	2A	2B	3A	3B
Age	N	Raw percentages						Cumulative percentages				
12:0	50	0	0	20	18	62	0	100	100	80	62	0
11:0	50	0	2	14	16	68	0	100	98	84	68	0
10:0	50	0	0	18	32	46	4	100	100	82	50	4
9:0	50	2	2	16	36	44	0	98	96	80	44	0
8:0	50	0	0	38	30	32	0	100	100	62	32	0
7:0	50	2	2	38	34	24	0	98	96	58	24	0
6:0	50	4	12	46	20	18	0	96	84	38	18	0
5:0	49	29	27	24	14	6	0	71	44	20	6	0
4:6	49	41	31	2	24	2	0	59	28	26	2	0
4:0	50	54	32	8	4	2	0	46	14	6	2	0
Total		132	108	224	228	304	4					
Median age		4:5	4:7	7:4	8:1	10:0	—					
Age of accession								4:2	5:2	6:7	9:9	—

●   ●   ●

The figures of Table 19 do not raise any further difficulty. The median ages stand at 4:5, 4:7, 7:4, 8:1, and 10:0 years, for stages 0, 1, 2A, 2B, and 3A, respectively. The slight difference between the ages of the first two stages is here again explained by the limitations of the sample. The gradation of median ages is thus regular enough to assume transitivity. The computation of ages of accession indicates a slow transformation of

Table 20

Sex differences on the questionnaire on floating and sinking

Age	Sex	N	0	1	2A	2B	3A	3B	X^2	df	
12:0	G	25	0	0	7	4	14	0	1.76	2	P>.01
	B	25	0	0	3	5	17	0			
11:0	G	25	0	1	6	6	12	0	9.44	2	P<.01
	B	25	0	0	1	2	22	0			
10:0	G	26	0	0	6	9	11	0	1.53	2	P>.01
	B	24	0	0	3	7	12	2			
9:0	G	25	0	1	6	11	7	0	5.38	2	P>.01
	B	25	1	0	2	7	15	0			
8:0	G	25	0	0	12	6	7	0	2.18	2	P>.01
	B	25	0	0	7	9	9	0			
7:0	G	25	0	0	11	10	4	0	1.90	2	P>.01
	B	25	1	1	8	7	8	0			
6:0	G	24	1	4	14	3	2	0	5.89	3	P>.01
	B	26	1	2	9	7	7	0			
5:0	G	25	8	7	4	5	1	0	2.07	3	P>.01
	B	24	6	6	8	2	2	0			
4:6	G	24	13	5	3	2	1	0	3.74	2	P>.01
	B	25	7	10	1	7	0	0			
4:0	G	25	10	9	4	1	1	0	2.87	2	P>.01
	B	25	17	7	1	0	0	0			
Total	G	249	32	27	73	57	60	0			
	B	249	33	26	43	53	92	2			
						Over-all X^2			36.76	22	P>.01

children's ideas about the floating of bodies: at the age of four, explanations are limited to the precausal level; around five years of age, explanations begin to include physical elements, but the structure of the reasoning processes is prelogical or contradictory; at about six and a half years of age, contradictions remain in the solution of only the most difficult problems; finally, around ten years of age, the reasoning is perfectly rigorous, even though it may still be based upon an imperfect or incomplete knowledge of the facts. The usual drop in the increase of percentages at the age of twelve is to be observed in stage 3A. As noted for some of the previous questionnaires, the phenomenon coincides with a somewhat late accession to this stage.

Table 20 shows the results grouped separately for boys and girls. For one age only (11:0), the difference is significant at the .01 level in favor of boys. This difference, however, seems to be exceptional, since the over-all X^2 is not significant.

In conclusion, it is interesting to compare these results with Deutsche's (1937). Among other things, she reports that her subjects almost never appeal to the heaviness of boats to explain their floating, and that answers based rather on the fact that boats are light are given at the same age. The number of protocols classified here in stages 2A and 2B is sufficient to show to what extent Deutsche's conclusion conflicts with the present findings: 226 children explain floating by contradictions of this kind and, in the very great majority of cases, the contradiction bears specifically on the weight of objects. Deutsche also seems to have observed only a few instances of finalism, magical causality, and dynamism. In the results presented here, these forms of precausality, mainly the dynamistic type, appear with striking frequency. Finally, according to Deutsche's interpretation, the principle of the floating of boats would be grasped by children of all ages: even though only one sixteen-year-old subject in her sample expressly compares the weight of the boat with that of an *equal volume* of water, the simpler comparison between the weight of the boat and that of water (with no reference to volume) is found at all age levels. In the present sample, this last type of comparison is made only by the older children. Contrary to Deutsche's contention, such answers do not in any way guarantee the exact understanding of the phenomenon, and frequently conceal dynamistic conceptions, a fact of which she does not seem to be at all aware.

Most of these divergences arise no doubt from differences in age between the two samples. The youngest of Deutsche's subjects had already reached the age of eight. Besides, the more detailed the questionnaire, the richer is the information it provides. Deutsche presented her subjects with only one question on floating, and indeed a very general one: *"Why do boats float on top of the water instead of sinking?"* Finally, too superficial an analysis of the answers involves the risk of drawing conclusions that are, to say the least, debatable. One of these would be to deny the existence of dynamism, although the comparisons made by children between the weight of water and that of the boat are almost always imbued with notions of this kind. The same type of analysis may also lead the investigator to claim that some of the answers fall outside of Piaget's categories (e.g., presence of air in the boat, and shape of the boat), whereas these very answers are specifically mentioned and described by Piaget on several occasions.

CHAPTER XIII

Interdependence of Precausal Notions

The analysis of results cannot be limited to the individual study of each questionnaire, but must be completed by a search for more general indications. The complete attainment of such an objective would, however, require a profile study of each subject's reaction to all five questionnaires. Such an analysis is almost impossible to undertake. The variety of the concepts under study, the differences noted in the evolution of each one of these concepts, and the great number of stages identified on the basis of each of the questionnaires—all these factors increase almost to infinity the number of possible profiles. Hence, it seems unpractical to aim at a complete reading of all of them. The diversity of these profiles would be so great that no definitive conclusions could be drawn from such an analysis. It would lead rather to an excessively long enumeration of varied behaviors from which it would not be easy to infer general tendencies.

The main problem raised by the comprehensive analysis of the results is that of the extent, or the general prevalence, of precausal beliefs. It may be asked, in the first place, whether the various beliefs grouped under the term precausality are of a wide enough scope to be thoroughly characteristic of the child's general attitude when he confronts reality. It may also be questioned whether there are sufficiently close mutual relationships among these beliefs to indicate the existence of a common factor which contributes to their individual development. According to several authors, precausal thinking should not be regarded as a general attitude of the child toward reality, since it seems to be only accidentally linked to the solution of certain particular and, indeed, rather exceptional, problems. In Piaget's opinion, on the contrary, the variability of the child's answers is in no way an argument against the existence, and even the universality, of precausal thinking. If the child does not always reason in the same way, it may be that he is questioned at a time when certain primitive beliefs have already disappeared. Progress cannot follow the same rhythm in all spheres. Thus, for instance, Piaget is not at all surprised to observe that more than half of his subjects resort to different levels of animistic thinking, according to whether they are questioned on the concept of life or on the existence of consciousness in things.

Carried to extremes, either of these two positions is untenable. To require uniformity and absolute consistency of reasoning from the child is to expect more of him than of an adult. On the other hand, to propound the total absence of relationships among the various beliefs of the same subject is to claim that these beliefs do not comprise a common mode of thinking. Therefore, only to the extent that a rather close relationship between the child's various conceptions is observed, can a conclusion be reached in regard to the parallelism of the evolution of each one of these conceptions as well as to the existence of an element common to all particular developments.

Table 21

Frequency of occurrence of various modes of precausal thinking in each one of the questionnaires

Questionnaire	Mode of precausal thinking				
---	realism	animism	artificialism	finalism	dynamism
Concept of dream	143	0	184	49	0
Concept of life	0	198	0	0	0
Origin of night	0	48	257	309	0
Movement of clouds	13	205	218	74	152
Floating and sinking	6	65	0	80	127
Total frequency of occurrence	162	516	659	512	279

The experiment reported here did not propose explicitly to verify the inclusiveness of precausal beliefs. It uses only five questionnaires and thereby reaches only a very restricted area of the child's thinking. Further, each questionnaire aims at exploring a different aspect of precausality; consequently, it cannot be expected that the child will base all his reasonings upon similar grounds. Notwithstanding these limitations, the results yield very valuable indications on the pervasiveness of precausal thinking in children. First of all, the various types of beliefs are all so frequently manifested that it is impossible to accord them a purely accidental or individual meaning. In this respect, Table 21, on the frequency of occurrence of various modes of precausal thinking in each one of the questionnaires, is particularly informative. It shows that animism, artificialism, and finalism are the types of beliefs most often expressed. In the instance of animism, it further displays a rather special phenomenon: answers to the questions on life are not more frequently animistic than are the explanations of the movement of clouds. This finding must no doubt be attributed to the fact that these two questionnaires are not equally difficult: the one on life is more abstract, and many subjects are classified in stage 0 because they did not understand the meaning of the questions. Realism and dynamism seem to be less widespread than other forms of precausal thinking. Realism is manifested almost exclusively in the explanation of dreaming. Indeed, in order to bring to light the child's confusion between what is subjective and objective, he must be questioned on very specific phenomena, of which dreaming is beyond doubt the most striking and least ambiguous example. The other questionnaires are less adapted to this purpose, and only the few magical beliefs which certain questionnaires elicit reveal indirectly an underlying core of realistic thinking. On the other hand, the relative scarcity of dynamism is largely explained by the excessive caution with which the protocols were assessed: only overt manifestations of dynamism were considered; we excluded all reasonings which, in all probability, are elicited by implicit dynamistic beliefs, as occurs, for instance, whenever the child appeals to the heaviness of objects to explain their floating. The same caution was exercised in the interpretation of finalistic answers. In the questionnaire on life, many children have recourse to the usefulness of objects to justify their answers. But, in such choices, it is often difficult to distinguish genuinely finalistic answers from those which are mere descriptions of the activity of objects. To avoid errors of interpretation, we preferred to disregard completely the finalism attached to the child's concept of life. The frequencies reported in Table 21 are therefore always minimal values.

The problem of the general pervasiveness of precausal thinking involves a second dimension. Once the frequency of each mode of precausality in the total sample is established,

Table 22

Distribution of subjects as to the number of
questionnaires in which various modes of
precausal thinking are manifested

Mode of precausal thinking	Number of questionnaires				Total
	4	3	2	1	
Realism	0	0	19	124	143
Animism	6	26	120	170	322
Artificialism	0	93	118	134	345
Finalism	1	26	104	222	353
Dynamism	0	0	46	187	233

it still remains to be seen if children have a tendency to resort
to the same type of explanation several times. Table 22 provides the necessary information on this aspect of the problem.
All the subjects who have given indications of precausal thinking are distributed according to the number of questionnaires
in which explanations of this kind occur. Thus, among the 322
children who speak in animistic terms, 170 do so in one questionnaire only, 120 in two, 26 in three, and 6 in four. The table
as a whole shows that 40 per cent of the children have recourse to the same form of precausal thinking in more than
one questionnaire. This proportion may seem small, but it
surely indicates a real tendency in the child to use the same
given type of explanation; this indication is all the more telling when it is recalled that the heterogeneity of the over-all
examination favors rather the opposite tendency. If several
questionnaires rather than one had been used to investigate
each of these forms of precausality, the results would have
been far less ambiguous, and would certainly confirm the
child's tendency to solve problems of the same kind in the
same way.

In spite of their diversity, the five types of primitive beliefs brought to light by the present examination are far from being independent. They constitute, in fact, the various possible forms taken by the thinking of a child who is still incapable of dissociating the external world from his own self. Therefore, in order to study the scope of the child's precausal thinking, it is very instructive to determine to what extent he manifests a tendency to use at least equivalent forms of causality. Some subjects, for instance, will systematically base their reasoning upon principles of objective causality, while others will always stick to precausal notions. Such a consistency, if it could be proven, would necessarily entail the recognition of a real unity in the child's thinking. To study this last dimension of the problem raised by the general consistency of the child's conceptions, the most simple procedure consists in correlating the results yielded by each one of the questionnaires, since precausality is characteristic of the most primitive stages while objective causality is observed in the more mature stages. When the results are expressed in terms of stages, that is, in hierarchical categories, the calculation of tetrachoric correlations yields the most accurate estimate of the relationship between two series of measurements. Each distribution is first reduced to a simple dichotomy based upon the value

Table 23

Tetrachoric correlations between
the five questionnaires

Questionnaire	1	2	3	4	5
1—Concept of dream		.76	.78	.72	.67
2—Concept of life	.76		.71	.59	.68
3—Origin of night	.78	.71		.69	.59
4—Movement of clouds	.72	.59	.69		.61
5—Floating and sinking	.67	.68	.59	.61	

nearest to the median, and dichotomies are then compared successively with one another. Table 23 shows the results of this analysis.

Coefficients range between .59 and .78, and indicate a real interrelation between the evolutions specific to each concept. Evidently, the child's various conceptions develop along close parallel lines. But, since these results are achieved by children of several age levels, higher correlations might have been expected, such as usually occur in most developmental tests. In fact, interrelations remain thus rather weak, in spite of the coefficients obtained, and the various forms of precausal thinking do not develop in a perfectly synchronous way. Indeed, a comparison of the individual development of each one of these beliefs has revealed large differences. It will undoubtedly be recalled, for instance, that realism is already outgrown at approximately six and a half years of age, that artificialism does not yield before nine, and that animism is still very persistent at twelve. It is not surprising, then, to observe, among most of the subjects from seven to twelve years of age, a dissociation between realism and artificialism, or animism. This lack of synchronism probably reflects the absence of systematization typical of the young child's thinking. He has no theory of the external world, and the conceptions he finally develops by himself are not organized in any way. He does not usually question himself on the various aspects of reality that the present examination tries to investigate, and does not spontaneously discuss them with his entourage. When questioned on these problems, however, he calls upon types of explanations that clearly manifest his natural tendency to think in a precausal way, as long as he has not succeeded in completely dissociating his own self from the external world. But, because the child's conceptions have no structure, his explanations should not be scanned for a logic and a coherence of which he is still incapable.

However, this lack of system in the child's thinking is not absolute. The correlations shown in Table 23 reveal a true interdependence among the several forms of primitive thinking. Thus, for example, the children who are the slowest in freeing themselves of artificialistic, finalistic, and dynamistic notions are also generally the last to reach the more mature stages of animism. To what should this interdependence be attributed? Chronological age is undoubtedly the main factor. In a developmental scale, it is a well-known fact that the magnitude of the correlations among various subtests depends generally on the range of chronological ages. These correlations are usually much lower when calculated for each age separately. This does not mean that chronological age is an artificial factor. In a scale of mental development, that is, in a scale consisting of problems which require the operation of truly intellectual processes, the series of chronological ages corresponds in fact to a series of levels in mental development. In other words, for the average subject, chronological age and intellectual maturity are contemporaneous and interdependent phenomena. In the present study, the influence of chronological age cannot be doubted. The subjects range from four to twelve years of age, and the correlations among the various forms of precausal thinking are calculated from the results yielded by children of all these age levels taken together. The interdependence of the children's various precausal beliefs is therefore largely explained by the considerable range of the ages sampled: the youngest generally think in terms of precausality, and the oldest in terms of causality. When, moreover, care is taken to correlate directly each one of the questionnaires with chronological age, the results are striking: coefficients rise to .86 for the explanation of dream, .74 for the concept of life, .82 for the origin of night, .76 for the movement of clouds, and .69 for floating and sinking. It can even be added that these coefficients are minimal estimates, for it must be recalled that the distributions of percentages describing the evolution of each precausal belief considered here are not always complete. It happens frequently that, in the development of a given concept, for instance, the artificialism attaching to explanations of the origin of night, the youngest among the children have already outgrown the most primitive stages. For other beliefs, especially for the animism inherent in the concept of life, the oldest children are still far from having reached the final stage. The influence of this factor is especially noticeable in the questionnaires on floating and sinking, on the concept of life, and on the movement of clouds, in which the distributions are the most truncated.

Is this quite close interdependence among precausal beliefs to be explained then solely by chronological age? Even if this hypothesis were accepted, the results would still refute the claim of several of Piaget's critics who deny the specifically infantile incidence of precausal thinking. It is all too evident that this form of thinking is mainly observed at earlier ages and recedes gradually in the course of development. The question, however, arises whether the influence of chronological age is exclusive, or only preponderant. If, for example, younger children are both more realistic and more artificialistic than their elders, is it simply because they are younger, or is it also because they have a natural tendency to use equivalent forms of precausal thinking simultaneously? Within the framework of the present study, even a control of chronological age would not provide a definite answer to this question. Due to the lack of synchronism that marks the evolution of the concept directly explored by the present questionnaires, the correlations calculated for each separate age would all be very low or very erratic, especially at intermediate ages. They could be higher at other ages, but this interdependence would then be explained only by the lack of discrimination usually observed at these extreme levels.

It must be pointed out, however, that the stage scale derived from each questionnaire is based exclusively upon the study of a particular concept and thus disregards parallel forms of precausality to which the children may often resort. This factor admittedly tends to obscure the picture. In fact, despite the time lags, a certain parallelism seems to exist even when the influence of chronological age is not taken into consideration. This is corroborated by the data already presented in Tables 21 and 22 (p. 233 and p. 235). These clearly indicate that any type of precausal reasoning is likely to appear in the explanation of any phenomenon. Despite Deutsche's and Huang's opinion, the level of the child's thinking is not exclusively determined by the nature of the problems put to him. On the contrary, the same types of explanation may recur when the child is confronted with very dissimilar phenomena. Table 21, for instance, shows that animism and finalism occur in four different questionnaires, artificialism in three, and dynamism in two. And again, upon examining the data in Table 22, it is striking to note that, among the total group of children who use a precausal form of thinking, 40 per cent resort to reasons of the same category in at least two questionnaires out of five. In this respect, animism and artificialism seem to be the preponderant forms of precausality among children.

The individual analysis of the protocols affords a still more direct confirmation of the reality of this parallelism. The data of Table 24 are very informative on this subject, even though several factors tend to reduce the amplitude of the phenomenon. This table does not, for instance, take into account subjects who were not given at least four of the five questionnaires, or subjects who were considered to be unclassifiable, or were classified in stage 0 even in only one of the five questionnaires. The precocious disappearance of the realism connected with the concept of dream, and the rigor used in the evaluation of dynamism and finalism, also contribute to elimi-

Table 24

Distribution of subjects according to number of
modes of precausality resorted to in the
whole series of questionnaires

Age	N	Number of modes of precausality											
		0	1	2	3	4	5	0	1	2	3	4	5
		Raw frequencies						Percentages					
11:0-12:0	50	4	14	6	16	9	1	8	28	12	32	18	2
10:0	49	4	2	15	18	9	1	8	4	30	36	18	2
9:0	47	0	2	11	15	16	3	0	4	23	32	34	6
8:0	43	1	2	6	12	21	1	2	5	14	29	49	2
7:0	44	0	0	6	8	24	6	0	0	14	18	55	14
5:0-6:0	52	0	0	3	10	19	20	0	0	6	19	37	48
4:0-4:6	17	0	0	0	0	3	14	0	0	0	0	18	82
Total	302	9	20	47	79	101	46						
Over-all percentage								3	7	16	26	33	15

nate many possibilities of interdependence. In spite of these
limitations, the results shown in Table 24 are most instructive.
At all ages, there are many subjects who, during the examination, invoke several different precausal reasons simultaneously. Even though the table gives no details, almost all possible combinations are likely to be met, not only in the
examination as a whole, but also in individual questionnaires.
For instance, in the questionnaire on the dream, one child
may be realistic, finalistic, and artificialistic, all at the same
time (e.g., "it's God who makes dreams and sends them to us
as punishment"). To explain the movement of clouds, another
child will resort to artificialistic, animistic, and dynamistic reasons, all at once (e.g., "it's God who orders the clouds to move;
the clouds obey and are aware of their movement"). Such

combinations are very numerous, and the younger the children, the more frequently this phenomenon is observed. Among the 302 subjects of various ages figuring in the analysis, 15 per cent call upon all of the modes of precausality that the present examination can possibly elicit, and 48 per cent call upon at least four out of five. As shown in the same table, these proportions are obviously much greater at lower ages, especially below seven years of age. It should be recalled, moreover, that the rapid recession of realism and the apparent scarcity of dynamism already tend to obscure the real interdependence.

Hence it is impossible to deny the presence of numerous combinations of beliefs in these protocols. Indeed, if the working out of a stage scale for each particular type of belief proved to be so difficult, it was mainly due to the frequency of these combinations. It need not be repeated that the correlations reported above do not take these facts into account. The stage scales on which these correlations are based systematically disregard all forms of precausality other than the one specifically studied by each questionnaire. Thus, for instance, the stages derived from the questionnaire on the dream describe the evolution of realism exclusively, up to the moment of its disappearance. Not until the third stage does the classification take into account parallel forms of precausal thinking that possibly occur in the explanation of the dream. The same principle applies to the analysis of the other questionnaires. In this perspective, even when the age dispersion is disregarded, the correlations observed certainly represent a minimal estimate of the possible parallelism among the child's precausal conceptions. A more minute study of individual protocols suggests that these various conceptions are at the very least complementary, if not absolutely contemporaneous and interdependent.

The opposite phenomenon would be difficult to explain. As

so aptly shown by Piaget's penetrating studies (1926, 1927), the intrinsic analysis of precausal notions leads to the postulate that they are all organically interconnected. In spite of their apparent variety, they all proceed from one and the same fundamental mechanism, the egocentrism or realism of the child. The primitive undifferentiation between the external world and the child's own self naturally entails an anthropocentric conception of the universe. According to this conception, external objects share the characteristics of man (hence animism and dynamism), and are earmarked for the service of man by the efficient will of God or of men themselves (hence finalism and artificialism). This interdependence does not, however, exclude the possibility of an asynchronic evolution of these several beliefs. It is normal that realism, under the most primitive guise of a gross confusion between what is objective and subjective, be the first to disappear as such; it would persist only through the other manifestations of precausality to which it has in fact given rise. On the other hand, artificialism and finalism are, by nature, complementary. To the extent that the existence of an object is justified by its usefulness to man, or by the use to which man can put it, the child will be led to imagine the intervention of a fabricating agent whose final intention is precisely to meet this need. As for dynamism, it is at first confused with animism. Energy, or the capacity to act by oneself, is in fact one of the most fundamental attributes of living beings. It is this capacity which the child most willingly confers upon numerous inanimate objects, more particularly upon those capable of movement, because it is so natural for him to interpret in terms of strength or energy the capacity of an object to move by itself, or to exert an influence upon its environment. Other attributes of living beings, especially those of human beings, such as consciousness, will, feelings, and the like, are easier to dissociate and, consequently, the child will arrive earlier at limiting them to certain classes of privileged objects. This is why dynamism is more enduring than animism, of which it is, in a sense, the natural continuation.

To sum up, it seems legitimate, with some reservations, to assume the existence of a common factor underlying the evolution of the beliefs investigated in the five questionnaires.

CONCLUSION

Precausality Reconsidered

This systematic replication of Piaget's experiments on the child's representations of reality confirms the existence of primitive beliefs of a precausal type. These beliefs are manifested with such frequency that they cannot be regarded as purely individual or accidental. Out of a total of 500 children, ranging from four to twelve years of age, 28.6 per cent use realistic terms at least once during the examination; 64.4 per cent, animistic terms; 69.9 per cent, artificialistic terms; 46.6 per cent, dynamistic terms; and 50.6 per cent, finalistic terms.

Of all the forms of precausality indicated by Piaget, phenomenism is the only one that is not clearly identified in the present analysis. This fact is rather surprising since phenomenism is the only mode of precausal thinking which is not contested by the investigators critical of Piaget's conceptions. Yet, it is easy to explain why the present findings would seem to be devoid of it. Whenever children confine themselves to mere descriptive statements, their answers are attributed to a lack of understanding. This procedure is doubtless debatable since it eliminates, at the start, a whole class of responses the analysis of which could be very instructive. But it has proven extremely difficult to ascertain whether the child's remarks constitute real attempts at an explanation or mere associations. Especially in the questionnaire on life, these descriptive answers entail reasoning processes that are too inconsistent to permit the identification of the child's operative criterion for distinguishing between living and nonliving objects. The same child, for example, will attribute life to the *sun "because it warms up,"* but will deny it to *fire* on exactly the same grounds. This inconsistency may be a characteristic or, more accurately, a consequence of phenomenism; but it may just as well mean that the child does not understand the questions at all. Since it is impossible to identify the exact meaning of these phenomenistic or descriptive answers, without getting involved in subjective interpretations, it was judged better to regard them as manifestations of a lack of understanding. It should not be inferred that this particular form of precausal thinking does not exist; but, for lack of more precise data, no definite conclusion can be reached concerning this question. At any rate, this procedure has no noteworthy effect on the analysis of the other modes of precausal thinking, or even on the classification of subjects within the particular stages of each questionnaire. There are only very few children—always among the youngest—who limit themselves to these phenomenistic answers. If phenomenism could eventually be distinguished from other manifestations of a lack of understanding, it would probably form an intermediate level between stage 0 and stage 1.

The answers to each questionnaire fall into three main stages, always preceded by a special category characterized by incomprehension or refusal to answer. These three general stages preserve the same significance within each scale: stage 1 is reserved for exclusively precausal explanations; stage 2 comprises subjects who simultaneously invoke both precausal and physical or objective causal factors; stage 3 marks the disappearance of the type of precausality with which the given questionnaire is specifically concerned. Only the stages derived from answers on floating and sinking do not conform entirely to these principles of classification: in this questionnaire, stages 0 and 1 have the same meaning as in the other scales, but later stages are worked out according to the rigor of the child's reasoning, and no longer according to the various types of explanation given by the child.

To provide further and finer gradation in this classification into four main categories, stages are sometimes divided into two or three substages. Explanations of dreaming are thus finally classified into seven levels; those of floating and sinking into six; those of the origin of night and of the movement of clouds into five; those of the concept of life into four. In spite of these numerous subgradations, stages are not always as homogeneous as may be desired. At the intermediate levels in particular, it was found very difficult to introduce, without being arbitrary, useful distinctions among a group of answers that represent all the possible degrees of transition between two opposite conceptions. Some answers, for example, show a continual oscillation between two levels of explanation. Others, but these much rarer, show a genuine progression during the examination: the child starts with an inferior level of explanation, but soon discovers its precariousness and ends up with the correct explanation. Most often, however, the relative importance of the various elements included in the child's explanation remains very difficult to assess, and any attempt at a differentiation involves interpretations that are too subjective not to be controvertible. No classification can be perfect, and it is preferable to admit to a lack of subtlety than to indulge in an excess of arbitrariness.

Not all the scales described by Piaget are found in the present classification. The differences noted are of two main types: either Piaget reserves a stage to answers too scarce or too ambiguous to characterize a real level of development (e.g., substantial formation of the night by dark clouds, explanation of life by the usefulness of objects, etc.), or else he does not provide a particular place for certain answers which are in fact truly typical and numerous enough to correspond to a normal level in the evolution of a concept (e.g., anthropomorphism related to the concept of life, artificialism in the explanation of the movement of clouds, etc.). These divergences, however, do not prevent a recognizable and fundamental resemblance between our scales and those of Piaget. In both investigations, the child's conception of the world develops from a level of pure precausality to a level of objective causality through intermediate steps in which the opposite conceptions are intermingled. The sequence of levels is thus basically the same. The differences in details may be accounted for by several explanations, of which the most obvious relates to sampling techniques. The collection of a representative group of children at each age level allows a more accurate assessment of the actual distribution of typical performances, of their possible equivalence, or even of their exact hierarchy. In this manner, the content of answers is not directly utilized for the delineation of stages, but rather for the recognition of the thinking processes underlying all responses that appear at a same given age. Stages can thereafter be inferred on the basis of these processes.

The precausal beliefs related to the five problems of the experiment are not altogether contemporaneous. Realism disappears at approximately six and a half years of age, artificialism around nine, animism and dynamism around ten. Since finalism is not the subject of a specific questionnaire, it is not possible to pronounce on its evolution. Despite this lack of synchronism, one can observe an unmistakable tendency among the youngest children to base their reasoning upon typically precausal principles. At four and four and a half, all the children tested who were capable of answering the questions resorted to these primitive notions. At these ages, at least, the preponderance, if not the universal character, of precausal thinking must be recognized. Generally, the correlations with chronological age indicate a clear decline of all forms of precausality as the children gradually grow older. Even if some of the oldest subjects have not yet reached the last stage in every scale, the evolutional rhythm of each of these notions is clearly enough recognizable to support the hypothesis that, after the age of twelve, precausal notions keep on receding until they become exceptional. The irregularities noted for the age of twelve, in three of the five scales, may be explained by a flaw in the sample, since they inevitably occur whenever accession to higher stages is somewhat tardy (after ten years of age), that is, whenever a slight mental retardation is more likely to exist. If this resurgence of primitive answers at the age of twelve were an indication of the reappearance of precausal notions in adults, the phenomenon would be, to say the least, abnormal, and would then perhaps derive from a change in the subject's attitude toward the questionnaire, or, exceptionally, from a pathological regression to infantile modes of mental functioning. In any case, in order to demonstrate that all these notions are exclusive to children, it would obviously be necessary to submit adolescents and adults to the same questionnaires. The decline observed until the age of twelve is nonetheless so clear that if it continued after that age or if it were followed by a recrudescence of primitive beliefs, the intervention of factors irrelevant to causal reasoning itself would have to be surmised.

All findings, therefore, point to the preponderance of precausal thinking in the child. Is it possible to ascribe these results principally to the examination procedure itself? It does not seem so. The examiners have always asked the same questions and, far from eliciting uniform answers, this standardization of the questionnaires has, on the contrary, given rise to a series of quite diverse explanations, which invariably ranged from pure precausality to total objectivity. Admittedly, some perhaps too suggestive questions might have been modified to advantage. Thus it would no doubt have been preferable to replace most of the "whys," which are always likely to prompt finalistic answers, by the more neutral "how is it that." This change of wording, however, might result in a mere substitution of artificialistic for finalistic answers. At any rate, it is certainly not possible to explain away all precausal responses by the wording of the questions. The fact that only the youngest subjects yield to the finalistic suggestion of the "why" makes it logical to suppose that these subjects are naturally inclined to think in finalistic terms.

The subject matter of the questionnaires is perhaps more likely to have a direct influence on the results. Although it is difficult to assess the importance of this factor, it certainly would be unjustifiable to maintain that the kind of problems presented to children compels them to answer in a precausal rather than in a causal way. The wide variety of solutions elicited by each questionnaire is obviously incompatible with such a claim. The fact that the child is questioned on a very specific aspect of the phenomenon undoubtedly favors certain types of explanations. Thus, when the subjects are asked to explain the origin of a celestial body, more artificialism than animism, realism, or dynamism is to be expected, since artificialistic beliefs are more naturally connected with the understanding of the origin of things. This is quite normal, for all the questionnaires were so designed as to elicit evidence of very specific conceptions. Under these conditions, the subject matter of the questionnaires has indeed an undeniable, but not a prejudicial, influence on the final results.

This factor may also affect the responses in another, but quite superficial manner. Thus the fact that the child is questioned on his conception of the world, rather than on simple physical phenomena, may give rise to beliefs that are somewhat remote from plain phenomenistic explanations. But whether they be phenomenistic, artificialistic, or realistic, and the like, the child's interpretations all have the same precausal origin. If the present study were meant to discover the relative importance of each type of precausal thinking in the child, it would obviously have to bear more extensively on objects from his immediate environment, since these objects are brought to his attention more frequently than the phenomena of nature. But the more basic issue of the very existence of precausal thinking had to be dealt with first.

There is a much more fundamental way—and this has hardly ever been pointed out—in which the subject matter of the questionnaires is likely to restrict the scope of the results. In the sphere of logical operations, the child's thinking is largely affected by the character of the objects with which it is concerned. It does not reach the operational level in all areas simultaneously, but is rather subject to horizontal time lags whereby the same intellectual structures are successively applied to different contents. The existence of these time lags in the evolution of logical thinking has repeatedly been demonstrated by Piaget. The simple problem of class inclusion, for instance, will be solved earlier or later depending on whether the elements of classes to be integrated are more or less endowed with properties that are readily accessible to perception or intuition. For example, the integration of the subclasses "boys" and "girls" into a general class "children" is easier to make than that of the subclasses "blue beads" and "red beads" into the class of "wooden beads." For the same reason, in the development of the concept of quantity, the conservation of matter is grasped earlier than the conservation of weight, even though both problems definitely call for operational thinking. Such operational thinking is indeed not perfectly achieved as long as it does not become independent from particular contents; but this condition is not met until the level of formal operations has been reached. At the preceding concrete operational level, the child's thinking remains subject to all sorts of time lags that are fostered by such factors as the nature of the problems, the child's personal experience, the effect of formal education on such experience, and so on. It is precisely the progressive resolution of these time lags that grants the child the capacity of extending a given logical structure to any content.

It may be inferred by analogy that, in the domain of causality, the child's intellectual evolution is subject to the same time lags as in that of logic, since the causal thinking here considered bears on conceptions of the world, or on physical causality, and thus remains, in its very nature, eminently concrete. It is therefore normal to find that some areas of reality are more easily or more rapidly objectified than others, according to the complexity of the phenomena, the child's experience, and the formal teaching he has received. Piaget himself very often notes the occurrence of these time lags within the child's beliefs. Some forms of realism, for instance, disappear earlier in the explanation of dreams than in that of thought. Our results also reveal similar time lags. The clearest instance is undoubtedly animism which persists much longer in regard to natural phenomena (e.g., sun, wind, clouds, etc.) than to mechanical objects (e.g., bicycle, automobile, watch, etc.). In the same way, the data on the origin of the wind, though incomplete, nonetheless indicate that precausal notions disappear more slowly in this context than in explanations of the origin of night. The presence of these time lags in the child's thinking leads to the recognition of a close dependence between results and contents of the examination. Had the children been questioned on other phenomena, the evolution of each of the precausal notions might have proved faster or slower according to the phenomenon chosen. In this sense, it would be true to say that the conclusions may not be extended beyond the areas explored by the questionnaires actually used. In view of the possible time lags, it must also be admitted that the ages of accession to the stages derived from these questionnaires have not the absolute value that would warrant generalization on the evolution of precausal thinking. Yet precisely because time lags, in this context, are of the horizontal and not of the vertical type, their presence would not support the claim that the infantile beliefs which have so clearly been brought to light are not essentially precausal.

To broaden unduly the scope of these reservations would, however, entail the danger of approaching the excess of certain investigators in whose opinion it is merely the content of questionnaires which accounts for the appearance of precausal notions. According to these authors, when children are questioned on phenomena that are very simple and most accessible to their daily experience, they will prove capable of logical or truly objective reasoning even at the age of three or four. Hazlitt's conclusions (1930) are particularly naïve in this respect. She infers the existence of logical thinking in children of less than five years of age, on the grounds that they succeed in solving generalization problems. For instance, she presented the subject with four trays on which were set, respectively, a *dog* and a *bird*, a *dog* and a *pig*, a *dog* and a *lamb*, and finally a *dog* and a *cow*. The subject had to find the common object in the four trays. If Hazlitt had paid closer attention to the procedure which the subjects used in solving this problem, she would certainly have noted, in the first place, that the so-called logical responses might easily have resulted from chance, since the common object on the four trays was presented four times more often than any other. She would especially have noted that a simple and purely intuitive apprehension could lead the child to give the correct answer without having to resort to any rigorous reasoning process, and without his even having understood the exact meaning of the question asked. In short, in this example, as in many others, the examiner unwittingly makes the task easier for the subject and, being convinced that only logical, or causal, reasoning can lead to the correct solution, he can but misjudge the real significance of the subject's answer. Almost all precocious solutions of a difficult problem may be explained by similar errors, and rare indeed are the investigators who seem to be aware of this. However, this possibility did not escape the attention of the shrewdest. Thus, in his excellent study on logical thinking, Morf (1957) presented children of various ages (from seven to eleven) with a series of problems requiring the use of formal reasoning for their real solution. Here is an example:

> "I think of an animal. If the animal has long ears, it may be either an ass or a mule. If my animal has a big tail, it is either a mule or a horse. Now, I want an animal with both long ears and a big tail. What can it be?" [p. 176].

The detailed analysis of the various procedures used by children to solve these problems allows Morf to make a clear distinction between genuine solutions credited only to the children who prove capable of formal thinking, and correct, but still intuitive, solutions which are sometimes within the reach of the youngest.

The present experiment also yields instances of such pseudo solutions. Especially in the first two sections of the questionnaire on floating and sinking, the purely intuitive attributes of weight and size may often be sufficient to answer for the facts—hence the advantage and the interest of having the child compare two objects (a large boat and a small marble) whose intuitive properties conflict with empirical observations. Then, if the child is really limited to primitive thinking, he cannot avoid contradictions which immediately reveal his prelogical mode of reasoning. The possibility of pseudo solutions is still more clearly demonstrated by the following example drawn from a questionnaire on the concept of speed, a questionnaire which has not been used in the present study on precausal thinking but was included in the complete battery given to the same children. Faced with two moving objects simultaneously traveling through two concentric courses of unequal length, the child was asked to designate the faster. Now the youngest subjects in the sample found the solution much more easily than their elders, but they inevitably failed as soon as they were compelled to discuss the elements of the situation. The only explanation they could give consisted in saying with strong conviction: *"you can see it," "it is because I see it going faster,"* and the like. These expressions convey unequivocally the intuitive and preformal quality of the child's solution. In such answers—to make use of a phrase coined by Gréco (1959) in a different, but analogous, context —it is the eyes of the body, not those of the mind, which seek and find the solution.

The danger of assuming the sure presence of logical or causal reasoning behind any correct answer is further strikingly illustrated by an ingenious experiment of Ausubel and Schiff (1954). Three groups of children of various ages (five to six, eight, and eleven) were asked to predict to which side a T-shaped scale, laden with objects of varying weights, would incline when the trays were released. Because the principle of the solution was not immediately understood by any of the children, the trials were repeated until the exact relationship was grasped. Each child was given two training series. In the first one, the relationship to be established was of a causal nature: the length of the arms, or the position of the weights, was what caused the tray to fall. In the second one, the principle involved no causal relation at all: it was rather the color of the objects which determined the movement of the trays. Interestingly enough, the youngest children learned the two series with equal facility, while the eight-year-old, and especially the eleven-year-old children had much more trouble in solving the problem in which the relationship was not really causal. Obviously if the five- or six-year-old child learned to use a right or wrong principle with equal facility, it was because he did not look for, or grasp, in either experiment a genuinely causal relationship. He learned, from simple observation and from memory, the outcome of each arrangement, and then based his predictions upon what he remembered from the previous experiments, without ever looking for a law that could account for varying results. This example clearly demonstrates the fallaciousness of such empirical learning; its external efficiency may lead to the belief that true concepts, or new and stable knowledge, have been acquired when in fact nothing of the kind has taken place. On this complex and delicate problem of the role of learning in the structuring of knowledge, Gréco (1959) has recently performed certain ingenious experiments. Some of his conclusions are very pertinent, and should be quoted here, at least in part.

a) Learning may give rise to the acquisition of empirical knowledge consisting in the ungrounded acceptance of observed facts —a knowledge which is accepted but not understood, limited to the situations being considered, and moreover rapidly lost;

b) but it may also give rise to mental structurings that have lasting and readily generalized effects;

c) however, these structurings generally remain incomplete; they are not extended to the group of mental transformations as a whole, and the schemata they supply do not therefore apply to a different situation; accordingly, we have to speak of partial (or inchoate) structurings, of "semi-logical" schemata, and of "quasi-concepts." A "quasi-concept" is then defined as an incomplete or unfinished concept, formed through a structuring process identical with that used in the elaboration of operational concepts, but the mobility and field of application of which remain limited [p. 176].

If even systematic learning can lead only to incomplete structurings, it becomes difficult to believe that the mere fact of using problems that are closer to the child's daily experience would be sufficient noticeably to lower the age of accession to causal or operational thinking. As the preceding examples show, premature solutions are almost always the result of simple empirical knowledge, intuitive reasoning, or any other primitive process. When an examiner fails to make a thorough inquiry into a child's interpretation, he may easily be led to mistake pseudo solutions for solutions that are specifically logical or causal.

The last problem to be discussed is that of the existence of real stages in the development of the child's conception of the world. It is accepted that the validity of an analysis by stages is essentially conditioned by the regularity with which performances typical of the various levels succeed each other. When this constancy in the successive order of performances is lacking, it is no longer possible to assume either the transitivity of stages or the continuity of mental development, and the very concept of stage loses all meaning. The study of this problem would require lengthy elaborations which lie beyond the scope of the present work; but the essentials may at least be summarized here. On the occasion of his study on analytic and synthetic connections, Piaget (1957) proposes a basic distinction between two ways of conceiving the bond that may unite several different performances in a given process of development.

It may be said, on the one hand, that two performances hold a relation of *filiation* when they have common characteristics and when the superior performance derives from the preceding through a process of transformation, the steps of which may be arranged in a series according to a constant order of chronological succession. This transformation implies an integration of the inferior performance into the superior. Development thus necessarily presupposes the transitivity of the various integration levels of these performances, in such a way that the action of external factors (e.g., previous teaching, ordinary learning, etc.) cannot modify the order of their chronological succession. The quality of continuity or discontinuity of this evolution will depend upon the number of intermediate performances which experimentation can reveal, provided that the measuring instruments do not artificially limit the possibilities of observation. Piaget's example of a continuous development through filiation is that of the acquisition of the concept of number: the elementary actions of the preoperational stages (classifications, seriations, etc.) are finally transformed, after a series of successive integrations, into reversible operations which indicate the starting point of numerical concepts.

On the other hand, development occurs through *substitution* when subsequent performances simply replace antecedent performances, under the almost exclusive influence of external factors, without internal similarities and necessary relationships between the first and the second. The order of successive levels of performance may therefore be upset by the action of external factors. The intermediate phases that may be observed are not the result of a process of successive integration of inferior, into superior, performances. The development is manifested rather through a twofold process: the progressive disappearance of the inferior performance and the correlative emergence of the superior which replaces the first, with or without overlapping. It is obvious that, in this type of evolution, the conditions of continuity and transitivity

CONCLUSION

of levels are not necessarily required. The example given by Piaget to illustrate this substitution process is precisely that of infantile artificialism which recedes gradually as naturalistic explanations of a causal type become more and more predominant.

In this perspective, the child's causal thinking would seem to develop through substitution rather than filiation. The present experiment clearly shows that, in effect, realism, artificialism, animism, and so on, are so many beliefs that disappear little by little to be replaced by more objective, or more physical, concepts. A rather long period is always observed during which primitive notions are still intermingled with explanations of a superior type, but nothing indicates that the superior performances are derived from a transformation or an integration of inferior performances. Physicalism is not the natural expansion of realism or of artificialism in the same sense that operational thinking, for example, is the prolongation and the consummation of preoperational thinking.

Does this mean that attainment of causal thinking is completely subject to influences of the external world, as if that attainment were, in the end, a phenomenon without antecedents, or a pure accident in the development of the child's mind? In other words, is it tenable that the child would never reach causality without the intervention of academic teaching, or inversely, that appropriate teaching would be sufficient to accelerate noticeably his accession to this form of thinking? It is difficult to admit that the disappearance of precausal thinking results exclusively from artificial or adventitious factors, as a hasty interpretation of Piaget's example might lead one to believe. It is mainly explained by the progressive dissociation of the child's own self from the external world. No doubt, this process of differentiation, which reveals itself in a steady progression toward socialization or objectivity in the child's thinking, is not a pure phenomenon of maturation, and requires the intervention of external pressures. But the pressures that are operative here originate in the necessary exchanges between the organism and its physical and social environment. These are registered at the very core of the natural process of adaptation, of which the complementary movements of accommodation and assimilation gradually bring the child to structuring, in one and the same course, his own self and the external universe. Measured in this perspective, the extent of the influence deriving from mere information imparted at home or at school is considerably reduced. This is indeed corroborated by the inefficacy of premature teaching: either the child quickly abandons the explanation received and reverts to his primitive schemata, or else he distorts the adult interpretation to adjust it to his own current beliefs. The same interpretation is also supported by the fact that many children substitute physicalism for precausal beliefs even before they are given any formal teaching, and that their explanations, no matter how inexact, show undubitable evidence of a personal quest for physical and objective concepts. It is perhaps at certain privileged moments of the evolution that external interventions are most likely to upset the natural order of development; but when this occurs, the disturbing influences are almost always detectable in the child's remarks, and are in fact too scattered to modify noticeably the results of a whole sample. Hence the ages of accession to stages preserve their essential significance and may be considered as really representing the various phases of mental development.

To summarize, the development of the child's causal thinking consists in a progressive substitution of physicalistic interpretations for primitive beliefs. This substitution takes place as the child progresses from initial egocentrism toward adult objectivity, that is, as he gradually succeeds in dissociating his own self from the external universe. Since this movement of socialization or differentiation is ultimately explained by a natural process of adaptation, it constitutes a genuine phenomenon of mental evolution, which can therefore be traced in a series of stages. If we further assume that these different stages are characterized by transitivity, it is not in the sense that each higher level implies a transformation or an integration of the preceding level, but in the sense that accession to the higher level presupposes at least a partial withdrawal from the preceding level, just as dissociation is always preceded by undifferentiation, and objectivity by egocentrism. For the same reasons, the evolution of causal thinking shows a certain continuity, at least on a functional plane; however, this continuity must be understood as meaning, not that natural causality would be the extension of precausality, as operational thinking is an extension of the preoperational thinking from which it derives, but as meaning that the transition from precausality to causality always involves an intermediate phase during which the two types of thinking intermingle. The present experiment clearly illustrates the course of this evolution. The transitivity of the stages remains to be verified, and the exact limits of the continuity mentioned above must still be more accurately defined. Longitudinal studies alone can provide conclusive solutions of these problems.

APPENDICES

APPENDIX A

Experimental Questionnaires

THE CONCEPT OF DREAM

Instructions

Ask the child each one of the following questions, trying always to make sure he understands it well. When necessary, change the wording of the questions, using terms more familiar to the child, but be very careful never to suggest more than is included in the instructions. Record all answers *verbatim*.

A. *General questions*

"Do you know what a dream is? Do you dream sometimes at night?"

B. *Specific questions*

1. *Origin of dreams*

"Tell me, where does a dream come from?

"Where are dreams made, where do they come from?

"Do they come from inside of you, or from outside of you?

"Who makes the dreams come?

"Is it you, or someone else? Who?"

2. *Location of dreams*

"While you are dreaming, where is your dream? Where does it go on, in what place is it?

"Is it inside of you, or in your room?"

(a) *If the dream is internal* (in the head, in the thought, etc.), say:

"If we could open your head while you are dreaming, if we could look into your head, could we see your dream?

"Why do you say that we could (not) see your dream?

"Then, where is it, in your head, your dream?"

(b) *If the dream is external* (in the room, on the wall, under the bed, close to the eyes, etc.), say:

"Is it in your room (on the wall, etc.) for real, or is it only as if it were there? Or does it only seem to be there?

"While you are dreaming, are your eyes closed or open?

"Then, where is the dream?

"When you dream that you are playing in the street, where is your dream? In the street, or in your room?"

(c) *In both cases,* go on with:

"Is there something in front of you while you are dreaming?

"Your mother, when she is in your room, can she also see your dream?

"And I, if I were in your room, could I see your dream?

"Why do you say that I could (not) see your dream?"

3. *Organ of dreams*

"Then, tell me, what do we dream with? Is it with our hands? With what, then?"

4. *Cause of dreams*

"What did you dream about, the last time?

"Why did you dream about that?"

If the child says he did not dream, ask him:

"Let's make believe you dreamed you had fallen and hurt yourself. . . . Why did you dream about that?

"Then, do you know why we dream? Why there are dreams?"

5. *Substance of dreams*

"What is a dream made of? Is it made of paper? Then, what is it made of?

"Can we touch our dreams? . . . Why do you say that we can (cannot) touch our dreams?
"Is a dream a thought, or is it a thing?"

6. *Reality of dreams*
"During the night, when you dream you are playing, are you playing for real?
"Is it the same as when you are playing during the day?
"Then, are our dreams true?"

THE CONCEPT OF LIFE

Instructions

Ask the child each one of the following questions, trying always to make sure he understands it well. When necessary, change the wording of the questions, using terms more familiar to the child, but be very careful never to suggest more than is included in the instructions. Record all answers *verbatim*.

A. *General questions*
"Do you know what it is to be alive, to be living? What does it mean?
"Give me the name of some things which are alive?"

B. *Specific questions*
1. *Individual objects*
   (a) "Is a *mountain* alive?
       "Why do you say it is (not) alive?"
   (b) Continue with the following objects, asking each time the same question as in (a):

(2) *the sun*	(9) *a bird*	(16) *the rain*
(3) *the table*	(10) *a bell*	(17) *a tree*
(4) *an automobile*	(11) *the wind*	(18) *a snake*
(5) *a cat*	(12) *an airplane*	(19) *a bicycle*
(6) *a cloud*	(13) *a fly*	(20) *a fish*
(7) *a lamp*	(14) *the fire*	(21) *a pencil*
(8) *a watch*	(15) *a flower*	

2. Comparisons

    (a) "Take the *rain* and the *fire*: is one of them more alive than the other?
        "Why do you say that it is the ... which is more alive?"

    (b) Continue with the following comparisons, asking each time the same questions as in (a):

        (2)   " ... the *wind* or a *bicycle?*"
        (3)   " ... a *fly* or a *cloud?*"
        (4)   " ... a *child* or a *cat?*"
        (5)   " ... a *flower* or an *airplane?*"

THE ORIGIN OF NIGHT

Instructions

Ask the child each one of the following questions, trying always to make sure he understands it well. When necessary, change the wording of the questions, using terms more familiar to the child, but be very careful never to suggest more than is included in the instructions. Record all answers *verbatim*.

A. *General questions*

    "Do you know what the night is? Tell me, what is night?
    "Why is it dark at night?
    "Where does the dark come from at night? What makes it night?"

B. *Alternate sections*

    In answer to the above questions, the child usually regards either one of three different phenomena as the origin of night: (1) *sleep*; (2) *clouds* (or black "air"); (3) the *disappearance of the sun*. According to the child's answer, proceed with the appropriate series of prepared questions listed in one of the three sections below.

    It may happen, however, that the child's initial answers do not fall exactly into one of the three categories suggested above. When this occurs, try to clarify the first response by using the child's answer in a question until his explanations indicate which of the three phenomena he considers as being the origin of night. For instance, ask: *"How does . . . [use the child's initial answers] . . . go about making the night?"* Whenever this is necessary, record each one of the additional questions and each one of the child's answers *verbatim*. Should the child change the category of his answer during the questioning, ask all the questions of the section corresponding to the new category.

Section 1: sleep

"Do you sleep, sometimes, during the day? Can we sleep during the day?

"Is it dark when we sleep in the daytime?

"Then, why is it dark at night?

"Why is it dark only at night?

"Are there times when it is night and you do not sleep?

"When you stay up late at night, is it dark outside?

"Then, how is it that it is dark when you do not sleep?"

Section 2: clouds (or black "air")

"Where do these clouds come from? What makes these clouds?

"How does . . . [the child's answer] . . . make the clouds? What does he make them with?

"Why do these clouds come only at night?

"The clouds at night, are they white or black?

"Can white clouds make it night?

"Why do you say that . . . [the child's answer] . . . ?

"During the day, are there clouds sometimes?

"Then why, when there are clouds in the daytime, is it not dark like at night?

"At night, is it black clouds which take the place of white ones, or white clouds which turn black?

"Where do the white clouds go at night?"

Section 3: disappearance of the sun

"Can you explain how it becomes dark when the sun is gone?

"Where does the sun go at night?

"Why does the sky become dark at night?

"Is the sun always there during the day? When it rains, do we see the sun?

"Then, why is it not dark like at night, when it rains?

"Then, why is it dark only at night?"

C. *Concluding questions* (to be asked of all children)

Ask all subjects, whatever their answers to the preceding questions may have been:

"Can we make the night in this room? If I pull the blinds down, is it going to be dark?

"Then, how is it? Where does the dark in the room come from?

"And the dark outside, what is it?

"When it is light, why is it light?

"What makes it day?"

THE MOVEMENT OF CLOUDS

Instructions

Ask the child each one of the following questions, trying always to make sure he understands it well. When necessary, change the wording of the questions, using terms more familiar to the child, but be very careful never to suggest more than is included in the instructions. Record all answers *verbatim*.

A. *General questions*

"Have you ever seen clouds moving forward?

"What makes them move?"

B. *Alternate sections*

In answer to the above questions, the child usually names either one of three different categories of causes behind the movement of clouds: (1) man (makes the clouds move as he walks); (2) God, celestial bodies, any meteorological phenomenon, even the clouds themselves, or man (without any reference to walking), etc.; (3) the wind. According to the child's answer, proceed with the appropriate series of prepared questions listed in one of the three sections below.

It may happen, however, that the child's initial answers do

not fall exactly into one of the three categories suggested above. When this occurs, try to clarify the first response by using the child's answer in a question until his explanations indicate to which of the three categories given above he ascribes the cause of the movement of clouds. For instance, ask: *"How does . . .* [repeat the child's answer] . . . *go about making the clouds move?"* Whenever this is necessary, record each one of the additional questions and each one of the child's answers *verbatim*. Should the child change the category of his answer during the questioning, ask all the questions of the section corresponding to the new category.

Section 1: man (as he walks)
   "Can you make them move?
   "When I walk and you stand still, do the clouds move?
   "And at night, when everybody is asleep, do the clouds move?"
      If yes:
         "But you just told me it's people who make the clouds move when they are walking?"
      If no:
         "Why don't the clouds move?"
   "Have you ever seen if the clouds move when you stand still?
   "Do they move when you stand still?"
      If yes:
         "Then, what makes them move?"
      If no:
         "Why don't they move?"
   "Why do the clouds sometimes move fast and sometimes move slowly?
   "Can the clouds go where they want? . . . Why can [can't] they go where they want?
   "Do the clouds know they are moving? Why do [don't] they know they are moving?
   "Do the clouds know it's we who make them move, when we are walking?

"Can the wind make the clouds move?"

If yes:

"How does the wind go about making the clouds move?

"Where does the wind come from?"

(then continue with section 3)

If no:

"Why can't the wind make the clouds move?"

Section 2: God, celestial bodies, etc.

"How does it [he, she, they] go about making the clouds move?

[*or,* "How do the clouds go about moving by themselves, all alone?"]

"Do the clouds move by themselves alone, or is there something to make them move?

"Do the clouds know they are moving?

"Do they know it's . . . [the child's answer] . . . who make[s] them move?

"Why do you say that they [do not] know it?

"And . . . [the child's answer] . . . does it [he, she, they] know it makes the clouds move?

"Can the clouds go where they want? . . . Why can [can't] they go where they want?

"But why do the clouds move?

"Why do the clouds move fast sometimes, and sometimes move slowly?

"Can the wind make the clouds move?"

If yes:

"How does the wind go about making the clouds move?

"Where does the wind come from?"

(then continue with section 3)

If no:

"Why can't the wind make the clouds move?"

Section 3: the wind

"Where does the wind come from?

"Can the clouds make wind?

"By moving, can the clouds make wind?

"When there is no wind, can the clouds move by themselves?

"Where does the wind come from?

"How is the wind made?

"Give me the name of some thing which can make wind?

"Why do the clouds move fast sometimes, and sometimes move slowly?

"Can the clouds go where they want? . . . Why do you say they can [can't] go where they want?

"Do the clouds know they are moving?

"Do the clouds know it's the wind that makes them move?

"And does the wind know it makes the clouds move?"

THE FLOATING AND SINKING OF OBJECTS

Material

1 rectangular plastic receptacle (3" x 3" x 4½");
2 cylindrical plastic receptacles (1¾" x 1" diam.);
1 wood cylinder to fit exactly into the cylindrical receptacle;
1 pair of tongs (to place the objects in, and remove from, the water);
1 plasticine ball about 1½" in diameter;
6 objects: a miniature boat (2" x ¾" x ¾"), a large glass marble (1" diam.), a small glass marble (½" diam.), a wooden bead (1" diam.), a nail (2"), a wooden peg (2" x 3/16" diam.).

Instructions

Fill the large receptacle about three quarter full of water and place it on the table in front of the child.

Problem 1 (floating and sinking of various objects)

Present the following items successively. The child can feel the weight of each item if he so desires. It is even advisable to let him place the objects in the water himself in order to increase his interest.

(a) *First, show the miniature boat* and ask:

"If I put this small boat in the water, will it remain on the water or will it sink, go to the bottom?

"Explain to me, why you think it will . . . [the child's answer]?"

Place the boat in the water and, if the child has predicted it would sink, ask:

"Why does it remain on the water, why doesn't it go to the bottom?"

(b) *Show the large marble* and ask:

"And this marble, will it go to the bottom, or will it remain on the water?

"Why do you think it will . . . [the child's answer]?"

Drop the marble in the water, and if the child has predicted it would float, ask:

"Why does it go to the bottom, do you think?"

(c) *Show the wooden bead* and proceed exactly as in (a).

(d) *Show the small marble* and proceed exactly as in (b).

(e) *Show the nail* and proceed exactly as in (b).

(f) *Show the wooden peg* and proceed exactly as in (a).

In all the preceding problems, as well as in the following, *if the child just explains the floating or sinking by the substance* the object is made of ("Because it's made of wood, because it's made of glass, of steel," etc.), *ask him each time to explain further*, saying, for instance:

"Why does it stay on the water when it's made of wood?

"Why does it sink, why does it go to the bottom when it's made of steel [iron], glass, etc.?"

Problem 2 (floating and sinking of similar objects)

(a) *Nail and wooden peg*

Take all the objects, except the nail and the wooden peg out of the water and then say:

"You see, there's only the small nail and the stick left. Then, tell me how it happens, how is it that the small nail went to the bottom and that the stick remains on top of the water?"

(b) *Small marble and wooden bead*

Take the nail and the woden peg out. Take the small marble and the wooden bead and put them (or have the child put them) in the receptacle, saying:

"And now, you see? The small marble went to the bottom

and the wooden bead remained on top of the water. How's that? Explain it to me."

Problem 3 (*sinking of a small marble in comparison with the floating of a large boat*)

Retrieve the marble and the bead, and ask simply:
"Have you ever seen a large boat? Then, tell me, why do large boats remain on the water?"
If the explanation is based on the movement of the boats (they move, they have a motor, sails, oars, etc.), ask again, before going on with the questionnaire:
"If the large boats didn't move, if they were standing still [if they didn't have a motor, oars, etc.], would they go to the bottom?
"Explain to me, why they . . . [the child's answer]?"
"Which is heavier: a large boat or a marble like this [hand the child the small marble]?
"Does a marble go to the bottom?
"And does a large boat stay on top of the water?
"Then, why does a large boat stay on top of the water, and a marble goes to the bottom?
"Which is heavier if you take them in your hands, the large boat or the marble?
"Then, why does the boat remain on the water?
"In a large lake, would the marble still go to the bottom?
"Explain to me, why you say that . . . [the child's answer]?"

Problem 4 (*difference in weight between water and wood*)

Take both cylindrical receptacles. Fill the first one with water (from the square receptacle) and put the wood cylinder into the other one. Show the two full receptacles but *do not let the child take them into his hands to feel the weight*. Then say: "You see, it's the same quantity [the same thing] of wood and water. The two small glasses are full so it's the same quantity in both. Which is heavier, do you think, this one or that one, the one filled with water or the one filled with wood?

"Why do you think it is the one filled with . . . [the child's answer]?"

Problem 5 (floating and sinking of plasticine)

Remove all objects from the square receptacle. Show the child the plasticine ball (he may weigh it if he wishes) and ask:

"If I put this in the water, will it remain on top of the water or will it go to the bottom?

"Explain to me, why you think that it will . . . [the child's answer]?"

Put the ball in the water. If the child's prediction was correct, make him realize he was right. If his prediction was wrong, ask him to explain why the plasticine ball went down to the bottom.

Then take the ball out, give it to the child, and say:

"Try to fix it so that it will remain on top of the water, so that it will float. Make something with the plasticine so that it will remain on top of the water. Can you do something to it so that it will remain on top of the water, so that it will not go down to the bottom?

"Then, try: what do you have to do, do you think, to make it float?"

Let the child work and record exactly everything he does (whether he tries to make smaller and smaller balls, whether on the contrary he tries to make the ball hollow, to form some kind of boat, etc.). When the child wants to test his answer by putting his construction in the water, let him do so but make a note of it. If the child then realizes he did not succeed in making it float and wants to try again, let him keep on trying with as many trials as he wishes during a *maximum five-minute* time period. However, make detailed notes of each one of these trials.

During these various attempts, try to make the child give, if he does not do so spontaneously, the reasons for the different transformations of the plasticine ball.

If the child does not succeed in making the plasticine float:

Gather all the plasticine and model it in the shape of a crucible (about 2″ in diameter and 2″ deep).

Set the crucible down on the water and question the child in the following way:

"You see, it floats now. Why does it float, do you think, when it's made like that? What makes it float, now?

"Why does a ball go down to the bottom, and this now remains on top of the water?"

If the child succeeds by himself in making the plasticine float:

Simply ask him to explain the phenomenon, saying:

"Explain to me, why it floats when it is like this. What makes it float?

"Why has the ball gone to the bottom a moment ago and this, now, remains on top of the water?"

Record all the child's answers *verbatim*.

APPENDIX B

Statistics on the Child Population of Montreal

Table 25

Distribution of Montreal children by age and occupational level of household head

Identification	Description	Younger than 6				From 6 to 13			
		No. in population	%	No. in sample	Total	No. in population	%	No. in sample	Total
1	Proprietary, managerial professional	20,707	12.66	6	10	23,219	15.47	8	12
		13,287	8.12	4		10,717	7.14	4	
2	Clerical	13,760	8.41	4	4	10,407	6.94	3	3
3	Commercial, financial	13,643	8.34	4	4	11,173	7.45	4	4
4	Manufacturing, mechanical, construction, transportation, communication	43,094	26.34	13	25	38,954	25.96	13	24
		15,791	9.65	5		15,598	10.40	5	
		21,362	13.06	7		19,293	12.86	6	
5	Service	9,753	5.96	3	3	9,760	6.50	3	3
6	Laborers	12,220	7.47	4	4	10,925	7.28	4	4
TOTAL		163,617	100.01	50	50	150,046	100.00	50	50

Table 26

Distribution of Montreal children (age: 0 to 24) according to number of children in the family
(Raw data)

Occupational level of household head	Only child	One sibling	More than one sibling	Total
1	16,155	30,572	51,052	97,779
2	6,349	9,640	17,451	33,440
3	6,178	10,282	17,168	33,628
4	31,959	50,902	131,399	214,260
5	4,804	7,304	17,662	29,770
6	4,810	7,100	21,639	33,549
Total	70,255	115,800	256,371	442,426

Table 27

Distribution of Montreal children (age: 0 to 24) according to number of children in the family
(Percentages)

Occupational level of household head	Only child	One sibling	More than one sibling	Total
1	16.50	31.26	52.24	100
2	18.98	28.82	52.20	100
3	18.37	30.56	51.07	100
4	14.95	23.74	61.31	100
5	16.13	24.52	59.35	100
6	14.33	20.96	64.71	100
Over-all %	16.55	26.64	56.81	100

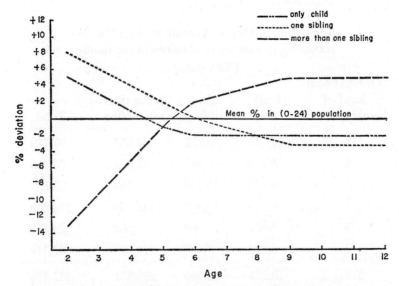

Fig. 2. Per cent deviation at each age level (2 to 12) from the percentage of identical cases of familial constellation (only child; one sibling; more than one sibling) in the general population (0 to 24 years of age). Through the use of this graph, the raw data of Table 27 are converted into the required proportions of the present sample (Table 28).

Table 28

Distribution of Montreal children by age (4 to 12), occupational level of household head, and number of children in the family
(Percentages corrected after demographical data)

Family Occup. lev.	Only child						One sibling						More than one sibling					
Age	1	2	3	4	5	6	1	2	3	4	5	6	1	2	3	4	5	6
4.0	18	20	19	16	17	15	35	33	35	28	29	25	47	47	46	56	54	60
4.6	17	19	18	15	16	14	34	32	34	27	28	24	49	49	48	58	56	62
5.0	16	18	17	14	15	13	33	31	33	26	27	23	51	51	50	60	58	64
6.0	15	17	16	13	14	12	31	29	31	24	25	21	54	54	53	63	61	67
7.0	15	17	16	13	14	12	30	28	30	23	24	20	55	55	54	64	62	68
8.0	15	17	16	13	14	12	29	27	29	22	23	19	56	56	55	65	63	69
9.0	15	17	16	13	14	12	28	26	28	21	22	18	57	57	56	66	64	70
10.0	15	17	16	13	14	12	28	26	28	21	22	18	57	57	56	66	64	70
11.0	15	17	16	13	14	12	28	26	28	21	22	18	57	57	56	66	64	70
12.0	15	17	16	13	14	12	28	26	28	21	22	18	57	57	56	66	64	70

Table 29

Distribution of Montreal French-speaking school children
by age (7 to 12), sex, and school grade[1]

(Raw data)

| Age | Sex | School grade | | | | | | | | | Total |
		1	2	3	4	5	6	7	8	Ungraded	
7:0	G	3405	2574	29	0	0	0	0	0	3	6011
	B	3543	2443	62	0	0	0	0	0	5	6053
8:0	G	466	3693	2700	69	3	1	0	0	4	6936
	B	550	3703	2557	71	2	0	0	0	22	6905
9:0	G	72	742	3465	2544	63	2	0	0	24	6912
	B	108	923	3452	2393	89	1	0	0	46	7012
10:0	G	21	190	989	3240	2013	63	3	0	42	6561
	B	29	287	1090	3211	1950	71	4	0	89	6731
11:0	G	7	59	295	1081	2688	1609	71	3	76	5889
	B	7	65	382	1221	2728	1456	106	2	117	6084
12:0	G	1	8	81	435	1131	2486	1376	54	145	5717
	B	2	30	120	553	1401	2395	1257	39	161	5958

[1] Statistics of the *Montreal Catholic School Commission* for 1955-56 for ages 8 to 12. For age 7, not included in the 1955-56 report, the 1951-52 data are used. Age is calculated as of January 1 of the current school year.

Table 30

Distribution of Montreal French-speaking school children by age (7 to 12), sex, and school grade[1]

(Percentages)

Age	Sex	School grade									Total
		1	2	3	4	5	6	7	8	Ungraded	
7:0	G	57	43	0	0	0	0	0	0	0	100
	B	59	40	1	0	0	0	0	0	0	100
8:0	G	7	53	39	1	0	0	0	0	0	100
	B	8	54	37	1	0	0	0	0	0	100
9:0	G	1	11	50	37	1	0	0	0	0	100
	B	2	13	49	34	1	0	0	0	1	100
10:0	G	0	3	15	49	31	1	0	0	1	100
	B	0	4	16	48	30	1	0	0	1	100
11:0	G	0	1	5	19	46	27	1	0	1	100
	B	0	1	6	20	45	24	2	0	2	100
12:0	G	0	0	1	8	20	43	24	1	3	100
	B	0	1	2	9	23	40	21	1	3	100

[1] See footnote, Table 29.

Bibliography

Abel, Theodora M. (1932), Unsynthetic modes of thinking among adults: a discussion of Piaget's concepts. *Amer. J. Psychol.*, 44:123-132.

Askar, R. M. (1932), Animism and the child's conception of the world: an experimental criticism and verification of Professor Piaget's inquiries into child animism. Unpublished M.A. thesis lodged in the University library, Birmingham, England.

Ausubel, D. P. & Schiff, H. M. (1954), The effect of incidental and experimentally induced experience in the learning of relevant and irrelevant causal relationships by children. *J. genet. Psychol.*, 84:109-123.

Bell, C. R. (1954), Additional data on animistic thinking. *Sci. Mon., N.Y.*, 79:67-69.

Binet, A. & Simon, T. (1908), Langage et pensée. *Année psychol.*, 14:284-339.

Bruce, Myrtle (1941), Animism vs. evolution of the concept "alive." *J. Psychol.*, 12:81-90.

Bureau fédéral de la statistique (1955), *Neuvième recensement du Canada, 1951.* Ottawa, Canada.

Commission des Ecoles catholiques de Montréal (1956), *Rapport de la Commission des Ecoles catholiques de Montréal, service de recherches et statistiques.* Montréal, Canada.

Crannel, C. W. (1954), The responses of college students to a questionnaire of animistic thinking. *Sci. Mon., N.Y.*, 78:54-56.

Dennis, W. (1942), Piaget's questions applied to a child of known environment. *J. genet. Psychol.*, 60:307-320.

————(1943), Animism and related tendencies in Hopi children. *J. abnorm. soc. Psychol.*, 38:21-36.

————(1953), Animistic thinking among college and university students. *Sci. Mon., N.Y.*, 76:247-249.

————(1957), Animistic thinking among college and high school students in the Near East. *J. educ. Psychol.*, 48:193-198.

————& Mallenger, Betty (1949), Animism and related tendencies in senescence. *J. Gerontol.*, 4:218-221.

————& Russell, R. W. (1940), Piaget's questions applied to Zuni children. *Child Develpm.*, 11:181-187.

Deutsche, Jean M. (1937), *The Development of Children's Concepts of Causal Relations.* Minnesota: Univ. Minn. Inst. Child Welf. Monogr.

Doll, E. A. (1953), *Measurement of Social Competence.* Princeton: Educational Test Bureau.

Gréco, P. (1959), L'apprentissage dans une situation à structure opératoire concrète. In: *Etudes d'épistémologie génétique. VII. Apprentissage et connaissance*, ed. P. Gréco & J. Piaget. Paris: Presses Universitaires de France, pp. 68-182.

Grigsby, Olive J. (1932), An experimental study of the development of concepts of relationship in preschool children as evidenced by their expressive ability. *J. exp. Educ.*, 1:144-162.

Havighurst, R. J. & Neugarten, B. L. (1955), Belief in immanent justice and animism. In: *American Indian and White Children: A Socio-Psychological Investigation*, ed. R. J. Havighurst. Chicago: Univ. Chicago Press, Chap. VI.

Hazlitt, Victoria (1930), Children's thinking. *Brit. J. Psychol.*, 20: 354-361.

Huang, I. (1943), Children's concepts of physical causality: a critical summary. *J. genet. Psychol.*, 63:71-121.

————& Lee, H. W. (1945), Experimental analysis of child animism. *J. genet. Psychol.*, 66:69-74.

Inhelder, Bärbel (1956), Criteria of the stages of mental development. In: *Discussions on Child Development. Vol. I: The Proceedings of the First Meeting of the World Health Organization Study Group on the Psychobiological Development of the*

Child, ed. J. M. Tanner & B. Inhelder. New York: Int. Univ. Press, pp. 75-86.

————& Piaget, J. (1955), *The Growth of Logical Thinking from Childhood to Adolescence.* London: Routledge and Kegan Paul, 1958.

Isaacs, Susan (1930), *Intellectual Growth in Young Children.* New York: Harcourt, Brace.

Jahoda, G. (1958a), Child animism: I. A critical survey of cross-cultural research. *J. soc. Psychol.,* 47:197-213.

————(1958b), Child animism: II. A study in West Africa. *J. soc. Psychol.,* 47:213-222.

Johnson, E. C. & Josey, C. C. (1931-1932), A note on the development of thought forms of children as described by Piaget. *J. abnorm. soc. Psychol.,* 26:338-339.

Jones, F. N. & Arrington, M. G. (1945), The explanation of physical phenomena given by white and Negro children. *Comp. Psychol. Monogr., 18,* No. 5.

Klingberg, G. (1957), The distinction between living and not living among 7- to 10-year-old children, with some remarks concerning the so-called animism controversy. *J. genet. Psychol., 90:* 227-238.

Klingensmith, S. W. (1953), Child animism: what the child means by "alive." *Child Develpm.,* 24:51-61.

Laurendeau, Monique & Pinard, A. (1957), Une méthode rationnelle de localisation des tests dans les échelles d'âge. *Can. J. Psychol., 11:*33-47.

Lowrie, D. G. (1954), Additional data on animistic thinking. *Sci. Mon., N.Y.,* 79:69-70.

Mead, Margaret (1932), An investigation of the thought of primitive children with special reference to animism. *J. Roy. Anthrop. Inst. Great Britain and Ireland,* 62:173-190.

Morf, A. (1957), Les relations entre la logique et le langage lors du passage du raisonnement concret au raisonnement formel. In: *Etudes d'épistémologie génétique. III. Logique, langage et théorie de l'information,* ed. L. Apostel, B. Mandelbrot, & A. Morf. Paris: Presses Universitaires de France, pp. 173-204.

Nass, M. L. (1956), The effects of three variables in children's concepts of causality. *J. abnorm. soc. Psychol.*, 53:191-196.

Osterrieth, P. et al. (1955), *Le problème des stades en psychologie de l'enfant*. Symposium de l'Association psychologique scientifique de langue française. Paris: Presses Universitaires de France.

Piaget, J. (1926), *The Child's Conception of the World*. London: Routledge and Kegan Paul, 1951.

———(1927), *The Child's Conception of Physical Causality*. London: Routledge and Kegan Paul, 1951.

———(1936), *The Origins of Intelligence in Children*, 2nd ed. New York: Int. Univ. Press, 1952.

———(1937), *The Construction of Reality in the Child*. New York: Basic Books, 1954.

———(1945), *Play, Dreams and Imitation in Childhood*. New York: Norton, 1951.

———(1957), Transposition du problème de l'analytique en termes génétiques. In: *Etudes d'épistémologie génétique. IV. Les liaisons analytiques et synthétiques dans les comportements du sujet*, ed. L. Apostel, W. Mays, A. Morf, & J. Piaget. Paris: Presses Universitaires de France, pp. 40-73.

———(1959), Esquisse d'autobiographie intellectuelle. *Bull. de psychologie*, 13:7-13.

Russell, R. W. (1940a), Studies in animism: II. The development of animism. *J. genet. Psychol.*, 56:353-366.

———(1940b), Studies in animism: IV. An investigation of concepts allied to animism. *J. genet. Psychol.*, 57:83-91.

———& Dennis, W. (1939), Studies in animism: I. A standardized procedure for the investigation of animism. *J. genet. Psychol.*, 55:389-400.

——— ———& Ash, F. E. (1940), Studies in animism: III. Animism in feeble-minded subjects. *J. genet. Psychol.*, 57:57-63.

———et al. (1942), Studies in animism: V. Animism in older children. *J. genet. Psychol.*, 60:329-335.

Simmons, A. J. & Gross, A. E. (1957), Animistic responses as function of sentence context and instruction. *J. genet. Psychol., 91*: 181-189.

Strauss, A. L. (1951), The animism controversy: re-examination of Huang-Lee data. *J. genet. Psychol.*, 78:105-113.

Voeks, Virginia (1954), Sources of apparent animism in studies. *Sci. Mon., N.Y.*, 79:406-407.

Author Index

Abel, Theodora M., 38, 283
Apostel, L., 285-6
Aristotle, 107
Arrington, M. G., 17, 32, 285
Ash, F. E., 286
Askar, R. M., 16, 24-5, 283
Ausubel, D. P., 22, 255, 283

Bell, C. R., 24, 38, 283
Binet, A., 33, 94, 283
Bruce, Myrtle, 18, 22, 24, 32, 46, 283

Chen, C. M., 38
Crannell, C. W., 38, 283

Dennis, W., 21-3, 25-8, 31-2, 35, 38, 43, 49, 53, 66, 68, 78, 131, 283-4, 286
Deutsche, Jean M., 17, 23, 25-30, 32, 43, 46, 48-9, 57, 229-30, 240, 284
Doll, E. A., 98, 284

Greco, P., 255-7, 284
Grigsby, Olive J., 22, 35, 284
Gross, A. E., 24, 38, 287

Havighurst, R. J., 22, 35, 284
Hazlitt, Victoria, 37, 253, 284
Henripin, J., 84
Herzfeld, E., 30
Huang, I., 17-20, 22-4, 26, 28, 30, 32-4, 37-8, 43, 46, 48-9, 57, 284

Inhelder, Bärbel, 8, 48, 94, 96, 204, 284-5
Isaacs, Susan, 16, 23, 25, 51, 285

Jahoda, G., 17, 20-1, 32, 285
Johnson, E. C., 16, 25-6, 28, 285
Jones, F. N., 17, 32, 285
Josey, C. C., 16, 25-6, 28, 285

Klingberg, G., 20, 23, 32, 49, 285
Klingensmith, S. W., 22, 32, 49, 285

Laurendeau, Monique, 47, 95, 285
Lee, H. W., 18, 26, 28, 32, 34, 49, 284
Lerner, E., 21, 35
Lowrie, D. G., 38-9, 40-1, 43, 285

Mallenger, Betty, 38, 284
Mandelbrot, B., 285
Mays, W., 286
Mead, Margaret, 17, 27, 285
Morf, A., 254, 285-6

Nass, M. L., 24-5, 286
Neugarten, B. L., 22, 35, 284

Osterrieth, P., 45, 52, 96, 286

Piaget, J., 1-5, 7-10, 14-18, 20-6, 28-35, 37-8, 40-1, 46, 48, 50-3, 55, 57-63, 66, 68-9, 72, 74, 78-80, 92-4, 96-7, 107, 112-3, 120-2,

289

Piaget, J. (*contd.*)

    127, 131-4, 137-8, 141, 150, 156-8, 160-1, 163-5, 172, 177, 183, 185, 190, 204-5, 219, 230, 232, 239, 243, 245, 247-8, 251-2, 257-9, 284-6

Pinard, A., 47, 95, 285

Russell, R. W., 21-8, 31-2, 35, 43, 47, 49, 52, 66, 68, 78, 131, 284, 286

Schiff, H. M., 22, 255, 283

Simmons, A. J., 24, 38, 287

Simon, T., 33, 283

Strauss, A. L., 32, 287

Tanner, J. M., 284-5

Voeks, Virginia, 32, 38-9, 40-1, 287

Wolf, K., 30

Yang, H. H., 38

Zietz, K., 22

Subject Index

Adherences, as used to describe pre-causal thinking, 10
Animism
  in adults, 37-44
  and concept of life, 131ff.
  definition of, 13, 66
  and floating and sinking, 74, 209-11
  and movement of clouds, 72-3, 189-99
  and origin of night, 172-8
Anthropocentrism, 12-3, 243
Anthropomorphism, 18, 21-2, 32, 40-2, 135-51, 196, 248
Artificialism
  and concept of dream, 106-7, 113, 124-5
  definition of, 12-5, 68-9
  and movement of clouds, 72-3, 184-5, 188-203
  and origin of night, 68-9, 160ff.
  see also Divine artificialism

Causal thinking; see Precausal thinking, Physicalism
Clouds (movement of)
  and artificialism, animism, and finalism, 72-3, 184-203
  as autonomous or influenced by

celestial bodies, 72-3, 192-6
  and dynamism, 72-3, 182-5, 189, 194, 198
  and magical thinking, 72-3, 185-6, 188-96
  and physicalism, 194ff.
  questionnaire on, 72-3, 268-71
  and realism, 188-9
  and religious teaching, 203
  and sex differences, 202-3
  and the wind, 73-4, 193-4, 197-201
Continuity of development
  and concept of stages, 48-9
  in relation to filiation or substitution, 257-9
Cultural differences, 16-22, 27

Decentration, 7-9
Divine artificialism
  and concept of dream, 106-7, 113
  and movement of clouds, 184-203
  and origin of night, 160-78
Dream (concept of)
  and divine artificialism, 106-7, 113
  and integral realism, 106-12
  and integral subjectivism, 62-6, 121-6
  and magical thinking, 116

This index does not claim to be exhaustive. It is meant only as an additional means of reference to the main concepts discussed in this book.

Dream (*contd.*)
  and mitigated realism, 112-21
  questionnaire on, 62-6, 263-5
  and sex differences, 129-30
  and various forms of precausal
    thinking, 124-5
Dynamism
  definition of, 13, 72
  and floating and sinking, 74-5,
    204ff.
  and movement of clouds, 72-3,
    182-5, 189, 194, 198

Egocentrism
  as basic to all forms of precausal
    thinking, 243
  definition and forms of, 7-10
  gradual disappearance of, 259-61
Examiners, 90-2

Filiation process, 257-9
Finalism
  and concept of dream, 124-5
  definition of, 12
  and floating and sinking, 74, 209-
    11, 219, 229
  and movement of clouds, 72-3, 189,
    194-9
  and origin of night, 68-70, 167-77
Floating and sinking
  and dynamism, 74-5, 204ff.
  and logical thinking, 74-5, 212ff.
  and magical thinking, 229
  questionnaire on, 74-6, 271-5
  and sex differences, 228-9
  and various forms of precausal
    thinking, 74-5, 209-11, 219, 229-
    30

Juxtaposition (mechanism of), 38,
  143

Learning (effect of), 22, 255-7
Life (concept of)
  and animism, 131ff.
  and anthropomorphism, 135-41
  based on general, 66, 144ff., or au-
    tonomous movement, 66, 147ff.

and juxtaposition, 143
lack of systematic criteria in the
  child's, 132-3
questionnaire on, 66-8, 265-6
and sex differences, 156-7
Logical thinking
  confused with precausal thinking,
    253-7
  and floating and sinking, 74-5,
    212ff.

Magical thinking, 11-2, 19
  and concept of dream, 116, 185-6,
    189-96, 229
  and floating and sinking, 229
  and movement of clouds, 72-3
  as related to realism, 234
Moralism, 19
  and concept of dream, 124-5
  and floating and sinking, 74, 209
Movement, as a criterion of life, 41,
  66-7, 144ff.

Night (origin of)
  and animism, 171-7
  and finalism and artificialism, 68-9,
    160-78
  and physicalism, 69-71, 171ff.
  questionnaire on, 68-72, 266-8
  and religious teaching, 161-3, 181
  and sex differences, 180-1
N'importequisme ("anythingness"),
  33

Pananimism, 20
Participation (feeling of), 11-2, 18
Phenomenism, 11-2, 17, 22, 30, 38
  apparent lack of, 245-6, 251
Physicalism
  and floating and sinking, 212ff.
  and movement of clouds, 73, 194ff.
  and origin of night, 69-71, 171ff.
Precausal thinking
  controversial evidence on, 16-23
  definition and forms of, 10ff.
  generality of, 231-4, 248-9
  as identified with logical or causal
    thinking, 17-20, 29-30, 252-7

Precausal thinking (*contd.*)
  infantile character of, 37-44
  as influenced by type of examina-
    tion, 23-6, by characteristics of
    subjects, 26-8, by techniques of
    analysis and topics investigated,
    28-36, 249-52
  interdependency of various forms
    of, 234ff., 248-9

Questionnaires
  choice of topics of, 58-61
  description of, 61-76, 263-75
  general structure of, 61-2, 77-9
  number of, 58-9

Realism
  and concept of dream, 106ff.
  definition of, 9, 62
  and movement of clouds, 188-9
  as related to magical thinking, 234
Regression, 43-4, 249
Results (analysis of)
  and ages of accession to stages,
    94ff.
  and identification of stages, 93-4
  and objectivity of scoring, 101-2

Sampling method
  critique of Piaget's, 80
  description of, 81-9
Sex differences
  and choice of questionnaires, 59-60
  and concept of dream, 129-30
  and concept of life, 156-7
  and floating and sinking, 228-9
  and movement of clouds, 202-3
  and origin of night, 180-1
Stages
  and age overlapping, 45-7
  and continuity of development,
    48-9

filiation or substitution of, 257-9
  order of succession of, 52-3
  and type of problems, 49-52
  see also Results
Subjectivism
  and concept of dream, 62-6, 121-6
Supernaturalism, 24, 161; *see also*
  Divine artificialism
Syncretism, 38, 193, 205, 219
Systematic thinking (lack of)
  due to the child's incoherence, 13-
    5, 132-3
  as related to type of problems, 49-
    52, 143, 212-20, 237ff., 251-3
  typical of intermediary stages, 33-4

Teaching (effect of), 161-3, 181, 185,
  203, 260
Testing
  conditions and place of, 90-1
  order of, 91-2
Timelags
  and content of questionnaires,
    251-3
  and levels of decentration, 7-8
Transitivity, 52-3, 98-100, 257-61
  and concept of dream, 126
  and concept of life, 154-5
  and floating and sinking, 227
  and movement of clouds, 201
  and origin of night, 179

Wind
  and movement of clouds, 73-4,
    193-4, 197-201
  origin of, 190

Zoomorphism, 135; *see also* Anthropomorphism